3

JEFFREYS

A New Portrait of England's "Hanging Judge"

By the same author:
ALFRED THE GREAT

Sir George Jeffreys, Recorder of London 1678–80

P. J. Helm

JEFFREYS

A New Portrait of
England's "Hanging Judge"

THOMAS Y. CROWELL COMPANY

NEW YORK · *Established 1834*

PRINTED IN GREAT BRITAIN

CONTENTS

Acknowledgements   9

1   Lions under the Throne: 'the Mouth of the City'
(1645–79)   11

2   The Salamanca Doctor and the Little Limping
Peer (1678–9)   36

3   Exclusion (1679–81)   55

4   The Royalist Counter-Attack (1681–3)   76

5   'From God the King, from the King the Law'
(1683–5)   95

6   A New King, and a Pillory'd Prophet (1685)   113

7   'Gaffer Scott's Vagabonds' (1685)   127

8   Lord Chancellor Jeffreys (1685–8)   146

9   'A Very Hard Game to Play' (1688–9)   168

10   'The Lies of this Age will be the History of the
Next'   184

Some Books   202

Index   203

ILLUSTRATIONS

Sir George Jeffreys, Recorder of London 1678–80.   *frontispiece*
Painting by an unknown artist. (National Portrait
Gallery)

facing page

Charles II, 1660–85. Painting by an unknown artist.
(National Portrait Gallery)   32

James II, 1685–8. Painting by Sir Godfrey Kneller.
(National Portrait Gallery)   32

The Popish Plot, 1678–9. Contemporary propaganda in
the form of packs of cards: on the King of Hearts Oates
is shown describing the Plot to Charles II. (British
Museum)   33

Oates in the pillory. (Mansell Collection)   48

Letter from Jeffreys to Sunderland, 5th September, 1685.
(Public Record Office)   49

Certificate for the transportation of two rebels from
Topsham to Virginia. (Public Record Office)   128

Lord Chancellor Jeffreys. Painting by Sir Godfrey Kneller.
(by kind permission of the Earl of Tankerville)   129

James, Duke of Monmouth. Painting by Sir Peter Lely.
(National Portrait Gallery)   129

Capture of Jeffreys at Wapping, 1688. A contemporary
print. (Mansell Collection)   144

Oak Room, Dorchester. Used as a court-room in 1685; John
Tutchin was sentenced here. (*Photo:* Leslie D. Frisby)   145

St. Mary's Aldermanbury; Jeffreys was eventually buried
in the chancel. (*Photo:* A. F. Kersting)   145

To

Norman and Pauline

ACKNOWLEDGEMENTS

Quotations from contemporary sources appearing in this book are mainly taken from:

Ailesbury, Earl of, *Memoirs*, Roxburgh Club, 1890

Burnet, Gilbert, *History of my own Times*, 6 vols., Oxford, 1833

Evelyn, John, *Diary*

L'Estrange, Roger, *Brief History of the Times*, 1687–8

Luttrell, Narcissus, *Brief Historical Relation of State Affairs*, Oxford, 1857

North, Roger, *Examen*; *Lives of the Norths*, 3 vols., 1890

Pepys, Samuel, *Diary*

Reresby, Sir John, *Memoirs*, 1875

State Trials, ed. Howell, 1840

Verney, *Memoirs*

The author wishes to thank the following, who have given him permission to draw on copyright material—Cassell and Co. Ltd.: Lord Birkenhead, *Fourteen English Judges*; Collins: Sir Arthur Bryant, *Samuel Pepys; The Years of Peril*; Eyre and Spottiswoode: S. Schofield, *Jeffreys of "The Bloody Assizes"*; George G. Harrap and Co.: H. Montgomery Hyde, *Judge Jeffreys*; William Heinemann Ltd.: H. B. Irving, *The Life of Judge Jeffreys*; William Hodge and Co.: J. G. Muddiman, *The Bloody Assizes*; Longmans, Green and Co. Ltd.: J. P. Kenyon, *Robert Spencer, Earl of Sunderland*; Macdonald and Co. Ltd.: G. W. Keeton, *Lord Chancellor Jeffreys and the Stuart Cause*; Methuen and Co.: J. Kemble, *Idols and Invalids*; A. D. Peters and Co.: Sir Arthur Bryant, *King Charles II; The Guardian*; the Brown, Picton and Hornby Libraries of the City of Liverpool; Sir Willoughby Aston, *Diary* —and to acknowledge his debt to them and to all the other sources referred to in this book.

The lies of this age will be the history of the next.
　　　Roger L'Estrange, Tory journalist and pamphleteer

What stratagems and devices, what ways and means, will not disaffected persons find out to blacken a government they have a mind to overthrow.
　　　　　　Robert Ferguson 'the Plotter', a Whig

We live in an age wherein men are apt to believe only on one side. They can believe the greatest lie if it makes for the advantage of their party, but not the greatest truth if it thwarts their interests. . . .
　　　　George Jeffreys, Tory, Lord Chief Justice

I

Lions under the Throne:
'the Mouth of the City'
(1645-79)

What a damned fool I was that I did not run away in time! Could
I not have had the wit of Petre, and put my ten thousand pound
bag of guineas under my arm and troop to Brussels? A dull beast
to stay to be thus noosed! Now, Petre, Pope and Judges, with your
dispensing scarlet, where are you to assist me? You will be damned
before you'll help me to a dead lift. I see, I see now, I was a dull
ass. Out upon it, to be thus outwitted! . . . Was it for this I per-
verted justice, and did things contrary to the law of God and man?
Oh, hub! Bub! Bub! Boo! What shall I do now? A PARLIAMENT!
A PARLIAMENT! . . . Curse my fortune that ever I should have
been born in a time of printing! They put my name in capital
letters, they have out my titles too, and seem to care no more for me
than for Balaam's ass. My purse and mace will not protect me; my
purse will serve to put my head in, after it is off; and my mace will
serve to stick it on afterwards!

The pamphlet, an *Address and Confession to both Houses of
Parliament*, was selling well in the spring of 1689. England had
just enjoyed a bloodless revolution. The Catholic James II had fled
and his place as ruler had been taken by the Dutch William of
Orange and his wife Mary—who was James's daughter. It was the
great age of political pamphleteering, and the dramatic change
in government had let loose a flood of fiction.

The *Address* was satirically attributed to the former Lord
Chancellor, Sir George Jeffreys, who was in the Tower. He had
not been brought to trial for any crime. He was dying, his
kidneys disintegrating. His own party, the Tories, were looking
for a scapegoat who might take the blame for their shortcomings;
his opponents, the Whigs, were out for revenge. The Jews used to
sacrifice two goats: one was sent into the wilderness with the sins

of the whole people laid upon it, the other was killed. It seemed not impossible that Jeffreys might play a double role.

At least one sentence in the *Address* was precisely correct: *Curse my fortune that ever I should have been born in a time of printing!* In Axe Yard, Westminster, a group of obscure scribblers working in a favourable political climate on the reputation of a man whose character had plenty of weaknesses, were busy creating the cardboard effigy of 'Bloody Judge Jeffreys'.

Some men attract myths as a magnet draws iron. In his lifetime Jeffreys was already the subject of impossible anecdotes. After his death even his physical remains were crusted with legend. According to one account his body was taken to Dorchester and walled up in a house where the first Monmouth rebels were sentenced. The tales did not come to an end as time passed, if anything they grew and proliferated. As recently as December, 1934, there were rumours that Jeffreys had been taken to Taunton and executed in the market-place. Then the headless body had been carried to Stocklinch, and buried in a vault there. When the vault was flooded, the coffin was seen to float. All this because in that month a vault at Stocklinch had been opened and found to contain a coffin shorter than usual, of a suitable length to contain a headless corpse.

In fact there is not a shadow of doubt that Jeffreys died a natural death and was eventually buried in the City of London. When even tangible evidence of this type can be disregarded, it is not surprising that equally fictitious interpretations of character and motive should survive. One of the fascinations of Jeffreys' life is that it touches on one of the cardinal historical questions; how do we know?

The assessment of Jeffreys also involves the historical discipline of seeing him in relation to his own age and not to ours. The seventeenth-century Tories are not the modern Conservative party; the Dissenters are not twentieth-century Methodists, but men whose philosophy was at best a solvent of the existing social order, at worst a programme for rebellion. To many, the Catholics are the agents of a French dictatorship.

This problem of historical perspective can be particularly confusing in the matter of seventeenth-century justice. Superficially, it was the same as today—the same robes, the same juries, the same ritual. These similarities, though, conceal a wealth of differences. What must, correctly, be felt as shocking from a twentieth-century standpoint must, equally correctly, be accepted as normal seventeenth-century procedure.

There is, for example, the matter of punishments. These were brutal in the extreme. They were not the peculiar whim of seventeenth-century judges, but part of the law and many of them continued to be imposed until the nineteenth century.

Even to lie in prison was to risk death. Gaol fever destroyed many of the prisoners after Monmouth's rebellion, but it was nothing new. A hundred years before, in 1577, five hundred prisoners had died during the assizes at Oxford from the disease, and in 1730 'some hundreds' died in Taunton itself. It was a virulent form of typhus, described by Griffith as 'a contagious, putrid, and very pestilential fever, attended with tremblings, twitchings, restlessness, delirium with, in some instances, early phrenzy and lethargy; while the victims break out often into livid postules and purple spots.'

Escaping gaol fever, one might fall a victim of the perjurer. Outside every law court stood men wearing inconspicuous tokens—often a wisp of straw—the prostitutes of the sessions. The cross-examination of witnesses by judges—an activity in which Jeffreys excelled—was undertaken in order to try to shake the composure of these perjured informers.

Convicted, the punishment could be a fine or a whipping. In many of the political trials the fines were so immense that they amounted to sentences of life imprisonment, since they could never be paid. Floggings of astronomical proportions became common after the Whippings Act passed in Henry VIII's reign. Seamen continued to be flogged to death in the nineteenth century, and even in civil courts it was not until 1821 that the number of strokes that could be imposed was limited to *three hundred*.

More severe, if more random in its effect, was the pillory. This was not merely a matter of standing with one's head and hands through a wooden board, the object of ridicule. It could become death by slow lynching. Sometimes the victim's feet did not touch the ground, sometimes his ears were nailed to the board. The spectators might throw what they pleased. For the popular victim friends would pack the space round the pillory and the hours spent there became something of a triumph. Benjamin Harris, a bookseller, whom Jeffreys prosecuted in 1680 and who was sentenced by Scroggs to the pillory, was saved in this way. On the other hand a hostile mob could destroy those in the pillory. In the eighteenth century an eye-witness described the horrible death of James Eagan and James Salmon as follows: 'The blows they received occasioned their heads to swell to an enormous size; and by people hanging on the skirts of their clothes they were nearly strangled. They had been in the pillory about half an hour when a stone struck Eagan on the head, and he immediately expired'. The pillory was not abolished until 1837.

The death penalty was common. One might be hanged for stealing five shillings. In London the hangings at Tyburn, then in the countryside but today the site of Marble Arch, provided a public entertainment. A foreigner, de Saussure, wrote in the early eighteenth century:

> Some time after my arrival in London I witnessed a spectacle which certainly was not as magnificent or as brilliant as the Lord Mayor's Show; ... I saw thirteen criminals all hanged at the same time. ... On the day of execution the condemned prisoners, wearing a sort of white linen shirt over their clothes and a cap on their heads, are tied two together and placed on carts with their backs to the horses' tails. ... In this way part of the town is crossed, and Tyburn which is a good half-mile from the last suburb, is reached, and here stands the gibbet. ... When all the prisoners arrive at their destination they are made to mount on a very wide cart made expressly for the purpose, a cord is passed round their necks and the end fastened to the gibbet, which is not very high. The chaplain who accompanies the condemned men is also on the cart; he makes them pray and sing a few verses of the Psalms. The relatives are permitted to mount the cart and take fare-well. When the time is up—that is to say about a quarter of an hour—the chaplain and the relations get off the cart, which slips from under the condemned men's feet, and in this way they remain all hanging together. You often see friends and relations tugging at the hanging men's feet so that they should die quicker and not suffer. ... All these scenes are most diverting, the noise and confusion is unbelievable, and can be witnessed from a sort of amphitheatre erected for spectators near the gibbet.

As late as 1833 a boy of nine was sentenced to this death for pushing a stick through a cracked window and stealing printers' ink to the value of twopence. In the following year gibbeting was abolished, but executions remained public until 1868.

For treason the penalty was death—death by torture. Those convicted were drawn to the place of execution on hurdles, hanged but cut down alive, and then disembowelled. Their heads were struck off and, together with their quarters, hung up in conspicuous places. Women were instead burnt to death. A strong man might live till the very end—it was reported that Collingwood, executed in the reign of Richard III, cried 'O Jesus, Jesus' after he had been disembowelled. In the eighteenth century Griffith described the preservation of the heads: 'I saw the heads when they were brought up to be boiled. The Hangman fetched them in a dirty dust basket, . . . put them in his kettle, and parboiled them with Bay-Salt and Cummin-Seed—that to keep them from putrefaction, and this to keep off the fowls from seizing on them.' The sentence remained unaltered till 1814, when the part that related to disembowelling was altered to death by hanging— but drawing, beheading and quartering remained on the statute book till 1870.

Those who refused to plead could not be tried and in cases of treason some remained mute, either because they feared the penalty or because their estates would be forfeit, leaving their families destitute. These suffered the *peine forte et dure*. Weights were placed on their body until they consented to stand trial, or died:

> The prisoner shall be remanded to the place from whence he came, and put in some low, dark room, and there laid on his back, without any manner of covering except a cloth round his middle: and one arm shall be drawn to one quarter of the room with a cord, and the other to another and his feet shall be used in the same manner, and as many weights shall be laid upon him as he can bear, and more.

In 1658 Major Strangeways, accused of having killed a man who wanted to marry his sister, was pressed to death. His friends hastened the end by jumping on the weights, but even so he did not die for ten minutes. The *peine forte et dure* was only abolished in 1827.

After considering these barbaric punishments, which the judges might not be able to mitigate, it is a relief to turn to the structure of justice. Here is the formal theatrical ritual, comfortingly familiar. But nothing could be more misleading than to assume that a seventeenth-century trial, because similar in its sequence of events, bore more than the most superficial resemblance to a twentieth-century action.

The great courts carried the same names: King's Bench, Common Pleas, Chancery. In the seventeenth century, though, the judges all sat in the same room, Westminster Hall, two hundred and fifty feet long and seventy feet wide. At the upper end was King's Bench, where the Attorney-General prosecuted in the great cases of treason, murder and felony. On the right hand of the entrance was Common Pleas, where civil cases were decided, and in the south-east corner was Chancery, presided over by the Lord Chancellor, the apex of the whole judicial system, the 'keeper of the King's conscience'.

All were at work simultaneously, their courts marked out by low partitions, and the open space between them was thronged with people: idle spectators or interested parties, 'humming' their disapproval or cheering a popular verdict; students from the Inns of Court, busily taking notes; pamphleteers, composing accounts, more or less inaccurate, in one of the newly constructed forms of shorthand; 'straw-men' waiting to destroy a man with their perjured evidence; solicitors, clerks and gaolers; men selling everything that might be wanted, from ink to food. All of them talking, jostling, clattering in and out. And over all, the stink of disease and unwashed bodies, so that the judges carried herbs to clear the air they breathed.

To control these courts successfully one had to combine the qualities and activities of leading actor, producer—and sergeant-major. There was no other way.

The judge had also another, to our eyes more sinister, role to play—that of a royal servant. In origin he was just as much the King's man as was the butler or the steward. One of the great constitutional debates of the seventeenth century concerned the position of the judges. Were they lions, guarding the common law, or were they, as Francis Bacon had maintained, '. . . lions, but lions under the throne, being circumspect that they do not check or oppose any points of sovereignty.' Bacon's was the conventional conservative view and though men were growing increasingly critical of it, Jeffreys and the vast majority of seventeenth-century judges adopted the traditional interpretation. They were by nature and training conservative, Jeffreys especially, but in any case they held their posts during the King's pleasure, able to be dismissed at any moment, servants in fact whatever they might be in theory.

Quite apart from his relationship to his royal master, the seventeenth-century judge was compelled by important differences in legal procedure to play what seems at first sight an improperly large part in many trials. In actions for treason and for felony the accused was not allowed counsel. He could himself cross-examine witnesses if he wished, and he might make a statement, but not on oath. In these circumstances the judge had to keep an eye on the prosecution, supervise the defence, and himself examine with the greatest severity any witnesses whom he suspected of committing perjury. It was his duty to excavate the facts and present his discoveries to the jury.

In political trials the pressures were naturally intensified—pressures from the judge; from the jury, firmly bent, according to their politics, on conviction or acquittal; from the crowd of spectators. In this last connection it is significant that the words *mob* and *sham* came into the language at this time. Sham (1677) is of unknown origin, perhaps it was connected with the Irish *Shamus*, since it was notorious that perjured witnesses were often from Ireland. Mob, recorded in 1688, was cant for the *mobile vulgus*, the excited crowd. When Titus Oates was tried for perjury in 1685 Jeffreys said to him 'We'll suffer none of your Commonwealth appeals to your Mobile'.

So much depended on the verdict: property, security, civil war or civil peace. Everyone concerned, judge and jury, counsel and mob, had prejudged the case. Whigs feared Papists, Tories feared Dissenters, as we fear subversive elements today. In a political trial the accused was on trial not only for the actions of which he was accused, but for his whole political philosophy; the tendency was to demand that the accused prove his innocence, and to accept too easily the proofs offered by the prosecution.

Even the record of these fierce political encounters is not free from party bias. The accounts were edited when they were first published—and in some cases re-edited later in a different direction. Collected in the *State Trials*, they provide the only evidence for many judicial activities, but they have been tampered with and are not necessarily reliable.

The universal acceptance of a brutal code of punishment; the anomalous position of the judge, part royal servant, part factfinder in chief; the constitutional cold war; the equation of religious dissent with political subversion—these are aspects of the seventeenth-century scene which the twentieth-century reader must keep constantly in mind when he considers the career of George Jeffreys.

In the early seventeenth century the Jeffreys family were

established as North Welsh landowning gentry of local importance in the marchlands of Cheshire and Shropshire. They claimed descent—a little problematically—from Tudor Trevor, Earl of Hereford, and *he* was said to be descended from the princes of Powys. But then every Welshman claimed royal ancestry. What is certain is that 'Judge' Jeffreys' grandfather, John Jeffreys I, was admitted a member of Lincoln's Inn in 1587, was later (1611) elected a Bencher, and became a judge on the North Wales circuit. He died in 1622 and by then held eight hundred acres, including Acton Park on the main road to Chester, now a suburb of Wrexham. The house stood until 1956.

Jeffreys' father, John Jeffreys II, was born in 1608. His wife, Margaret Ireland, was the daughter of Sir Thomas Ireland, of Beausay, near Warrington. Ireland was a well-to-do lawyer, a Sergeant-at-Law, and the editor of *Coke's Reports*. John and his wife Margaret settled down at Acton Park in 1631 and raised a family of seven children. John outlived most of his family, dying in 1691 and stoutly declaring shortly before his death 'that he had always studied the welfare and happiness of his children, and had never been guilty of an unkind or unjust act to any of them'.

John Jeffreys prospered, in a small-scale, provincial way. He inherited land at Eyton to the south of Wrexham, and bought more near Shrewsbury. When that town got a new charter in 1638 he became a member of the Council.

When the Civil War started in 1642, Shrewsbury became the royalist headquarters in the west, the recruiting centre for Wales, and for a time Prince Rupert's headquarters. It fell to the parliamentary forces in February 1645, when the war was almost at an end. It is probable that John Jeffreys helped to defend the town, and it is certain that his brother Edward fought on the royalist side with the rank of captain.

In the troubles many parish registers were destroyed and no record of George Jeffreys' christening now exists, but it is likely that he was born some time between October, 1644 and May, 1645. He was the fifth son of John and his wife Margaret. George, with his four brothers (John, Edward, Thomas and William) entered Shrewsbury Grammar School on 17th November, 1652. By that time Charles I had been executed and a republic had been in existence for three years. As a royalist Jeffreys' father presumably had to lie low for a time, but he had not, like many Cavaliers, been ruined. He seems to have been able to trim his sails a little to the new wind, for in 1654 he became a burgess of the town, and in the following year he was elected High Sheriff of Denbighshire. Perhaps his wife Margaret, 'a very pious good woman', had a hand in the matter, for she was a friend of Philip Henry, a well-known Dissenting minister. Henry, at the request of his mother, examined George Jeffreys and 'commended his proficiency'.

In 1659, when he was about fourteen, Jeffreys left Shrewsbury and was sent to London, to study at Paul's School. (St. Paul's, but the Puritans had dropped the 'Saint'.) Jeffreys was at St. Paul's for two years. The High Master was Dr. Samuel Cromleholme who, as a junior master, had taught Samuel Pepys. In his diary the latter wrote of his former schoolmaster, 'Lord! to see how ridiculous a conceited pedagogue he is, though a learned man, he being so dogmatical in all he does and says.' He disapproved of 'Mr. Crumlum's' drinking habits and added that he felt sorry for his wife 'a pretty woman, never yet with child, and methinks looks as if her mouth watered now and then upon some of her boys.'

Cromwell had died the year before Jeffreys came up to London. For eighteen months he ruled England from his grave, but gradually the Commonwealth rule collapsed in disorder and in 1660 Parliament invited the late King's son, Charles II, to return from Holland, where he was living in exile. The new King, under whom Jeffreys was to make his name as a lawyer and a judge, was then thirty years old.

He is (wrote a contemporary) somewhat taller than the middle stature of Englishmen; so exactly formed that the most curious eye cannot find any error in his shape. His face is rather grave than severe, which is very much softened whensoever he speaks; his complexion is somewhat dark, but much enlightened by his eyes, which are quick and sparkling. Until he was near twenty years of age the figure of his face was very lovely, but he since grown leaner; and now the majesty of his countenance supplies the lines of beauty. His hair, which he hath in great plenty is of a shining black, not frizzled, but so naturally curling into great rings that it is a very comely ornament. His motions are so easy and graceful that they do very much recommend his person when he either walks, dances, plays at pall mall, at tennis, or rides the great horse, which are his usual exercises. To the gracefulness of his deportment may be joined his easiness of access, his patience in attention, and the gentleness both in the tune and style of his speech; so that those whom either the veneration for his dignity or the majesty of his presence have put into

an awful respect are reassured as soon as he enters into a conversation.
(Sir Samuel Tuke, *A character of Charles II.*)

In 1661 Jeffreys was transferred to Westminster. The school was
royalist, as was the headmaster, the great Dr. Richard Busby, who
yet begged that he might not have to uncover in the King's
presence for fear of destroying his pupils' awe of him. (Dr. Busby
need not have worried. It was said that his old pupils still used to
turn pale when they passed his marble monument in Westminster
Abbey.) He was a great scholar as well as a great disciplinarian,
able to read Euclid in Arabic and the Bible in the language of the
Red Indians of Massachusetts.

Jeffreys, like all seventeenth-century schoolboys, spent most of
his time on Greek and Latin. The textbooks at Westminster had
been written by Dr. Busby himself and years later Jeffreys still
remembered the Doctor's work. Commenting on a badly constructed indictment he quoted the rule that the relative must
always refer to the last antecedent, adding 'or else Dr. Busby (that
so long ruled in Westminster School) taught me quite wrong.'
And in 1687 Lord Chancellor Jeffreys at the height of his career
gave £12 'for the education of two poore schollers at the schoole
in Westminster.'

A close connection existed between Westminster and Trinity
College, Cambridge, and in March, 1662, Jeffreys entered
Trinity. He was up for a year (it was common practice for would-
be lawyers to spend only a year at the University before proceeding to the Inns of Court), and then, in the following May, he
was admitted a member of the Inner Temple. On both sides of his
family there were strong precedents for the adoption of a legal
career, and his cousin John Trevor—known to all as 'Squinting
Jack'—had recently become a barrister of the Inner Temple.

From 1663 to 1668 Jeffreys kept his terms and ate his dinners
and prepared his work. Life there was very like life in the
twentieth century at Oxford or Cambridge, the students dining
in Hall and living as a single community. There was one important difference, there were no written examinations. The students
were expected to attend discussions, read prescribed texts, abridge
former cases and make notes on current ones. They thronged
Westminster Hall where the great Courts sat, and some judges
would use a case for demonstration purposes in the way that a
modern surgeon uses an operation. Roger North, a contemporary
of Jeffreys and himself a lawyer, wrote:

I have known the Court of King's Bench sitting every day from eight to twelve and the Lord Chief Justice Hale managing affairs of law to all imaginable advantage to the students, and in that he took a pleasure or rather pride; he encouraged arguing when it was to the purpose and used to debate with counsel, so as the court might have been taken for an academy of sciences as well as a seat of justice.

North goes on to say that Hale's expositions were so popular with the students that even if one got there at six in the morning one could not be sure of getting a good place.

Very little is known of Jeffreys' years as a student. Later, when he had become famous, the legends grew up: that he was kept short of money by his family; that nevertheless he spent his time drinking and rioting; that he went to Kingston Assizes in 1666 disguised as a barrister and there spoke so brilliantly that the court broke into spontaneous applause. There is no evidence for any of these stories; for instance, his income seems to have been quite adequate—£40 per year from his grandmother and £10 from his father, figures that compare satisfactorily with Francis North's income of £60 a year.

The one hard fact during these years is that Jeffreys married, but once again the details are clouded by uncertainty. The story ran that he courted a rich heiress, using as go-between the girl's cousin, Sarah Neesham. It was arranged that the heiress should elope, but her father got wind of the affair, discovered letters, locked his daughter up, and dismissed Sarah. She went to a friend's house in Holborn and from there wrote to Jeffreys. He hurried round, found her in a state of collapse, proposed, was accepted, and at once married her. The story reads suspiciously like something out of a romance—Richardson might have used the plot. One must disregard unsubstantiated tales favourable to Jeffreys as firmly as one dismisses those unfavourable to him.

The indisputable facts are these. Jeffreys married Sarah Neesham. She was twenty-three years old, the daughter of the Reverend Thomas Neesham, rector of Stoke D'Abernon. Her father had died in 1661 and she brought Jeffreys a dowry of £300. They were married on 23rd May, 1667, at All Hallows, Barking, and set up house at Number 79 Coleman Street, close to the Guildhall. The marriage seems to have been a happy one. Sarah died in 1678 and Jeffreys married again, but when he himself was dying he asked that he might be buried 'as near as may be to my former wife'.

By the end of 1668 Jeffreys was a qualified barrister, and a father. In appearance he was below average height, slight in build, with dark hair and brown, heavy-lidded eyes. It was a face that perhaps betrayed his Welsh origins, and in temperament too he was very Celtic—sensitive, mercurial, quick to get into a passion, up one moment and down the next, an accurate mimic and fond of a good story.

Jeffreys took over for a large premium (£230) chambers in King's Bench Walk, the first floor on No. 3 South. As a newly qualified barrister he was not allowed for three years to accept any briefs for the three great courts that sat in Westminster Hall. Meanwhile he practised in the City courts: the Court of the Lord Mayor and Aldermen at Guildhall; the Recorder's Court at Old Bailey; and the Middlesex Justices' Court in Clerkenwell at Hicks' Hall. The cases in all these courts were largely of the type that would be known today as police court work.

To succeed in the jungle of Restoration London one needed influence, ruthlessness and ability—in that order. Jeffreys possessed the last two to a high degree. He had a strong voice and he used this together with his large dark eyes to great effect in cross-examination, for which he soon discovered that he had a knack. 'He was,' said a contemporary, 'of bold aspect and cared not for the countenance of any man.' Reputation came swiftly, aided by self-advertisement and by various little tricks of the trade. Roger North describes how Jeffreys used to meet attorneys for a drink in the coffee-houses and inns, having previously arranged with his clerk that the latter should, after a few minutes, hurry in with a message that he was wanted in his chambers. 'Let them stay a little,' Jeffreys would throw out in an off-hand manner, 'I will come presently.' The attorney would be suitably impressed. It was all very good for business.

It was essential, though, to have influential friends—and that was not easy for an unknown provincial from the far west. Nevertheless, before those first three years were up Jeffreys had acquired some useful contacts. His ability attracted attention, while his amusing conversation and easy *bonhomie* made him a good fellow, worth helping.

The greatest of Jeffreys' patrons at this time was the influential Sir Matthew Hale, Lord Chief Baron of the Exchequer. Hale was an upright Puritan—it was said that in thirty-six years he had never missed going to Church twice on Sundays—scrupulously

impartial, of penetrating judgement and with a unique fund of
legal knowledge; '. . . his manner of hearing patient, his directions pertinent, and his discourses copious and, though he
hesitated often, fluent . . . his stop for a word by the produce
always paid for the delay, and on some occasions he would utter
sentences heroic . . . he was allowed on all hands to be the most
profound lawyer of his time,' Roger North considered. Hale
gave Jeffreys much sound advice.

> The student [he wrote] must observe a method in his reading and
> study, for let him assure himself, though his memory be never so
> good, he shall never be able to carry on a distinct, serviceable
> memory of all, or the greatest part he reads, without helps of use or
> method; yea, what he hath read seven years since will, without the
> help of method or reiterated use, be as new to him as if he had scarce
> ever read it. A method, therefore, is necessary, but various, according
> to every man's fancy.

Whether or not he acted on Sir Matthew's words, Jeffreys certainly became well-known for his formidable memory. In return
for the old man's practical hints Jeffreys would, says Roger North

> by little accommodations administer to him in his own house after
> his own humour, as a small dinner, it may be a partridge or two upon
> a plate, and a pipe after, and in the meantime diverting him with
> satirical tales and reflections upon those who bore a name and
> figure about town.

Jeffreys also enjoyed the influential friendship of several of the
City magnificoes. The greatest of these was probably Sir Robert
Clayton, who had risen from scrivener's boy to merchant banker
and was now 'vastly rich'. Clayton was Sheriff in 1671 and later
was to be Lord Mayor of London (1679–80) and M.P. for the City.
   Then there was a group of London business-men called
Jeffreys. They were not directly related to George, but one may
suspect a certain clannish 'London Welsh' attitude in the coinci-
dence of names. One was Sir Robert Jeffreys, known to Pepys as
'a merry man', who became Lord Mayor in 1685. Another was
John Jeffreys. His two nephews John and Jeffrey Jeffreys were two
of the five executors of George Jeffreys' will. Their uncle was an
Alderman and one of the richest of the City merchants—when
he died in 1688 he left a fortune of £300,000, an immense sum
for those days. In the Great Fire of 1666 he lost £20,000 worth of
tobacco from his warehouses and his friends never let him forget
the fact, calling him 'the Great Smoker' for the rest of his life.

These men were all Tories, as was another of Jeffreys' contacts, Sir Thomas Bludworth. Sir Thomas was a Levant merchant, who also had interests in Africa and in the East India Company. Jeffreys later took his daughter as his second wife. Sir Thomas was an ineffectual fusspot. An anonymous analysis of 1672 hits the nail squarely on the head when it describes Sir Thomas as 'a zealous person in the King's concernments, willing, though it may be not very able, to do great things.' He had had the bad luck to be Lord Mayor at the time of the Great Fire and the occasion had found him out, for 'he, having been drinking overnight and loath to rise, said, when called between sleep and waking, he could piss it out.' When he discovered the true state of affairs he lost his head; Pepys, who thought him 'a silly man' saw him crying 'like a ranting woman, "Lord! what can I do? I am spent: people will not obey me. I have been pulling down houses, but the fire overtakes us faster than we can do it".'

With the help of these varied patrons, Jeffreys took his first step towards the heights. In 1671 the office of Common Serjeant of the City fell vacant and he was chosen to fill it. It was the second judicial post in the City and a plum for an ambitious young barrister still in his twenties. The Common Serjeant joined the Lord Mayor's retinue at meetings of the Council in Guildhall, sat on the bench in the City courts, and pronounced the judgements of the King's judges at the Old Bailey. It was not the end of a legal career in the courts since it was possible to combine the work of a judge in the City with that of an advocate at Westminster. In addition the office carried with it a comfortable house and garden in Aldermanbury, Cheapside, opposite St. Mary's Church.

Jeffreys held the post of Common Serjeant until 1678. During these years he was involved, in a minor capacity, in the trial of Lodowick Muggleton. The proceedings are of importance as a first example of the way in which later Whig historians blackened the reputation of Jeffreys.

Muggleton was a tailor, described as having high cheekbones, a low brow, a projecting chin, and long straight 'murky' hair. He was also the fanatic head of his own private sect, the Muggletonians. In 1650 he and his cousin, John Reeve, had become convinced that they were the two witnesses referred to in the eleventh chapter of Revelation:

I will give power unto my two witnesses, and they shall prophesy.
... And if any man will hurt them, fire proceedeth out of their
mouth, and devoureth their enemies: and if any man will hurt them,
he must in this manner be killed.

Rival prophets got short shrift from Muggleton. One, being
told 'that proud spirit of thine, which said it was God, must be
thy Devil', instantly recanted and retired into private life.
Another received only a note *We pass sentence upon you of eternal
damnation*—and was so alarmed that he fled immediately to
Holland. Clearly, Muggletonians did not believe in toleration.

In January, 1677, Muggleton was tried at the Old Bailey on a
charge of blasphemy. The trial itself did not directly concern
Jeffreys, being conducted by the judges of King's Bench, but
when Muggleton was found guilty it was his duty to pronounce
sentence.

More than a hundred and fifty years later Macaulay wrote as
follows:

He (Jeffreys) was hardly less facetious when he passed judgement on
poor Lodowick Muggleton, the drunken tailor who fancied himself
a prophet. 'Impudent rogue!' roared Jeffreys, 'thou shalt have an
easy, easy, easy punishment!' One part of this easy punishment was
the pillory, in which the wretched fanatic was almost killed with
brickbats.

Macaulay's general treatment of Jeffreys will be considered
later, but here two particular points should be noticed. First,
Jeffreys had not 'passed judgement', he had only announced the
judgement of his superiors. Secondly, there is no official account
of what Jeffreys actually said. Macaulay's description is taken from
Muggleton's own account of his trial which—given Muggleton's
character—could hardly be unbiased. Muggleton wrote that
Jeffreys was

a reprobate devil, and he shall be recorded here on earth to the end
of the world a damned devil. For that body of his, which now is his
heaven, which clothed itself in scarlet and sat in the judgment seat
against me, shall be in hell. And that lofty, bawling spirit of his shall
be his devil, the one shall be as fire, and the other as brimstone
burning together to all eternity. And he shall remember ... that he
gave judgement upon me ... and I am sure the God of heaven will
not deliver him from these eternal torments.

Clearly this is not a report of the trial, but a prophetic denunciation. It tells us nothing of Jeffreys' character, for the judges on

King's Bench were similarly castigated by Muggleton and he even called his own counsel 'a deceitful knave'. He outlived Jeffreys and spent his old age writing his autobiography in the style of Revelation. His followers, the Muggletonians, survived into the present century and still sang

I do believe in God alone,
Likewise in Reeve and Muggleton. . . .
None salvation-knowledge hath,
But those of Reeve and Muggleton.

City influence had given Jeffreys a good start in his career, but it could only take him one step higher on the legal ladder, to the office of Recorder. That would be the limit of City preferment and Jeffreys knew it. The Court of King Charles at Whitehall was the fountain of higher honours. Soon Jeffreys began to make influential friends there as he had once done in the City. Ambition advised it, his presence in the Westminster courts placed him close to Whitehall, and his own High Tory principles were more welcome at Court than in the Whig-dominated City.

If the Court could be of use to Jeffreys, he too could be of use to it. He was making a reputation for himself at Westminster Hall as a lawyer who could win cases by strong cross-examination. People commended his 'bold presence, fluent tongue, audible voice and good utterance', and he was 'courted to take fees, breviates (briefs) were thrust into his hands in the middle of cases by parties who perceived that things were going ill with them.' It was not only as a lawyer, though, that the Court became interested in Jeffreys. It was very valuable to know the exact state of opinion in the City and Jeffreys, from his point of vantage as Common Serjeant, was well placed to supply the information. By its very nature the evidence for this is scanty—a hint here, an obscure letter there—but it seems to represent the visible fraction of an iceberg of small services.

The anonymous report on the characters of the Aldermen and Common Council of the City in 1672 was probably based on information supplied by Jeffreys, for most of his friends got a good press. The Lord Mayor is described as 'a person almost void of understanding, but not of will. He is very weak in the one, but most perverse in the other. He employs abundance of time, but does no business', but Sir John Robinson, a friend of Jeffreys and a fellow Welshman 'hath been most industrious in the civil government of the City, watchful to prevent anything that might reflect any prejudice or dishonour upon the King's government, happy in dispatch of business to the great contentment of the people.'

Then there is a mysterious little letter to Sir Richard Browne, the Clerk of the Council, written by Jeffreys from the Inner Temple on 5th April, 1672.

SIR,—I have caused a diligent search to be made from the beginning of 1668 till this time, and you may be assured there is none; fear not; keep all things close, excuse haste and the rudeness of this address made by

Your most faithful servant,
GEORGE JEFFREYS

So Jeffreys began to move into Court circles and to find new patrons, some of them very potent indeed. There was Mr. William Chiffinch, the Secretary and Keeper of the King's Closet —and the King's confidential agent, a man who had made of closet intrigue an exact science. 'This Mr. Chiffinch was a true secretary as well as a page,' wrote Roger North, 'for he had a lodging at the backstairs which might have been properly termed the spy-office; where the King spoke with particular persons about intrigues of all kinds.' His method was to make his visitors drunk, with the aid of 'salutiferous drops', then he 'discovered men's characters which the King could never have obtained by any other means.' The repository of innumerable secrets, it has been said that Chiffinch's greatest service to Charles was that he did *not* write his memoirs.

Very different from this secret agent was the Breton Louise de Querouaille, the King's mistress—or one of them. The foundations of her fortune were a pretty face and an ability to burst into tears at the right time. She bore Charles a son, the future Duke of Richmond, and in 1673 was naturalized and created Duchess of Portsmouth. Sir Robert Browne had known her parents and he may have formed the link between the Duchess and Jeffreys, or the common factor may have been Sir William Scroggs, a later Lord Chief Justice. Whatever the means, common gossip was in no doubt as to the consequences. A lampoon anatomized Louise de Querouaille as

Monmouth's tamer, *Jeff's advance*,
Foe to England, spy of France,
False and foolish, proud and bold,
Ugly, as you see, and old.

In the same year in which Louise became a Duchess, Charles appointed a Yorkshireman, Sir Thomas Osborne, to the post of Lord High Treasurer, by which he became in effect chief minister. As Earl of Danby, Osborne ruled England for Charles until 1678 and for a time was able to control Parliament; he 'neglected the great men, who he thought raised their price too high; and reckoned that he could gain ten ordinary men, cheaper than one of those' wrote a contemporary. In his reckoning Jeffreys could provide valuable information.

In 1676 Jeffreys had clear proof that the Court would do more for him than the City could. The office of Recorder fell vacant. It was given, not to Jeffreys, but to William Dolben, 'an arrant peevish old snarler', a nonentity whose claims lay in the fact that he was the son of the Archbishop of York and had powerful friends at Court.

Jeffreys learnt his lesson. He made himself useful to Danby. The following letter concerning parliamentary feeling towards the chief minister was written in February, 1677:

MY MOST HONOURED LORD—I did design an earlier trouble to your Lordship rather than be thought unmindful of returning my dutiful acknowledgement of the many favours you were pleased to confer upon me: but there fell nothing within the narrow compass of my intelligence worthy of your consideration, or wherein I could imagine you were much concerned. Nor do I at present find any such momentous design against your Lordship as should need affect the meanest of your thoughts. I only beg favour to acquaint you with, what I doubt not but you have already been advertised of, that to-morrow there are some few (for I cannot understand, though I have been inquisitive, that there are many concerned in it) that design to try some reflections on your management of the Excise (a month later Danby obtained from the Commons a renewal of the additional Excise) and have been inquisitive in that affair in order thereunto; . . . I cannot perceive that you are materially aimed at . . . I beg leave to assure your Lordship that I will with all zeal and industry embrace all opportunities wherein I may manifest myself to be a loyal subject to my King.

My Lord, Your Lordship's most grateful, faithful
and obedient servant,
GEORGE JEFFREYS.

It would be wrong to see Jeffreys as a Faustian figure, selling his soul to the Mephistophelian king in exchange for the power and the glory of this world. He and Danby saw eye to eye on these

matters, loving the Church and loathing Dissent, seeing in the
union of Crown and Church the only sure foundation of strong
conservative government. To attack the Church was to aim at
the destruction of the State, and *vice versa*. The analysis was correct to the extent that in the seventeenth century religious dissent
normally went hand in hand with political extremism.

For his services George Jeffreys was knighted at Whitehall in
September, 1677, becoming at the same period a K.C., and being
elected a Bencher of the Inner Temple in the following January.
The tide was beginning to run strongly in his favour—but the
City scribblers were not impressed. They wrote

> George from the Courts has knighthood got
> Bestowed upon him for his bawling,
> A royal mark for caterwauling.

There was more to come. In August, 1678, Jeffreys entertained
the King and the Duchess of Portsmouth at his new house of
Temple Bulstrode in Buckinghamshire. The royal party drove
over from Windsor and the lawyer from the provinces sat at
dinner with his king, who drank to him 'full seven times'. (Each
toast would have to be returned, but Jeffreys was well able to cope
with that side of the entertainment.)

The news of the King's visit set legal circles in London buzzing
with gossip, it was even suggested that Jeffreys was to become
Lord Chancellor of Ireland. In fact the King made it possible for
Jeffreys to be the next Recorder of the City. He retired Mr.
Justice Twisden of King's Bench with a pension of £500, and
promoted William Dolben to the vacancy. Next the Court of
Aldermen received a letter recommending Sir George Jeffreys as
the new Recorder, and in October he was duly elected 'freely,
unanimously, and by scrutiny'. The City, of course, were not
sorry to have someone, whom they still regarded as their man, in
royal favour.

As Recorder Jeffreys held the chief judicial post in the City. It
was his duty to pass sentence on prisoners convicted at the Old
Bailey sessions, and to act as spokesman for the City Council on
official occasions. He was well able to carry out these duties, his
strong voice and even stronger assurance made them a positive
source of pleasure to him. In his capacity as spokesman Jeffreys
frequently referred to himself as the 'Mouth of the City' and
when the differences between the Tory Recorder and the Whig

Council became more obvious, his opponents seized on this with delight and nicknamed him 'Mouth'.

One of Jeffreys' first duties was to attend the Christmas Sessions at Old Bailey in December, 1678. The Lord Chief Justice, Sir William Scroggs, presided over the trials of about thirty prisoners. At that time it was the custom for those found guilty to be brought back at the end of the Sessions and sentenced in groups, when they would be reminded of the enormity of their crimes and urged to repent. This was the Recorder's duty, and the Sessions Papers contain reports taken down in shorthand, and possibly improved a little during transcription, of the addresses delivered by Jeffreys on this occasion.

Six people were condemned to death: their crimes included murder, clipping the coinage, and the ravishing of a child of eight. The murderer was a bailiff; he had killed a man who had tried to prevent him carrying out his duties. To him Jeffreys spoke as follows:

> One of you stands convicted of that most horrid crime, murder, blood which cries out to Almighty God for vengeance, murder, I cannot but say without any provocation, which is not only an offence against the law of God, but even against nature, for one man to destroy another without provocation. If there were no such thing as a God in heaven or justice upon earth, Nature itself teacheth a man not to be barbarous to his own likeness. Therefore it will become thee to use all the tears thou canst shed to wash away the blood thou hast spilt, and that will not be enough to take off thy guilt, for nothing but the precious blood of our dear and blessed Lord and Saviour, the Lord Jesus Christ, can save a man that is guilty of so great and horrible a wickedness as shedding innocent blood.

The second group consisted of ten people, three men and seven women, convicted of various forms of petty larceny—crimes which did not carry the death penalty. Here is the second occasion on which one can compare the record with the use that Macaulay made of it. Jeffreys' recorded words were

> You, the prisoners at the bar! I have observed in the time that I have attended here, that you, pickpockets and shoplifters, and you other artists which I am not so well acquainted with, which fill up this place, throng it most with women, and generally such as she there, Mary Hipkins, with whom no admonitions will prevail. They are such whose happiness is placed in being thought able to teach others to be cunning in their wickedness, and their pride is to be thought

more sly than the rest; a parcel of sluts who make it their continual study to know how far they may steal and yet save their necks from the halter, and are so perfect in that as if they had never been doing anything else. But take notice, you that will take no warning, I pass my word for it, if ever I catch you here again I will take care you shall not easily escape. And the rest of these women that have the impudence to smoke tobacco and guzzle in alehouses, pretend to buy hoods and scarves only to have an opportunity to steal them, turning thieves to maintain your luxury and pride; so far shall you be from any hope of mercy if we find you here in the future that you shall be sure to have the very rigour of the law inflicted on you. And I charge him that puts the sentence into execution to do it effectually, and particularly to take care of Mrs. Hipkins, scourge her soundly; and the other women that used to steal gold rings in a country dress; and, since they have a mind to it this cold weather, let them be well heated.

Your sentence is that you be taken to the place from whence you came, and from thence be dragged tied to a cart's tail through the streets, your bodies being stripped from the girdle upwards, and be whipt till your bodies bleed.

This was the normal sentence, customary in the seventeenth century, though intolerable in the twentieth. Now consider how Macaulay rewrote the affair:

There was a fiendish exultation in the way in which he Jeffreys pronounced sentence on offenders. . . . Thus, when he had the opportunity of ordering an unlucky adventuress to be whipped at the cart's tail, "Hangman," he would exclaim, "I charge you to pay particular attention to this lady! Scourge her soundly, man. Scourge her till the blood runs down! It is Christmas, a cold time for Madam to strip in! See that you warm her shoulders thoroughly!"

It was by such passages that the Whig myth of 'bloody' Jeffreys was perpetuated.

Three lesser offenders remained to be dealt with. Momford, a soldier, had got drunk, boasted that he was a Catholic, and declared that he hoped to see all Protestants burned or drowned. This was careless talk with a vengeance; '. . . you must not think drunk or sober to revile the Protestant religion and go unpunished for it . . . You are an excellent man no doubt at a faggot,' commented Jeffreys. Momford was fined £100 and committed to Newgate till payment was made.

The last two prisoners were two brothers, Thomas and John Johnson, found guilty of stealing lead from the roof of Stepney

Church. They were lucky to have been caught before they had
taken off five shillings' worth, for in that case they would have
been hanged. Jeffreys was able to end the Sessions on a light note:

> You are brethren in iniquity, Simeon and Levi. I find you are not
> Churchmen the right way. But you are mightily beholden to the
> Constable; if he had given you but half an hour longer, you had been
> in a fair way to be hanged. Your zeal for religion is so great as to
> carry you to the top of the Church. If this be your way of going to
> Church, it is fit you should be taken notice of ... good men meet
> there to pray against such offences, not to commit them as you did.

The brothers were fined £20 each and bound over.

These Sessions are well documented, they provide a valuable
check on the methods of Jeffreys' Whig denigrators and they are
a random sample of one type of work that was to engage Jeffreys'
energies during the next eighteen months. Another branch of his
activities was his work as an advocate. An amusing case occurred
soon after his election as Recorder. Jeffreys was retained by the
Stationers' Company in an action against a group of people who
had infringed the Company's monopoly by printing a Psalter,
which they had had the impudence to call 'the King's Psalter'. The
case came before the Privy Council, where King Charles himself
was presiding. Jeffreys seized his opportunity and glanced,
wittily and obliquely, at the King's reputation as a manufacturer
of illegitimate children. The infringers of copyright, he said, 'have
teemed with a spurious brat, which being clandestinely mid-
wived into the world, the better to cover the imposture they lay
it at your Majesty's door.' Charles appeared delighted with the
metaphor murmuring, 'This is a bold fellow, I'll warrant him.'

Jeffreys was becoming a man of wealth, a man of property. As
early as 1676 he had bought Temple Bulstrode, a well-timbered
estate of 800 acres in Buckinghamshire, within striking distance of
London. Soon he added to it the neighbouring manor of Fulmer,
and spent considerable sums on the repair of Temple Bulstrode
itself. An eighteenth-century engraving shows it as a country
house of medium size—there are fourteen windows on the ground
floor—with a pleasant classical exterior. After Jeffreys' death the
house passed to his son-in-law, Charles Dive, who sold it in 1706
to the first Earl of Portland, William Bentinck, who had come
over with William of Orange. A century later the property

James II, 1685-8

Charles II, 1660-85

The Conspirators Signeing ỹ
Resolve for killing the King.

Father Conyers Preaching agᵗ
ỹ Oathes of Alejance & Supremacy

Dʳ Oates receiues letters from
ỹ Fathers to carry beyond Sea

Dʳ Oates discouereth ỹ Plot
to ỹ King and Councell.

The Popish Plot, 1678–9. Contemporary propaganda in the form of packs of cards: on the King of Hearts Oates is shown describing the Plot to Charles II

passed to the Duke of Somerset. The house was pulled down and rebuilt in 1862, and now the park is built over.

Jeffreys' wife Sarah did not share her husband's prosperity for long. She died on 14th February, 1678, at their town house in Aldermanbury and was buried four days later in the Wren-built church of St. Mary the Virgin, Aldermanbury. She had borne Jeffreys six children, four boys and two girls, of whom the eldest boy, John, and the two girls, Sarah and Margaret, survived. Although Jeffreys married again, his first wife held his heart and eventually he was buried, as he wished, beside her.

During these years, Jeffreys was launching out in many directions. Papers discovered in a Buckinghamshire outhouse over two hundred and fifty years later proved to be part of his private accounts. They show him entertaining in the grand manner, and yet at the same time carefully investing part of his earnings each year. As early as 1669, when he had only been a barrister for twelve months, he was able to buy a sixth share in the *Dextra*, a London vessel probably engaged in trade with the West Indies. In the following year he bought property at Sydalch, Denbighshire, making a part payment of £100 to G. Gwillim on 22nd June, 1670, and a further payment of £240 in the following September.

Jeffreys spent considerable sums on his houses at Bulstrode and Fulmer, and on his official residence in Aldermanbury. Bills in 1676 for repairs to Temple Bulstrode and the 'Letel house at Jarats Cras' (Gerrard's Cross) include such items as £45 spent on bricks, '67 foot of Dutch tyles', and '3000 Lath nayles'. His house in Aldermanbury and his sets of chambers (he had acquired a second set, opposite his first, in 1679) were repaired yearly. He must over the years have laid out in all a sum approaching £10,000.

Jeffreys was also spending money on books and paintings. There is a record of several pictures commissioned from the foreign artist Michael Fortin, and of a drawing of Chief Justice Scroggs. His own portrait as Recorder, painted when he was thirty and now in the National Portrait Gallery, probably hung in his official residence in Aldermanbury.

Part of Jeffreys' account with his bookseller John Starkey, 'at the sign of the Mitre' in Fleet Street, has survived for the period August, 1677–August, 1679. It totals £13 19s. od. and records the purchase of an eclectic selection of books—legal works, novels, plays, historical and theological volumes. On legal matters he bought Dalton's *Country Justice, Coke of Littleton*, the *Statutes of Ireland*, Hackworth on *The Liberty of the Subject* and on *Parliaments,* and the newly passed *Habeas Corpus Act*. Historical and religious books included Rushworth's *Historical Collections*, Burnet's *History of the Reformation*, Spratt's *Sermons* and Barrow's *State of the Greek Church*. Most interesting, perhaps, for the light they throw on Jeffreys' private tastes are the novels and plays: amongst the former were a French novel, *Pharamond*, and *Don Quixote*, while the latter consisted of the collected works of Beaumont and Fletcher, works by Dryden and Ben Jonson '7 New Plays' and the collected plays of Shakespeare, this last costing £2. (In Lady Ivy's Case—see p. 108—Jeffreys referred to *Henry IV, Part I*; Act V, Sc. iv., saying to counsel: 'Ask him what questions you will, but if he would swear as long as Sir John Falstaff fought I would never believe a word he says.')

In 1679 Jeffreys is recorded as buying 'one Persian Coate', 'one ffrocke ditto', several dimity vests and one flowered silk gown—in preparation for his second marriage?

For, eighteen months after the death of Sarah, Jeffreys married again, on 10th June, 1679. His wife, Lady Ann Jones, was the young widow of a Welsh knight, and the daughter of Jeffreys' City friend Sir Thomas Bludworth. A letter from Sir Thomas written shortly before the wedding illustrates, with its muddled thinking and arch postscript, the character of Jeffreys' father-in-law.

Thorncroft
6 May 79

SIR,

Your messenger brought me a real cordial at a time I needed it, having had trouble added to my indisposition. To think of the dull and unmannerliness of my servants to see to such weather and not provide a coach for you, which I and my wife called for, though it was too late and past redemption which we count all to be a crime; but we hope you, being so well versed in pardon and we in succeeding to mention, you will add this to the rest that you allow.

The repetition of the reality and sincerity of your affection to your mistress is to me, and I do believe to all her relations, without any the least cloud or question, and hath my hearty prayers that it may have a happy and hearty return whereof I see not to the contrary, God giving his blessing which I shall never cease to implore, my interest therein being so great. The great mutations that are like to be and disputes are matters of weighty consideration to sober minds; God order all for the best, though my fear is we see not the worst of things or times.

If my health doth compel me to stay my company and keep your mistress from you till Monday (as I believe it must), I pray put it upon my score who will promise to redeem it for time to come to your better advantage and satisfaction; and if in the meantime your joys be not so full as people give you, make it up with thinking that the time will come.

And if to this favour and trouble you will add the relation of what passes and to send it to my house, to be sent to me on Saturday, though it be any time before 9 o'clock at night, it will get a conveyance to me Sunday morning and quicken my devotion to the Almighty for public peace, and to you and your temporal and eternal joys and peace.

Sir,
Your most affectionate friend and servant,
THO. BLUDWORTH.

My wife desires her respects may be joined to mine, but for the rest of my company I leave them to themselves being of age.

The marriage was not a great success. Ann had a bad reputation as a 'brisk young widow'. City gossip fathered their first child on his cousin 'squinting Jack Trevor, than whom no man ever had a worse squint'. From the date of birth it is quite possible that the child was Jeffreys', but the rumour indicates his wife's reputation.

She was also said to be a shrew. The City skit *A Westminster Wedding, or the Town Mouth: alias the Recorder of London and his Lady* neatly linked the two accusations in one verse:

> 'Tis said when George did dragon slay,
> He saved a maid from cruel fray:
> But this Sir George, whom knaves do brag on,
> Missed of the maid and caught the dragon.

A nice story, unfortunately probably apocryphal, recounts that Jeffreys, cross-examining a woman, snapped: 'Madam, you are very quick in your answers!' The witness flashed back: 'As quick as I am, Sir George, I was not so quick as your lady.'

Whatever the truth of the matter, Lady Ann Jeffreys does not seem to have played a large part in her husband's life, and when he fell from power she made no effort to help him. She bore him seven children, three sons and four daughters, of whom two, Mary and Christian, survived infancy.

2

The Salamanca Doctor
and the Little Limping Peer
(1678-9)

While Jeffreys was thus establishing himself, apparently securely, in society, the first act was taking place in the final struggle for power between King and Parliament.

The honeymoon period between the restored Charles II and his 'Cavalier' Parliament had come to an end at about the time that Jeffreys was appointed Common Serjeant of the City. Since then the various elements on either side had begun to cluster and cohere, at least for the time being, into two groups, the Tories and the Whigs.

Those who were soon to be called Whigs included at least half a dozen different interests. There were the old Presbyterians who had destroyed Charles I and had then been cheated of the fruits of victory, first by Cromwell and then by the Restoration of Charles II. There were the more radical men, superannuated republicans and aristocratic political theorists, the 'old Oliverians' who still hoped for the end of all monarchy and the triumph of the 'Good Old Cause'. They were strong in London, Bristol and the textile towns of the West Country. There were also adventurers who, looking for room at the top, clustered round the Duke of Monmouth, Charles II's illegitimate son, and took their tone from Sir Thomas Armstrong, the dissolute swashbuckler who was Monmouth's wicked angel. Most important of all the groups, because they were the largest and the most moderate, were those who termed themselves the 'Country opposition'. They were united by the politics of resentment—resentment at Court corruption, at their own poverty, most of all at exclusion from power. Two classes of men made up the party, country gentlemen who had been disappointed of office in 1660, like the former royalist

George Speke, and the City merchants, conscious of their economic power and determined to hold political power also—determined to feel that control of the country's wealth and of the government's prerogative of taxation were both securely in their hands.

Clearly there was no lack of discontented elements. What was required was a man with the influence and ability to weld them into a unit, as 'King' Pym had welded the opposition to Charles I forty years earlier. Such a man was in fact already at work.

Anthony Ashley Cooper, Earl of Shaftesbury, had had a checkered political career. During the Civil War he had served on both sides; after the victory of Parliament he had married into the parliamentary establishment; then at the Restoration he had supported the King and had been created Lord Ashley. He had been a member of the Cabal, the inner ring of Charles II's government, and in 1672 had been made an earl and Lord Chancellor. Within two years it had become clear that the 'little limping peer' would only serve the King if the King would serve Parliament, and he had been dismissed from all his offices.

Shaftesbury was a natural oligarch, consistent only in fighting to extend the privileges and freedoms of his own class and of its allies, the devotees of commercial imperialism. Although opposed for these reasons to royal despotism he was in no sense a democrat —in fact he wanted to reduce the electorate to one quarter of its existing size.

After his dismissal the 'great little lord' at once set to work to recreate the old Country party of the days before the Civil War, and once more men found themselves engaged in the dangerous business of choosing sides. Shaftesbury was a political genius and from 1678 to 1688 England danced to the tune he piped. He created a Whig party, he destroyed absolute monarchy, and in the process brought down James II and—among others—Chancellor Jeffreys, though Shaftesbury himself was dead before those ten years were half over.

How did he do it? By political organization and its concomitant, political corruption. In 1674 Shaftesbury moved from Exeter House in the Strand to Thanet House in Aldersgate Street in the City. From there he held the threads of his political net, while his campaign headquarters were at the Green Ribbon Club, in the King's Head Tavern, Temple Bar.

Shaftesbury's strength lay partly in this political machine and

partly in his own knowledge of England and of people's character. He was able to be all things to all men, for he himself was a
bundle of contradictions. Thus he was a free-thinker but drew
support from the Low Church and the Dissenters. He would
support the demands of the poor, though down in Dorset he was
himself an enclosing landlord with no regard for the rights of
those who were not strong enough to oppose him. He was the
patron of the political philosopher John Locke while at the same
time he was an able rabble-raiser and a libertine—'the greatest
whoremaster in England'.

Lord Peterborough thought him:

> ... as proud as Lucifer, and Ambitious beyond whatever entered
> into the designs of any Man; impatient of every Power but his own,
> of any Man's reputation; false to that degree, as he did not esteem
> any Promise, any Engagement, any Oath, of other use than to serve
> a purpose, and none of these of consequence to bind a Man further
> than it was his interest.

While Shaftesbury was constructing his political machine, the
King was involved in a war with France which made him depen-
dent on Parliament for supplies. A Court party must be created by
influence, by propaganda, by bribes, that would balance Shaftesbury's Country party. The management of the Commons was
the job of Jeffreys' patron, Danby:

> He was a positive and undertaking man: so he gave the king great
> ease, by assuring him all things would go according to his mind in
> the next session of parliament. And when his hopes failed him, he
> had always some excuse ready to put the miscarriage upon. And by
> this means he got into the highest degree of confidence with the
> king, and maintained it the longest of all that ever served him. . . .

This is the testimony of an enemy, Bishop Burnet, it is nevertheless clear that such a man would not be an equal match for the
great Shaftesbury. By 1675 the Country party had grown to such
a strength that Parliament was split neatly down the middle.
In that year a Commons committee rejected the financial requests
of the King by 172 votes to 165, figures that probably represent
Shaftesbury's maximum strength.

Then, in the summer of 1678, the European war came to an
end. Now Charles had troops that would no longer be needed
overseas, and he had the money which parliament had voted for
the continuation of the war. Burnet summed up the situation:

The party against the court gave all for lost. They believed that Lord Danby, who had so often brought his party to be very near the majority, would now lay matters so well as to be sure to carry the session. And many did so despair of being able to balance his numbers, that they resolved to come up no more, and reckoned that all opposition would be fruitless, and serve only to expose themselves to the fury of the court.

And then the Bishop innocently continues

But of a sudden an unlooked for accident changed all their measures.

The 'unlooked for accident' was the Popish Plot which ushered in ten years of bitter party warfare, powered by judicial attack and counter-attack.

In 1678 something was needed to hold the Country party together. Shaftesbury knew that there were 'two enchanting terms which at the first pronunciation could, like Circe's intoxicating cups, change men into beasts, namely *Popery* and *the French interest*'. These were subconscious emotions, appealing to irrational hopes and fears. Half England, remembering the Civil War, feared the levelling republicanism of militant Dissent, while the other half dreaded the establishment of a Catholic dictatorship on the model of contemporary France.

It was clear to Shaftesbury that a good plot was what was required, a spy scare based on the disclosure of foreign Catholic interests. Something could no doubt be arranged for, as David Ogg has observed, 'Plotting was one of the sparetime occupations of the seventeenth century, one of the undesirable things that have disappeared with washed faces and outdoor games.' London hummed with the murmur of informers, notably the Irish 'MacShams' ready to swear against either side—or both. Perjurers, the 'straw-men', paraded like street-walkers outside the law courts, their profession discreetly advertised by a wisp of straw stuck in their shoe-buckles.

As matters turned out, however, Shaftesbury was spared the labour of concocting a sham plot, for one fell ready to hand, and all he had to do was to direct the production. On Tuesday, 13th August 1678, Christopher Kirkby, an amateur chemist who was attached to Danby's household, stopped the King as he was ambling in St. James's Park that morning. What he had to say did not disturb Charles unduly, but he advised Kirkby to see the invaluable Chiffinch. Before long the Council found themselves examining an indictment of forty-three articles, drawn up by two informers, Israel Tonge and Titus Oates.

Tonge was a diffuse, eccentric man in his fifties, the rector of St. Michael's, Wood Street, an amateur educationist (he had written papers on how to teach children to write), an amateur botanist (he had examined the flow of sap in plants), an alchemist and a strong anti-Catholic.

Oates was a more powerful, and a much more sinister, figure. Twenty-seven years old, he had already acquired many dishonours. He had been expelled from school, 'spewed out' from Cambridge, convicted of perjury, dismissed from a chaplaincy in the Navy where 'If his Coat had not Pleaded for his Neck, he might have Stretch'd.' He was in genuine Anglican orders, and to these had added a bogus degree as a Doctor of Divinity at the university of Salamanca. More recently he had attended the Jesuit college at St. Omer, where he was known as 'a perpetual Makebate' (creator of strife). To these miscellaneous qualifications he added those of supreme self-confidence, boundless effrontery, a complexion variously described as 'purple' and 'rainbow-coloured', and—so it was said—the largest chin in England. As a result of this last, when his great mouth was opened in denunciation it appeared to be in the exact centre of his face '. . . and a Compass there would sweep his Nose, Forehead and Chin within the Perimeter.' In the days before he became notorious his appearance was otherwise unremarkable: 'his hair was cut off, close cropped to his Ears, and an old White Hat over his Head, and a short gray Coat over like a Houseman's Coat.'

The Salamanca Doctor had landed in England on 23rd June, 1678. By 6th September he and Tonge had manufactured their indictment, soon swollen to eighty-one articles to which was added a list of nearly 120 'conspirators'. The gist of all this paperwork was that Oates knew of a Popish Plot, organized by the Jesuits, the first object of which was to murder King Charles—two Jesuits, Grove and Pickering, were to try to shoot him with silver bullets, four 'Irish Ruffians' had been engaged to stab him, while if all else failed the Queen's physician, Sir George Wakeman, would arrange to poison her husband. The rest of the Plot was similarly lavish. The French and Spanish governments were providing money, forty thousand Irish were waiting the signal to rebel, English Protestants were to be massacred wholesale, and as a final touch Westminster was to be fired by 'Tensbury

Mustard-balls'. All this would clear the way for the King's brother, James Duke of York, to take the Crown. The Plot had been concocted at a Jesuit 'consult' held at the White Horse tavern in the Strand on 24th April, 1678, at which Oates had luckily been present.

Or so he said.

In fact Oates was not even in England on that day, as was later to be shown.

The Plot was a complete fabrication, but it gave form to the inchoate fears of half the nation and it was eagerly taken up by Shaftesbury. It was just what he needed and he gave it all the backing of his organization: 'I will not say who started the Game, but I am sure I had the full Hunting of it.' Of course, he was not taken in by Oates. Roger North, commenting that Shaftesbury 'was the Dry-Nurse, and . . . took Charge of leading the monstrous Birth, till it could crawl alone' added that when the Earl was asked how people could be brought to believe such nonsense, he replied 'the more Nonsensical the better; if we cannot bring them to swallow worse Nonsense than that, we shall never do any good with them.'

On 28th September Oates and Tonge made depositions on oath concerning the truth of their accusations before a London magistrate, Sir Edmund Berry Godfrey. By this time the names of the accused included twenty-four English Jesuits, nineteen foreign ditto, twelve Scottish ditto, ten Dominicans, nine Benedictines, three Carmelites, two Franciscans, four English laymen, four Irish ditto, and two archbishops. The Council did not know what to think. The Secretary, Henry Coventry, wrote

If he be a liar he is the greatest and adroitest I ever saw, and yet it is a stupendous thing to think what vast concerns are like to depend upon the evidence of one young man who hath twice changed his religion.

The King was quite sure that the Plot was false. He cross-examined Oates closely and repeatedly caught him out on matters of fact—as for instance when he asked Oates what kind of a man Don Juan (whom Oates claimed to have met) was. Oates answered that he was tall and dark, this being the popular picture of a Spaniard. Charles laughed, 'I know him very well. He is fat, short and fair.' Charles also told Bishop Burnet that he believed Shaftesbury was behind the whole business.

Others asked, pertinently, what Oates had been doing at the

Jesuit consult. Why had he pretended to be a convert in the first place? When this was put to him

> Titus turn'd his Cane in his Hand, Advanc'd the Head of it to the Tip of his Nose; Laid his Head upon one Shoulder; and then smiling opened his Mouth and said (with a Tone and Accent peculiar to himself) 'I have heard (says he) that the Jesuites are a Subtile sort of People. Are they so! (said I to my self) But I shall go near to be too Cunning for 'em; for Nothing (an't please ye) but a Diamond can cut a Diamond; and so I went among 'em!'

The doubters were convinced.

Evidence of the danger was needed. It was soon forthcoming. Ten days after he had taken the depositions of Oates and Tonge, Sir Edmund Berry Godfrey left his house on Saturday morning. He did not come back. On the following Thursday evening a baker and a farmer noticed a stick and a pair of gloves on Primrose Hill, Hampstead. They soon found the body of Godfrey, prone. His own sword had been driven through him with such force that it projected six inches on the further side. His hat, wig and money were there, but his cravat and pocket-book were missing. At the inquest the jury brought in a verdict of wilful murder.

For Oates and Shaftesbury the death conveniently provided evidence of the Plot. Clearly, they claimed, the Jesuits had struck to close Godfrey's mouth.

In fact the case was not so simple as it seemed at first sight. The inquest showed that Godfrey was dead *before* his sword was thrust through him. It appeared too, that he had not eaten for some time. There were marks on his neck which suggested that he had been strangled, and there were strange bruises on his body.

Who killed Sir Edmund Berry Godfrey? There is not space here to discuss all the possible answers to that question.[1] It is fairly clear that Godfrey had been strangled and that afterwards somebody had arranged for his body to be carried to Primrose Hill, spitted with his own sword, and left there. Two things are certain: that there was no conceivable way in which these actions could have helped the Plot, supposing one had existed; and that the murder occurred very conveniently from the point of view of Shaftesbury and Oates.

The City was seized with a spy mania. Propaganda poured out, often of a very esoteric nature. There was, for instance, an

[1] They are summarized in David Ogg's *England in the Reign of Charles II*, pp. 579–84.

advertisement for a wall sheet: *The Jesuits' manner of consecrating both the persons and weapons employed for the murdering of Kings and Princes; and Sir Edmund Berry Godfrey's made visible ... plain or painted, and with rollers, being a neat ornament for Gents' houses.* Old stock was reissued—*An Account of the Bloody Massacre in Ireland* had been printed in 1641, but now sold well to gullible apprentices, who took it for up-to-date. It was suggested—perhaps satirically—that Jesuits should be hunted down like wolves:

> ... let that wholesome statute be reviv'd,
> Which England heretofore from Wolves reliev'd:
> Tax every shire instead of them to bring
> Each year a certain tale of Jesuits in;
> And let their mangled quarters hang the Isle
> To scare all future Vermin from the Soil.
>
> (*John Oldham*)

Mr. Choqueux, a fireworks manufacturer, must naturally be planning to blow up Parliament. His premises were searched, and he was lucky to escape with a reprimand. (The fireworks had been in store since the festivities at the Restoration eighteen years earlier.)

Although Catholics formed probably not more than two per cent of the population, the hysteria affected high and low alike. The City Chamberlain lamented 'I do not know but, the next morning, we may all rise with our throats cut.' Lady Shaftesbury carried a pistol in her muff for her protection—and her husband took care that everybody should know it. At a lower social level Stephen College 'the Protestant joiner', did a roaring trade in 'Protestant flails', life-preservers with a little jointed arm which people might use against the unknown conspirators. North wrote, sarcastically, of these weapons:

> our Sparks ... intended to be Assailants upon fair Occasion; and had, for that End, recommended also to them a certain Pocket Weapon, which, for its Design and Efficacy, had the Honour to be called a Protestant Flail. It was for Street and Croud-Work, and the Engine, lurking perdue in a Coat Pocket might readily sally out to Execution; and so by clearing a great Hall, or Piazza, or so, carry an Election by a choice way of polling, called knocking down. The Handle resembled a Farrier's Blood-stick, and the Fall was joined to the End by a strong nervous Ligature, that, in its Swing, fell just short of the Hand, and was made of *Lignum Vitae*, or rather, as the Poet termed it, *Mortis*.

In due course more was to be heard of the Protestant joiner.

To the doubtful murder of Godfrey was now added a successful ednunciation. Oates' Plot had been a medley of Protestant fears, underworld rumours, and shrewd guesses, to which he had annexed a great deal of gossip and some semi-accurate information picked up while he was at St. Omer, including the fact that the Duchess of York's secretary, Edward Coleman, was in touch with the French court.

Coleman was a natural target. Burnet records that 'he went everywhere, even to the gaols among the criminals, to make proselytes' (to the Catholic church). He had deep-set, mournful eyes, and always wore a black peruke—an appearance that naturally suggested fasting and fanaticism. In reality he was a harmless, conceited man. His conceit proved his undoing. For years he had been corresponding with the French court, and keeping all the letters, for no very good reason. The gist of this correspondence was that, from the French point of view, the Duke of York was a better bet than King Charles and that therefore Louis XIV would be well-advised to keep the Duke supplied with money. Everyone was trying to get gold from Louis—King and Duke, Whigs and Tories—but Coleman's letters contained sentences which, taken out of their context, could be used to support Oates' accusations.

Coleman was arrested, his correspondence was discovered, and Oates was able to point to such passages as—'we have here a mighty work on our hands, no less than the conversion of three kingdoms, and by that perhaps the subduing of a pestilent heresy which has domineered over part of this northern world a long time.' *A mighty work*, clearly this referred to his Popish Plot, said Oates.

Parliament met on 21st October and, as Burnet says, 'It may easily be imagined in what temper they met.' The five Catholic lords denounced by Oates (Arundell, Belasyse, Powis, Peters and Stafford) were at once committed to the Tower, and a resolution was passed 'that there has been and still is a damnable and hellish plot, contrived and carried on by Popish recusants for the assassinating and murdering of the king, and for subverting and rooting out and destroying the Protestant religion.' The 13th November was declared by Parliament a solemn fast day, and the good work was completed with a bill disabling Papists from sitting in either house, from which James, the heir to the throne, was only excepted by a majority of two—a whisper of things to come.

The Plot was afloat. The Whig party was in the ascendant. The first steps had been taken that were to lead eventually to the revolution of 1688. The infernal machine that had been set in motion was to destroy James, the Duke of Monmouth, Shaftesbury and, among many others, Jeffreys himself. Oates survived—though by the narrowest of hairs breadths—and lived to play a large part in the creation of the myth of 'bloody Jeffreys'.

Titus Oates, having addressed the Commons on the first day of the session, had been allotted at their request a suite of rooms in Whitehall, an armed guard and a pension of £1,200 a year. On Sunday, 24th November, Oates accused the Queen of knowing of the Plot to poison Charles. The King stood by her: 'They think I have a mind to a new wife, but for all that I will not see an innocent woman abused,' he declared. Charles was prepared to go to any lengths to protect his wife and his brother, but for the rest the law must take its course, and Oates ruled all—'for behind that blood-stained and accusing finger lay the powers of Parliament, packed juries and frightened judges, and the howling mob'.[1] So wrote a twentieth-century historian, but contemporaries, once their delirium was passed, spoke in much the same terms:

> He was now in his trine Exaltation, his Plot in full force, Efficacy and Virtue . . . he had the Impudence to say to the House of Lords, in plain Terms, that if they would not help him to more Money, he must be forced to help himself. He put on an Episcopal Garb (except the Lawn Sleeves), Silk Gown and Cassock, great Hat, Sattin Hatband and Rose, long Scarf, and was called, or most blasphemously called himself, The Saviour of the Nation. Whoever he pointed at was taken up and committed, so that many People got out of his Way, as from a Blast, and glad they could prove their two last Years Conversation. The very Breath of him was pestilential, and, if it brought not Imprisonment, or Death, over such on whom it fell, it surely poisoned Reputation, and left good Protestants arrant Papists, and something worse than that, in Danger of being put in the Plot as Traitors.

On Tuesday, 26th November, as a curtain raiser, the first of Oates' victims, William Stayley, a Catholic goldsmith's son who had been found guilty of uttering threats against the King's life, was hanged. On the following morning the much more important

[1] Bryant, A., *King Charles II* (London, 1943); p. 268.

trial of the Queen's secretary took place. Coleman appeared before the Lord Chief Justice, Sir William Scroggs. The Crown was represented by the Attorney-General, Sir William ('Bull-faced') Jones—a man who believed so implicitly in the Plot that he had had his own cellar emptied of firewood lest the Papists should use it to burn the house—the Solicitor-General, Sir Francis Winnington, and Mr. Recorder Jeffreys. The latter played a small part in this, the first of the long series of political trials that was to dominate England for the remainder of his life. It was his duty to read the indictment and call the witnesses:

> May it please you, my lord, and you gentlemen of the jury, Mr. Edward Coleman, now the prisoner at the bar, stands indicted for high treason, and the indictment sets forth that the said Edward Coleman, endeavouring to subvert the Protestant religion and to change and alter the same, and likewise to stir up rebellion and sedition among the King's liege people and also to kill the King, did on the 29th of September in the twenty-seventh year of the reign of our Sovereign Lord the King, at the parish of St. Margaret's, Westminster, in this county, compose and write two several letters to one Monsieur La Chaise, that was then servant and confessor to the French King, and this was to procure the French King's aid and assistance to him and other traitors, to alter the religion practised and by law established here in England to the Romish superstition.

When Oates was called it fell to Jeffreys to request that he might give his evidence in his own way without interruption. This Scroggs allowed, warning Oates:

> You are to speak the truth and the whole truth; for there is no reason in the world that you should add any one thing that is false, I would not have a tittle added for any advantage or consequences that may fall, when a man's blood and life lieth at stake; let him be condemned by truth; you have taken oath, and you being a minister, know the great regard you ought to have of the sacredness of an oath, and that to take a man's life away by a false oath is murder, I need not teach you that.

Thus admonished, Titus Oates proceeded to perjure himself and destroy Coleman.

The evidence seemed conclusive. Scroggs summed up, making his own feelings quite clear. He referred to the general assumption that all Jesuits—and indeed all extreme Dissenters too—approved of regicide, adding piously 'I hope I shall never go to that heaven where men are made saints for killing kings.' It had been proved that Coleman was in touch with Jesuits, need one say more? The faggot and the dagger were their methods of conversion, he said, and concluded, with a side glance at Guy Fawkes—'our execution shall be as quick as their gunpowder, but more effectual.' The verdict was almost inevitable. Coleman was executed on 3rd December.

The Plot was now fairly launched. The Tory journalist, Roger L'Estrange, wrote sardonically:

> The populace, mellow as tinder to take fire on the least spark, ran amuck at Christianity itself and bore down everything that stood betwixt this and hell. There was never such a competition between Divine Providence on the one hand and the World, the Flesh and the Devil on the other for the preserving or destroying of a nation.

But to the vast majority Oates was 'the Saviour of the Nation'.

The witch hunt was on. For the first six months of 1679 the Plot trials continued in unbroken sequence. Oates lorded it through the corridors of power in Whitehall. Now he sported a coat-of-arms and traced his descent from John of Gaunt's family. Ordinary citizens, their apprehensions fanned by weekly sermons —'it is easier to chain up the damned spirits in hell than such blood-thirsty monsters'—grew hot at the rumours. Spanish galleons were bound for Milford Haven. Catholic armies had landed at Purbeck and the two forces would now combine to march on London. Not a word of truth in it. On Sunday, 12th January, a great dark-ness covered London for half an hour and Sir Edmund Berry Godfrey's ghost was seen to walk in the Queen's Chapel while Mass was being celebrated—but Roger North maintained the darkness was only a combination of fog and smoke, an early example of London smog.

The next batch of trials took place at the Old Bailey and Jeffreys, as Recorder, was this time on the bench. Five men were arraigned, but two were sent back to Newgate prison when the informer 'Discoverer' Bedloe decided, a little inexplicably, not to give evidence against them. Scroggs came from Westminster to conduct the trial of the other three: Ireland, a Jesuit; Pickering, a secular priest; and Grove, a Catholic gentleman.

Oates' story was that Pickering and Grove had attended the Jesuit consult and had been ordered to assassinate the King. He declared he had often seen them during the summer, skulking around in the bushes at St. James's Park, carrying screwed pistols (an awkward weapon for this sort of work, half-way in size between an ordinary pistol and a carbine), loaded with silver bullets which they had 'champed' so that, on the dum-dum principle, the jagged metal might cause incurable wounds.

Scroggs, ironically as future events were to show, declared the Plot scarcely believable

> ... it is almost impossible for any man either to make such a story or we to believe it when told. I know not whether they [the Papists] can frame such a one; I am sure no Protestant ever did, I believe, nor never would invent such a one to take away their lives.

Yet, on reflection, to Catholics anything was possible—

> We know their doctrines and practices too well to believe they will stick at anything that may effect those ends ... whatever they command is to be justified by their authority; if they give a dispensation to kill a king, that king is well killed. This is a religion that quite unhinges all piety, all morality, all conversation, and is to be abominated by all mankind.... They eat their God, they kill their King, and saint the murderer....

It is hardly surprising that the jury found all three men guilty and that Scroggs congratulated them on their verdict: 'You have done, gentlemen, like very good subjects, and very good Christians—that is to say, like very good Protestants. And now much good may their thirty thousand masses do them!'

As Lord Chief Justice from 1678 to 1681, Scroggs played the leading part in the Popish Plot trials. Like Jeffreys he has been blackened by the pamphleteers. They wrote, for instance, that he was '... the son of a one-eyed butcher near Smithfield Bars, and his mother a big fat woman with a red face like an ale-wife ...' when in fact his parents were perfectly respectable gentry from Oxfordshire! Other charges that he was debauched and drunk should therefore be taken with more than a pinch of salt—they were common form in the political warfare on both sides. North writes of Scroggs:

> He was a Man that lay too open; his Course of Life was scandalous, and his Discourses violent and intemperate. His talent was Wit; and he was Master of Sagacity and Boldness enough; for the setting off of which, his Person was large, and his Visage broad. He had a fluent expression, and many good Turns of Thought and Language. But he could not avoid Extremities; if he did ill, it was extremely so, and if well, in Extreme also.

TESTIS OVAT

TITUS OATES,
From a rare Print.

Oates in the pillory

195

80

Letter from Jeffreys to Sunderland, 5th September, 1685 (*see pages* 139–40)

That is probably the worst that can be safely believed of Scroggs—there are obvious parallels with the character of Jeffreys himself. As Recorder it was the latter's duty, as usual, to announce the sentence of the court. It has already been seen how Macaulay was able to colour Jeffreys' words. Lord Campbell in his *Lives of the Chancellors* (1857) provides another example of the manner in which the Jeffreys myth was perpetuated. Speaking of this trial, Campbell wrote:

> And then came from his delighted lips, the hurdle, the hanging, the cutting down alive, and other particulars too shocking to be repeated.

The contemporary punishment for treason is shocking, almost unbearably so:

> That you, the Prisoners at the Bar, be conveyed hence to the place from whence you came, and from thence that you be drawn to the place of Execution upon Hurdles, that there you be severally hanged by the Neck, that you be cut down alive, that your Privy Members be cut off, and your Bowels taken out and burnt in your view, that your Heads be severed from your Bodies, that your Bodies be divided into Quarters, and those Quarters be disposed at the King's pleasure: And the God of infinite Mercy be merciful to your Souls.

Those were the details that Lord Campbell was too mealy-mouthed to set down. But it was not Jeffreys' fault that he had to pronounce them. The sentence remained current until 1848, only a few years before Lord Campbell wrote. With regard to the phrase 'his delighted lips', one must note that Jeffreys spoke to the prisoners in much more moderate terms than those that Scroggs had used.

> God forgive you for what you have done! and I do heartily beg it, though you don't desire I should. Poor men, you may believe that your interest in the world to come is secured to you by your Masses, but do not well consider that vast eternity you must ere long enter into, and that great Tribunal you must appear before, where his (Pickering's) Masses will not signify so many groats to him, no not one farthing. And I must say it, for the sake of those silly people whom you have imposed upon with such fallacies, that the Masses can no more save thee from future damnation than they do from a present condemnation. . . . I once more assure you, all I have said is in perfect charity. I pray God forgive you for what you have done.

There followed the formal sentence of execution.

4

Next month three men, Green, Berry and Hill, were tried and convicted for the murder of Sir Edmund Berry Godfrey. The evidence was largely supplied by two professional informers who had thrown in their lot with Oates: Prance and Bedloe. The latter said with engaging ingenuousness: 'I have been a great rogue; but had I not been so I could not have known these things I am now about to tell you.'

In June a further batch of 'plotters' was tried: Whitehorne, provincial of the Jesuits in England; his colleagues, Fenwick, Harcourt, Turner and Gavan; and a Catholic barrister, Langhorne. The trial followed the now-established pattern and Jeffreys, as Recorder, again pronounced sentence. He spoke particularly of his professional colleague, Langhorne:

> There is one gentleman that stands at the bar, whom I am very sorry to see, with all my heart, in that condition, because of some acquaintance I had had with him heretofore; to see a man who hath understanding in the law, and who hath arrived at so great an eminency in that profession as that gentleman hath done, should remember that it is not only against the rules of all Christianity, but even against the rules of his profession, to attempt any injury against the person of the King.

The prisoners asked that their friends might be allowed to visit them. 'Yea,' agreed Jeffreys, 'it is fit that they should have the comfort of their friends and relatives; and God forbid but we should do all we can to make their passage as comfortable as may be. . . . You know you are under the public notice of the world; therefore you must use the liberty that is granted to you with that moderation and prudence that it is fit to use such a privilege with, for I shall not deny you any lawful favour.'

Langhorne asked that his clients might be allowed to see him. 'I would not deny Mr. Langhorne anything I could grant him. If it be any business that any person would have an account of, which you have been concerned in for them, they may be permitted to come to you.'

The gaoler, Captain Richardson, interposed to say that by the regulations nobody might speak to the prisoners unless he were present.

'Yea, my lord, I hope my wife and children may,' Langhorne objected.

'Yea, God forbid,' said Jeffreys, 'but he should have his wife and children with him.'

'Or any others that come about business.'

'Yes, with the caution I have given you.'

When one reads Jeffreys' words to Langhorne and his reasonable attitude to the prisoners' requests one cannot but be struck by the fact that these bear no relation to the 'delighted' judicial monster of Macaulay and Campbell. On the contrary Jeffreys seems to have gone out of his way to be reasonable—and this at a time when the Plot fever was at its height and when it was not merely unpopular but dangerous for a public figure to show himself unbiassed.

Now Shaftesbury and Oates flew higher, their ultimate objectives still being the King's Catholic brother, James, and the King's Catholic wife, Catherine of Braganza. As early as the previous November Oates had drawled in the tones that he affected 'Aye, Taitus Oates, accause Caatherine, Quean of England, of Haigh Traison.' He had accused the Queen's physician, Sir George Wakeman, of plotting to poison Charles. In the middle of July, 1679, Wakeman came up for trial together with two more priests, Marshall and Corker, and a layman, Rumley.

The trial opened at the Old Bailey in an even tenser atmosphere than usual. This was the critical one. If Wakeman were found guilty it would be difficult—probably impossible—to protect the Queen any longer. After the Queen it would be James's turn. The succession to the throne would be altered; the Whigs would have won. Before the Bench, headed as usual by Scroggs and including Mr. Recorder Jeffreys, Oates told his story.

From his account it would appear that everyone had been very careless. Wakeman had written to a fellow Catholic, Mr. Ashby, advising him to take a milk diet and a course of the waters at Bath —casually adding the interesting news that the Queen had just agreed to help to poison the King! A few days later, Oates continued, he had heard through an open door at Whitehall the Queen saying 'that she would assist them in the propagation of the Catholic religion with her estate, and that she would not endure these violations of her bed any longer, and that she would assist Sir George Wakeman in the poisoning of the King.' Wakeman might be in court, but it was clear from this who was really on trial.

Wakeman cross-examined Oates. He recalled that the latter had failed to recognize him at a meeting of the Privy Council, saying he had never seen him before in his life. Oates replied he

had been tired that day and that the light had been in his eyes—
excuses he had used already at Coleman's trial. Wakeman pressed
his slight advantage, pointing out that the interviews Oates
claimed to have had with him were all said to have taken place in
the presence of men who had since been executed—and could not
therefore be called as witnesses.

At this point it suddenly became clear to Oates that there had
been a change in the judicial attitude. To his amazement, Scroggs
began to press Wakeman's questions.

'My lord,' said the bewildered Oates, 'I desire I may have leave
to retire, because I am not well.'

The request was refused.

After the other informers had been cross-examined by Scroggs,
Oates was recalled. He did what he could to change his evidence
to suit the changing wind, protesting, 'God forbid that I should
say anything against Sir George Wakeman, for I know nothing
sure against him.'

In spite of this *volte face* the Bench persisted: if Oates had seen
incriminating letters written by Sir George, why had he not
charged him with them when they met before the Privy Council?
By this time Oates had completely lost his self-assurance. All he
could say was that he had been too tired to do so.

'What!' roared Scroggs. 'Must we be abused with we know
not what? It did not require such a deal of strength to say, "I saw
a letter under Sir George's hand."'

Oates twisted again. Now that he came to think of it, he *had*
charged Sir George.

'Then why,' demanded Scroggs, 'was the prisoner allowed to
remain at liberty if you charged him?'

'To speak the truth, they were such a Council as would commit
nobody.'

It was a most dangerous remark and Jeffreys seized the opportunity, like the great cross-examiner he was, to underline it.

'That was not well said,' he pronounced slowly.

Wakeman dotted the '*i*'s. 'He reflects on the King and the
Council.' And Scroggs sharply added, 'You have taken a great
confidence, I know not by what authority, to say anything of
anybody.'

Oates said no more.

One of those accused with Sir George took heart and described
the Plot witnesses as 'villains in print, preferment tickles them,

rewards march before them, and ambition, which greedily follows, beckons them to lie, though God and conscience tell them they are unjust. . . .' This was a little too much for Scroggs, who launched into an attack on all Papists:

'If we look into the Gunpowder Treason, we know how honest you are in your oaths, and what truth there is in your words; to blow up King, Lords and Commons is with you a merciful act, a sign of a candid religion: but that is all a story with you; it is easier for you to believe that a saint, after her head is cut off, went three miles with her head in her hand and to the place where she would be buried, than that there was a Gunpowder Treason.' However, he summed up in the prisoners' favour, concluding, 'Let us not be so amazed and frightened with the noise of plots as to take away any man's life without reasonable evidence.'

The judges then retired for supper, leaving Mr. Recorder Jeffreys to take the jury's verdict. After about an hour they returned and asked him if they could bring in a verdict of 'concealment of treason'.

'No,' Jeffreys replied correctly, 'you must either convict them of treason or acquit them.'

'Then take a verdict,' replied the foreman. It was one of not guilty.

'Down on your knees!' cried Captain Richardson, the Newgate gaoler.

'God bless the King and this honourable bench,' the prisoners prayed.

And well they might. The acquittal of Sir George Wakeman marked the turning point in the Popish Plot. It was not the end of Oates, whose career continued to be entwined with that of Jeffreys, and Plot trials went on for a while, especially in the provinces. But the judges had withdrawn their support from the informers 'and now', as Bishop Burnet wrote, 'the witnesses saw they were blasted.' It was a victory for the Crown—and for the forces of reason and justice.

How had it been gained? Scroggs had been down to Windsor immediately before the trial and there he must have received from Charles more than a hint that the King would not tolerate an attack on his Queen. That, and Oates' own words, had done the trick.

Now half the nation saw that they had been deceived. Attacks on Oates commenced. A print was sold showing him as a monster,

Mamamouchee Musty, half Protestant doctor and half Turkish soldier:

> His Mouth's the Centre of Protesting face.
> Cravatt his Neck doth, yet unstretch'd, Environ,
> His Rascall Side is guarded with cold Iron.
> Here Cloak, there Coate, his equall Deference Show
> To Calvin Lack and Lack of Leyden too.
> Whilst one hand holds a Flail, the t'other Sword,
> It paints a Modern Holder-forth oth' word.
> Button'd Schismatic Cassock, Girded, notes
> An Odd Amphibious Animal like O ——
> Who for a Doctorship nere paid Ten Groates
> But length of Chin betrayes his Want of Sense
> Which makes him Ape and Irish Evidence.
> View him all ore: he's Quaker, Presbyter,
> Musulman, Jesuite, and for Him, not Her.

The other half of the nation continued to believe in the Plot. Scroggs was not popular with Shaftesbury's 'brisk boys' from Wapping. Half-dead cats were thrown into his carriage, and the apprentices chanted

> Our Juries and Judges to shame the Plot
> Have traitors freed to prove it not,
> But England shall stand when they go to pot,
>   Which nobody can deny.

The Whig grandees had nevertheless suffered a severe defeat. 'If Oates and Bedloe are not to be believed,' one of them lamented, 'our business is at an end.' He need not have despaired. There was another shot or two in Shaftesbury's locker.

3

Exclusion
(1679-81)

While these stirring events were taking place on the public stage, with Jeffreys playing his part in them, his private affairs continued to improve. His income has been estimated to have been at this time about £5,000 a year. In January, 1679, he was offered the post of Solicitor-General to James, Duke of York. This was not a government appointment, but an honorary private one, giving Jeffreys the position of legal adviser to James. It placed him a step nearer to the heart of power; if all went well, James would one day be King of England. Meanwhile the Duke, under attack from Shaftesbury and Oates, found it prudent to go abroad to Brussels and the Hague, leaving his affairs in the capable hands of his new Solicitor-General. In view of the political situation, there was danger in Jeffreys' acceptance of the appointment, but there was also the possibility of great advancement— and Jeffreys was always a bold man.

On Sunday, 26th January, 1679, about ten o'clock in the evening, fire broke out in Pump Court in the Temple. The wind took the fire up Middle Temple in the direction of Fleet Street. The Lord Mayor arrived, but the members of the Inn would not let him enter their private domain. The water in the pipes was frozen and, though buckets were passed from hand to hand, and the pumps fed with beer from nearby cellars, the fire threatened to engulf the Inns of Court, Fleet Street and the Strand. That it did not do so was largely due to the energetic action of Jeffreys and some other Benchers. They obtained gunpowder from a nearby grocer and blew up a group of buildings in Hare Court, making a fire-break which the fire could not cross.

Great crowds had collected and, by one of the ironies of history, they included the Duke of Monmouth, and also Lord Feversham, who was to command the royal army at the Battle of Sedgemoor.

Feversham was hit on the head by a falling beam and his skull had
to be trepanned. The Duke must have been standing a little further
off, for he was heard to remark jocularly that 'he never met with
people so willing to be blown up as these lawyers'!

When the Plot trials were still in full flood, Shaftesbury and the
Country Party carried the struggle against the Court into Parliament. Influenced by Oates' revelations, the 'Cavalier' parliament,
which Charles had kept for eighteen years, had attacked Danby in
December, 1678. To save his chief minister Charles had prorogued
the assembly and a month later had dissolved it, remarking genially that parliaments were like cats 'they ever grow cursed with age.'

In February, 1679, elections for a new parliament were held,
perhaps the first to be fought on party lines—or at least on a clear-
cut issue. Men used the names of Whig and Tory as party labels.
Originally the Tories were dispossessed Irish who descended from
their hiding-place in the hills to cut the throats of English settlers.
(The word is derived from the Irish for a 'pursuer'.) It was an obvious insult to hurl at the Court, at all Papists and crypto-Papists.
It is, in the nature of things, impossible to say who first popular-
ized the word, but Oates has a strong claim to the title. The informer, 'Discoverer' Bedloe, had asserted that he had letters from
Ireland 'that there were some Tories to be brought over' to England to murder him and Oates. Defoe wrote that Oates, with his
genius for propaganda, seized on the name:

> The Doctor, whose zeal was very hot, could never hear any man
> after this talk against the Plot, or against the Witnesses, but he
> thought he was one of these Tories, and call'd almost every Man a
> Tory that oppos'd him in Discourse; till at last, the Word Tory
> became Popular, and it stuck so close to the Party in all their Bloody
> Proceedings, that they own'd it, . . .

It did not take long for the Tories to find a suitable riposte. The
Whiggamores were Scottish Presbyterians, outlaws in the Southern Uplands of Scotland. Soon, as Burnet observed, 'All that
opposed the Court came in contempt to be called Whiggs.'

The new Parliament of Whigs and Tories met in March, 1679,
and at once it became clear that Danby could not rely on the support of more than thirty or forty members. In the following
month a bill of attainder was introduced against him. He surrendered his offices and was placed in the Tower where he remained,
safe but immobilized, for about five years.

The fall of Danby affected Jeffreys' position a little. His patroness, the Duchess of Portsmouth, made haste to transfer her interests from Danby to one of the rising stars, young Robert Spencer, Earl of Sunderland, and Jeffreys, as part of her property, was included in the new alliance. Sunderland was a Tory, and a sparkling one. Good-looking, rich, treacherous, his dress and his manners set the fashion at Court. His drawl, 'Whaat maaters who saarves his Majesty, so lang as his Maajesty is saarved' was famous—even Titus Oates modelled his accent on that of Sunderland.

The Whigs were triumphant. The Plot had enabled them to get control of the new Parliament, and that control had made it possible for them to break the King's chief minister. The next step must be against James, Duke of York, the man who would in the normal course of events succeed to the throne—for Charles had no legitimate children. (He had, it was true, an illegitimate son, the thirty-year old Duke of Monmouth, but for the moment few were inclined to look to him.)

The main objective of the Whigs was to exclude James from the succession. In this the Plot might play its part, but there was another line of attack. On 1st May, 1679, Richard Hampden (son of that John Hampden who had refused to pay Ship Money to Charles I) introduced the first Exclusion Bill in the Commons. By this the succession was to be regulated so that the Crown would pass as though James were dead to the next heir—his eldest daughter Mary, who was married to the Dutch ruler, William of Orange. In this way the Whig leaders would at one blow get rid of James the apostle of absolute monarchy and at the same time would ensure that the next ruler owed her position to them.

The Bill passed its second reading in the Commons by a majority of two to one. Charles acted promptly to save his brother. Parliament was immediately prorogued, and was dissolved in July, 1679, without having met again.

In the autumn Charles again tried to provide himself with an amenable parliament. The acquittal of Sir George Wakeman had broken the Plot, perhaps the country would now return a Tory majority. The hope was illusory; the Whig party machine was much too efficient. A contemporary pamphlet set out the Whig strategy in its sub-title: 'England's Great Interest in the Choice of this New Parliament; Rather take a Stranger if recommended by an unquestionable Hand, than a Neighbour ill affected to your interest. 'Tis not pleasing a Neighbour, because rich and powerful, but saving England that you are to eye.'

It was clear to the King that the new Parliament would be no more tractable than the old one had been, so it was immediately prorogued and did not meet until October, 1680, twelve months later. Meanwhile Charles replaced Danby by a group of young advisers—Lawrence Hyde (39 years old), Sidney Godolphin (35), and Jeffreys' new patron Sunderland (38). The Whigs, contemptuous of their youth, called the new men 'the Chits'.

The collapse of the Plot trials, the attempt to exclude James from the succession, the King's refusal to keep his new Parliament in session—these startling events all combined to sharpen political animosities to an extent reminiscent of the dangerous days just before the Civil War. It is against the background of these sharp and cutting antagonisms that the next stage in Jeffreys' career must be seen.

Hitherto he had been able to advance his own fortunes by working both for his patrons at Court and his masters in the City. He was attached to the Court, a legal adviser to the Duke of York, but he was also an official servant of the City of London, now predominantly Whig. In the new political climate it was no longer possible to serve two masters.

Jeffreys now took the most important decision of his life. The majority of Aldermen supported the new policy of Exclusion, but their Recorder became a Tory. What else could he have done? Oates had shown himself an unscrupulous perjurer; Whiggism was, at least potentially, treason. Religious dissent was tainted with republicanism. Shaftesbury had killed Catholics, soon the King would kill Whigs. In choosing the Tory side Jeffreys followed his real principles—or prejudices—for he was by inclination a natural High Tory Anglican.

Almost immediately Mr. Recorder had to show his colours. The autumn of 1679 was marked by a wave of petitions, begging Charles to summon the Parliament he had prorogued. From all parts of the country, but especially from London itself, they poured in to Whitehall, their signatures often illegible marks resembling, as one Courtier remarked, 'vermin in the bed of the Nile'. It was a put-up job, of course, and *Petitioners* soon became an alternative party label for the Whigs. The Clerk of the Council was quite clear about this.

> Observe [he wrote] how the plot begins to foment. There are printed here in one form a multitude of petitions, dispersed into the several counties and confided to certain gentlemen therein to go

from parish to parish and, not only to gather hands, but to set down those that refuse, that there good qualities may in convenient time be known.

Clearly this was a poll from which it was dangerous to be absent. In London itself tables and pens, ink and forms, were placed in the taverns and at the Royal Exchange and it was rumoured that the petition was finally a hundred yards long. The argument used was that Parliament alone could 'apprehend and understand the symptoms of all Diseases which could threaten the Body Politic. Without Parliament, Popery would be introduced and the people made slaves if not hanged at their doors; the French power was to do it.'

The Council summoned before them the Lord Mayor, Sir Robert Clayton, and the City Aldermen. Clayton protested that 'they knew of no course they might take by law to suppress this inconvenience.' Jeffreys, present as the City's Recorder, suggested that the King might easily act by Royal Proclamation to 'prohibit the framing and presenting any such Petitions, and command all Magistrates of the Peace to punish all persons acting contrary.' In the end his suggestion was adopted in a modified form, warning the public of the dangers of petitioning 'in a seditious and tumultuous manner', but not forbidding the practice altogether.

Jeffreys had crossed his Rubicon. He had supported the Court against the City in an unequivocal manner, and on a clear-cut issue. He would no doubt lose his position in the City, it therefore behoved him to strengthen his connections with the Court. Whitehall, for its part, was glad to use his talents.

Meanwhile the Whig political machine continued to function powerfully. The political temperature was kept at fever-heat. The campaign reached a climax on 17th November, the anniversary of Queen Elizabeth's accession. After dinner Shaftesbury and the Whig grandees appeared on the balcony of the White Horse Tavern and addressed the crowd. Then they smoked a pipe or two and tolerantly watched the procession they had organized as it passed below them.

First came 'Six whistlers to clear the way'. These were followed by:

A bell-man ringing and shouting, 'Remember Justice Godfrey'.

A dead body, representing Sir Edmund Berry Godfrey, in the habit he usually wore, the cravat wherewith he was murdered about his neck, with spots of blood on his wrists, shirt and white

gloves, riding on a white horse, one of his murderers behind him
to keep him from falling, representing the manner he was
carried from Somerset House to Primrose Hill.

A Jesuit giving pardons very freely to those who would murder
Protestants.

Six Jesuits with bloody daggers.

A consort of wind music called The Waits.

Four Popish bishops in purple and lawn sleeves.

The Pope's chief physician with Jesuit's powder (quinine) in one
hand and an urinal in the other.

Lastly, the Pope, preceded by silk banners with bloody daggers
painted on them for murdering heretical kings, and behind him
his counsellor the Devil.

Two hundred thousand people watched the procession, at the end
of which the Pope's effigy was duly burned beneath the statue of
Queen Elizabeth.

To live always at concert-pitch is tiring and perhaps the
Whigs kept up the tension too long. Moderate men like Halifax
longed for peace and quiet; 'I confess,' he wrote, 'I dream of the
country as men do of small beer when they are in a fever.' The
Court judged it might venture on a small counter-attack. Jeffreys
was employed to conduct the prosecution of two Whig pamphleteers, Harris and Smith.

Late in 1679 Benjamin Harris, a City printer, had published 'An
Appeal from the Country to the City for the Preservation of His
Majesty's Person, Liberty, Prosperity, and the Protestant Religion'. The loyal title concealed the usual Whig programme
(except that Monmouth was mentioned as a possible successor)
including a plea for Exclusion and a warning that if James came to
the throne those who had bought monastic lands would be ex-
propriated. 'Any who have estates in abbey lands, who desire to
beg their bread and relinquish their habitations and fortunes to
some old, greasy bald-pated abbot, monk, or friar, then let him
vote for a Popish successor.'

Jeffreys opened the case for the Crown before Scroggs at the
Guildhall in February, 1680. Everyone, he said, appeared to think
they could attack James. If Harris had been writing about an ordinary tradesman he would never have dared to write as he did, but
now, it seemed, anything might be written 'under the dissem-
blance of a pretence for the Protestant religion'. The defence did
not attempt to deny the authorship, but called witnesses to Harris's

character, to show that he was a quiet man. Jeffreys retorted that this was irrelevant: 'A bookseller that causes a factious book to be printed, or reprinted if it was printed before, is a factious fellow.' Scroggs agreed. The jury enquired if they might find Harris guilty only of *selling* the book. Scroggs answered that they must find a straight verdict of guilty or not guilty. Still the jury could not agree. Jeffreys suggested that in that case they might prefer to give their verdict individually. Appalled at this suggestion, they hastily found Harris guilty, and he was fined £500 and ordered to stand in the pillory for one hour.

Two days later the second pamphleteer, 'Elephant' Smith (so called from his sign of the Elephant and Castle), came up for trial. Smith had printed 'Observations upon the Late Trial of Sir George Wakeman &c.,' said to be written by 'Tom Ticklefoot, the Tabourer, late Clerk to Justice Clodpate.' 'Clodpate' was Scroggs and the pamphlet claimed that the Chief Justice had been persuaded by the King to acquit Wakeman for '. . . by all that is good it was my old master Clodpate's desire, peace be with him! always to sham up an evidence when anybody had been with him the morning before.'

When Jeffreys opened the case for the Crown he commented:

> I know that every word I utter is taken in short-hand to be commented on as persons' humours shall steer them; but I do think, as being the mouth of the City of London, it is my duty to speak thus much, that I hope, nay, I may dare confidently affirm, that the generality of the City of London, all good men and men of abilities, are for the King and Government as it is now established by law.

At this the spectators gave a loud 'hum'—the contemporary equivalent of hissing.

He went on to paint a lively picture of the Whig patrons of Harris's shop, where 'after they have blackened their mouths with tobacco and smoke' if they do not 'rail against the Church and Government, they are looked upon straight as not Protestants'. Jeffreys was in good form, and when a printer admitted that he had worked on the book at night, he picked up the point: 'Ay, it was a deed of darkness, and so fit for night work.' He considered the title of the book; '. . . persons begin to grow wonderful witty in the beginning of their books in hopes to ensnare people to read them and to prevail upon them so far to make them believe there is something extraordinary by the title.'

'Elephant' Smith was defended by Mr. William Williams, of

whom more will be heard later. He was forced to admit that the libel was 'sufficiently infamous', and that Smith was the author, but he pleaded that he was 'a languishing, sick and dying man'. 'I am,' said Jeffreys ironically, 'for a sinner's repentance with all my heart.' Smith suffered only a light fine: he was, of course, perfectly well, and it was not long before he and Jeffreys met again. Parliament showed their support very clearly by soon appointing Smith as their official printer.

Jeffreys was rapidly making clear his own allegiance. He had attacked the practice of petitioning, he had successfully prosecuted two Whig propagandists. Now, in April, 1680, he played a leading part in a counter-attack against the Petitioners. If the Whigs humbly petitioned the King that parliament might be called, why should not other citizens submit petitions humbly *abhorring* the notion that any pressure should be put upon the King in such a matter? And so, on 17th April, two petitions of this type were presented. The first 'Abhorrers', as they were soon called, were Jeffreys himself and Francis Wythens, a barrister and one of the two M.P.s for Westminster. The idea caught on. In the words of a contemporary, 'The train took and the frolic went all over England'. The strength of the Abhorrers was shown to be greater than the Whigs had suspected; the Exclusion campaign had suffered a set-back.

The Abhorrers naturally had their reward. Francis Wythens was knighted the very next day. And on 30th April Jeffreys was appointed Chief Justice of Chester.

Chester was a little realm in itself with its own High Court. The palatinate jurisdiction covered Jeffreys' home area—one in which the Petitioners had been very active. Perhaps the sight of a favourite son returning loaded with honour (and a salary of £500 a year) might teach the local gentry where their true interest lay.

On 12th May, Jeffreys, with ten others, was admitted to the rank of Sergeant-at-Law. The Sergeants wore a black patch on their wigs, had the sole right to practise in the Court of Common Pleas and were the men from amongst whom were drawn the judges of the common law courts (Common Pleas, Exchequer, and King's Bench), and the King's Sergeants, who acted as public prosecutors in State trials. The new men performed

the ceremony of walking in their coifs from Westminster to Gray's Inn (the Lord Chief Justice being of that Inn) with a great train of gentlemen of the long robe out of all the societies of law, and afterwards entertained the nobility and judges very splendidly at Sergeants' Inn Hall in Fleet Street.

It was the custom for the new Sergeants to give rings, inscribed with some appropriate sentiment, to the King and to certain officials. Jeffreys chose for his the phrase *A Deo rex, a rege lex.* 'From God the King, from the King the law'—it was, of course, a tactful compliment, but it was more than that. It summed up succinctly Jeffreys' political philosophy. Kings were kings by Divine Right, and the law was their instrument. This was generally accepted in Europe (notably in France), but in England the Civil War had made such a doctrine obsolescent. Fifty years earlier the Lord Chancellor, Francis Bacon had maintained that judges were lions—but lions 'under the King's throne'. To realize that Jeffreys still honestly held this view, is to understand his whole attitude towards the functions of a judge and the powers of a king.

Promotion had come quickly to the first Abhorrer, and there are some signs that it went to his head. Seventy years ago Irving, in the first impartial life of Jeffreys, made a shrewd analysis of his character:

> ... success was fraught with danger to a man of Jeffreys' temperament. He possessed one of those extreme dispositions that charm us in the artist but depress us in the Judge—a temperament passing in one moment from the height of self-satisfaction to the utmost depths of gloom and depression, over-confident in success, unduly prostrate in failure, intemperate, emotional. In the artist, emotion of this kind is translated into his work and lends it passion and intensity. But Jeffreys was a lawyer, not an artist, and, had he confined himself strictly to the exercise of his profession, might have learnt to subdue his dangerous tendencies towards an emotional expression of life. Unfortunately, he belonged to that class of lawyers who were politicians first and men of law afterwards, ambitious of power and preferment, using their legal career as a stepping stone to the great places in the State. The furious excitement of politics in Charles the Second's reign had much in common with the artistic temperament.... For that reason its effect on Jeffreys would be exciting in the extreme....[1]

Jeffreys had his full share of what is called—perhaps a little unfairly—the Celtic temperament. He was a man of strong emotions; when he was up, he was up; when he was down, he was down—and all the world might know it. His Welsh pulse raced

[1] Irving, H. B., *The Life of Judge Jeffreys*, London, 1898; p. 111.

or limped in time to changing circumstances. His anger would come blazing out of a clear sky as the adrenalin was pumped into his system. He could not suffer fools. If he thought he was right, then there was no room for argument, to dispute with him was to attack the authority of the King, of the Law—and of Jeffreys. These traits became increasingly obvious as this Dantonesque figure (in the previous autumn Charles Hatton had said of him, 'He hath, in great perfection, the three qualifications of a lawyer; Boldness, Boldness, Boldness') found his hands more truly on the controls of power.

That summer at the Kingston Assizes, he argued with the Judge, Baron Weston, complaining that he was being 'curbed in the management of his brief'. He was very properly rebuked by Weston, and the Judge's words are significant: 'Ha! Since the King has thrust his favours upon you, in making you Chief Justice of Chester, you think to run down everybody; if you find yourself aggrieved, make your complaint. Here's nobody cares for it!' Jeffreys retorted, 'I have not been used to make complaints, but rather to stop those that are made.' It was said that he wept with frustration, and the word went round in legal circles that 'Sir George Jeffreys behaved very ill at Kingston Assizes'.

During the summer and autumn of 1680 Jeffreys was closely involved in three trials connected indirectly, and each in rather different ways, with the dying Popish Plot. The first was the trial of Mrs. Cellier, 'the Popish midwife', said to be implicated in the Meal-Tub Plot. This oddly-named affair had come to light in the preceding November and was wrapped in such a web of double-talk that even today the real motives of those involved are not entirely clear. A gentleman on the fringe of the underworld, Thomas Dangerfield alias Captain Willoughby, 'a subtle and dexterous man, who, Burnet said 'had gone though all the shapes and practices of roguery', claimed to have discovered a great Presbyterian plot. Then, when interest had been aroused, he declared that the Catholics had fabricated the whole affair to discredit the Presbyterians. This plot within a plot included documents said to have been found in a meal-tub at Mrs. Cellier's.

The Meal-Tub Plot created a sensation, but never caught on as the original Popish Plot had done. A Lancashire J.P., with hard Northern sense, divided the population of England at this time into knaves, fools and wise men; the first made plots, the second believed them, the third saw through them. People were becoming sceptical of the professional informers, the 'Irish MacShams' who 'hearing that England was disposed to hearken to good swearers' came over 'with bad English and worse clothes, and returned well-bred gentlemen, well-caronated [coronetted], periwigged and clothed' having sworn away half-a-dozen lives.

Jeffreys conducted the prosecution, but there was really no evidence against Mrs. Cellier. One of the witnesses against her re-fused to give evidence, while she, with considerable forethought, had investigated Dangerfield's past and was able to produce records of sixteen previous convictions. Jeffreys tried, with no success at all, to argue that these must refer to somebody else. Dangerfield had been provided with a Court pardon, but there was an error in the wording—and the case ended with Mrs. Cellier's acquittal and Dangerfield's arrest. The whole looking-glass affair had in itself little importance, but it was symptomatic of the times—and both Mrs. Cellier and Dangerfield were to re-appear in Jeffreys' life at a later date.

The second case was that of Henry Care, brought before Scroggs in July and accused of publishing a libel in 'The Weekly Pacquet of Advice from Rome'. Care had hinted (as 'Elephant' Smith had done) that Scroggs had been bribed to secure Sir George Wakeman's acquittal. In the 'Pacquet' there was a mock advertisement for an incomparable medicament called:

'The Wonder Working Plaister', truly Catholic in operation, some-what akin to the Jesuit's powder, but more effectual . . . [which] makes justice deaf as well as blind, takes spots out of deepest stains, helps poisons and those that use them, and stifles a plot as certainly as the itch is destroyed by butter and brimstone.

Jeffreys opened the case for the prosecution.

Such is the age that we live in, that a man that hath wit enough to libel any man in the government, thinks he hath licence enough to expose that man to public knowledge also. . . . he thinks he can scratch *the itch* of the age, and that he may libel any man in the Government if he can but call him a Papist or popishly affected, let a man never be so honest, let a man be never so much for the support of that religion that every honest man ought to support—that is, the Protestant religion as it is established by law—without going to Rome or Amsterdam for assistance.

As usual the crowd in the court followed the speeches with all the attention that today might be given to a Test Match, applaud-

5

ing a good hit, or 'humming' their disapproval. They disapproved strongly of the prosecution, and Jeffreys had a stab at them in his final speech, '. . . whoever it is, who is bound by his oath to go according to the evidence shall acquit this man, he must be of humming conscience indeed.' After an hour, the jury brought in a verdict of guilty and were congratulated by Scroggs; 'You have done,' he said, 'like honest men.'

The third trial, also in July, was that of John Giles, at which Jeffreys presided in his capacity as Recorder. Arnold, a Monmouthshire magistrate, had come up to town and one evening had gone to call on a lawyer living in Bell Yard, off Fleet Street. He said that as he entered the yard two men, wearing long cloaks, had attacked him and that he had recognized one of his assailants, John Giles, a Catholic.

Jeffreys probed hard at Arnold's claim to have identified Giles, concluding by saying

It is not to be expected that a man in your circumstances should be extraordinary precise in circumstances. Therefore it is asked you that, according to the best of your apprehension, you might acquaint the court with those circumstances that may be remembered by the jury, that they may see there is no injury done to the prisoner at the bar, but that right be done on both sides. . . .

The circumstantial evidence was against Giles. He had bought a rapier only the day before the attack, and on the morning afterwards gone down to Monmouthshire and there, when he had later heard of the affray, he had exclaimed 'God damn him, he had armour on'. Arnold claimed he had heard an identical exclamation in the inn yard when he was defending himself.

Giles tried to show that he had an alibi but his witnesses were unconvincing, though their testimony provided some light relief. A friend, Howell, said Giles was abed by eleven, well before the attack took place—but it was shown that Howell had drunk a great deal of brandy that night. 'After two pints of brandy,' Jeffreys commented genially, 'I wonder he can remember anything.'

Another witness for the defence was the chambermaid at the inn, Elizabeth Crook, who was said to have made Giles' bed soon after ten. The Crown countered with the evidence of another guest, Richmond, who claimed that he had come into the bedroom while Elizabeth Crook was there and had not left again till after midnight, at which time Giles had not yet appeared. His evidence reads like the first draft for a scene in a Restoration comedy.

RICHMOND (to Elizabeth Crook): Was I not in the chamber when you made the bed?

WITNESS: No, I don't remember you.

RICHMOND (to Recorder): My lord, when this maid came to make the bed I went into the room after her and had some discourse with her. We leaned together in the window, and I told her I was in love with her. I told her if she liked it I would marry her the next morning. I did it to make merry—for, indeed, I am a married man.

RECORDER: What time of night was it?

RICHMOND: About twelve o'clock.

RECORDER (to witness): If you forget your other sweethearts, can you remember this? Do you remember now he was there?

ELIZABETH CROOK: I remember he was there.

GILES (to Arnold, who had burst out laughing): Mr. Arnold, pray do not laugh at my witnesses and make May games at them. It is not the part of a gentleman.

CROWN COUNSEL (to witness): What time of night was it that he was making love to you?

ELIZABETH CROOK: I think about ten o'clock.

CROWN COUNSEL: Time passed merrily away with you, then.

RICHMOND: It was twelve o'clock.

ELIZABETH CROOK: Why do you say so? Our house was all quiet presently after eleven.

RICHMOND: Why will you say so? Were we not singing and roaring together?

RECORDER: Come, do not be angry. You were not angry when you were making love together.

The jury found Giles guilty, he was pilloried three times and fined £500.

A shorthand account of this trial was made and certified by Jeffreys as correct. Sir James Stephen, the nineteenth-century jurist, considered that the trial was conducted 'with conspicuous fairness and decency'. It is significant that the trials in which Jeffreys is said to have behaved unfairly are usually those of which no official account has survived.

Contemporary opinion thought poorly of another case over which Jeffreys presided at the same sessions, in which a Catholic magistrate, Doughty, was found guilty of killing a coachman named Capps with his rapier. Capps had in fact survived the attack and had died a few days later of a fever. No report of the case has survived, not even the name of the judge, but a number of mysterious rumours have done so. It was said that Jeffreys had obtained a conviction in order to oblige his patroness the Duchess of Portsmouth. One of the aristocratic Verney family wrote 'Jeffreys is extremely cried out against about Justice Doughty's being convicted of murder. Some say he and Mrs. Wall, the Duchess of Portsmouth's woman lay their heads together to have it so,' while a common broadsheet thought it knew the reason:

> But though they fret and bite their nails and brawle,
> He'll slight them all and go kiss dear Nelly Wall.

In the autumn of this year 'Elephant' Smith, the Anabaptist printer convicted of libel earlier in the year, appeared before Jeffreys for a second time, on a similar charge. He had composed a pamphlet in which he complained that it cost so much to keep up the social activities of a sheriff that a poor man could not afford the expense—'debauchery is come to that height that the fifth part of the charge of the shrievalty is in wine, the growth of another country.' It was a mild enough libel and the Grand Jury threw out the bill by the established process of endorsing it *Ignoramus*—('we take no notice of it', an endorsement showing that they considered the evidence insufficient to warrant the case going before a petty jury).

At the Old Bailey Jeffreys had the bill presented again, and again the Grand Jury rejected it. 'God bless me from such jurymen,' Jeffreys exploded. 'I will see the face of every one of them and let others see them too. I will hear them repeat every man of them their own sense of this bill, thus exposing them to all possible contempt.'

Each of the seventeen Grand Jurors then had to declare 'Ignoramus' under the heavy-lidded glare of Jeffreys. After they had done so the Recorder sent for 'Elephant' Smith.

'Mr. Smith, you have the countenance of an ingenious person; show yourself as you seem to be,' Jeffreys said blandly, '. . . and confess, and try the grace and favour of this Court, and shame the jury that hath brought in a verdict contrary to plain evidence.'

Smith refused to rise to the bait.

'Sir,' he replied, 'my ingenuity hath sufficiently experienced the reward of your severity already formerly; and besides, I know no law commands me to accuse myself, neither shall I; and the jury hath done like true Englishmen, and worthy citizens; and blessed be God for such a just jury.'

Francis Smith was remanded to the next session, but in the end the proceedings against him were quietly dropped. At first sight the case seems of only moderate interest, but in effect Jeffreys had been doing his best to frustrate a new tactic in the judicial battles that were now being fought. Shaftesbury and his legal advisers knew that, if a Grand Jury declared there was no case, endorsing the bill *Ignoramus*, there was little that could be done about it. And who decided the composition of a Grand Jury? The Sheriffs. It began to appear that the outcome of the political struggle might easily turn on the election of the two Sheriffs of the City of London.

In the previous July these annual elections had taken place as usual and the Whigs, stealing a march on their opponents, had swept the board. The new Lord Mayor was Sir Patience Ward, a republican, and the new Sheriffs—elected by a majority of two to one—were Shaftesbury's nominees, Henry Cornish and Slingsby Bethel. (Of the latter, North said that he '. . . used to walk about more like a corn cutter than Sheriff of London. He kept no house, but lived upon chops, . . .') In effect the judicial machinery of the City had fallen into Shaftesbury's hands.

The importance of Jeffreys' action and the significance of his failure now became clear. If he had succeeded in shaking the Grand Jurymen or in persuading 'Elephant' Smith to plead guilty he would have won for the Crown a victory comparable in importance to the acquittal of Wakeman, or the counter-petitioning of the Abhorrers. He had failed, and the Whigs seemed to have spiked the Tory guns. From now on the judicial officers of the Crown might expect to find their efforts frustrated by packed 'Ignoramus' juries. The victory at the City election in July had made it certain that every Grand Jury would give whatever decisions Shaftesbury chose.

In the summer of 1680 the Whig cause had seemed to be losing ground, but now, in the late autumn and early winter, the tide had once more carried Shaftesbury high. The election of the London sheriffs had been one victory, the acquittal of Smith had been another. In August and September the Duke of Monmouth had been encouraged to go on a triumphal progress through the disaffected west country. Most important was the fact that Charles

II was now very short of money and could no longer postpone the meeting with that fourth Parliament of his that had remained in a state of suspended animation, prorogued but not dissolved, for almost exactly a year.

On 21st October parliament assembled. Charles, in his speech from the throne, asked for money to strengthen the defences of Tangier, and pleaded for unity, 'that which I value above all the treasure in the world . . . is a perfect union among ourselves. . . . I have done all that was possible for me to do to keep you in peace while I live and to leave you so when I die.'

It was no use. The Whig attack was mounted. Shaftesbury controlled the City and, up-stream, the parliament at Westminster. There Mr. William Williams, the Recorder of Chester, the same man who had clashed with Jeffreys during the first trial of 'Elephant' Smith, was elected as Speaker, and then the Commons got down to business. This was to be, not the granting of supply, but an advance on two fronts, one the preparation of a second Exclusion Bill, the other an attack on the Court's supporters.

Lord Chief Justice Scroggs was impeached, together with two other judges. So was the middle-of-the-way 'trimmer', the Marquis of Halifax. Sir Francis Wythens, one of the original Abhorrers, was expelled from the House of Commons. In this purge it was not likely that Jeffreys would be overlooked. A Commons committee was set up to investigate the conduct of the Recorder, and a few days later Pepys' clerk wrote to his master that the Committee was 'swinging Sir George Jeffreys off, as they will anybody else that come in their way'.

The Chairman of the committee, John Trenchard, Recorder for Taunton, an extreme Whig and a recently elected member of Shaftesbury's Green Ribbon Club, presented the report that recommended Jeffreys' removal. Naturally the Whigs had no sympathy for the Recorder who had deserted them: 'what sticks with me,' said Sir Robert Clayton, 'is his officiousness at the council table.' One of the members for Chester, Henry Booth (later Lord Delamere), another strong Whig, gave his account of Jeffreys' behaviour during the preceding summer when, as Lord Chief Justice of Chester, he held the Assize there:

'. . . who I must say behaved himself more like a jack pudding clown than with that gravity which beseems a Judge; he was mighty witty upon the prisoners at the bar; he was very full of his jokes upon people that came to give evidence, not suffering them to

declare what they had to say in their own way and method, but
would interrupt them, because they behaved themselves with more
gravity than he; and, in truth, the people were strangely perplexed
when they were to give in their evidence; but I do not insist upon
this, nor upon the late hours he kept up and down our city; it's
said he was every night drinking till two o'clock, or beyond that
time, and that he went to his chamber drunk; but this I have only
by common fame, for I was not in his company; I bless God I am
not a man of his principles or behaviour; but in the mornings he
appeared with the symptoms of a man that overnight had taken a
large cup. But that which I have to say is the complaint of every
man, especially of them who had any lawsuits. Our Chief Justice
has a very arbitrary power in appointing the assize when he pleases;
and this man has strained it to the highest point; for whereas we
were accustomed to have two assizes, the first about April or May,
the latter about September, it was this year the middle (as I remember) of August before we had any assize; and then he despatched
business so well that he left half the causes untried, and, to help
the matter, has resolved that we shall have no more assizes this
year.'

At first sight a formidable indictment, but when one analyses it,
setting aside rumour (*it's said*), and prejudice (*I bless God I am not
a man of his principles or behaviour*), nothing remains but the complaint that Jeffreys had held only one Assize instead of two and
that therefore half the causes had had to be postponed to the next
year. But it was not until the last day of April that Jeffreys had
been made Chief Justice of Chester, too late for the Spring
Assize. Booth was well known for choler; Clarendon said of him
'A little thing puts him in a passion'.

Jeffreys' real crime, in the eyes of the Whigs, was that he had led
the Abhorrers against the petitions for the immediate summoning
of parliament. Of that there could be no doubt, and in due course
the Commons' *Journal* recorded:

Resolved, That Sir George Jeffreys, Recorder of the City of London,
by traducing and obstructing petitioning for the sitting of this
Parliament, hath destroyed the right of the subject.

Ordered, That an humble address be made to His Majesty to
remove Sir George Jeffreys out of all public offices.

Ordered, That the Members of this House that serve for the City
of London do communicate the vote of this House relating to Sir
George Jeffreys, together with their resolutions thereupon, to the
Court of Aldermen for the said City.

Jeffreys anticipated his dismissal. On 2nd December the Court of Aldermen of the City of London noted:

> Sir George Jeffreys, Knight, Sergeant-at-Law, Recorder of this City, did freely surrender up unto the Court his place of Recorder, of which surrender the Court did accept and allow.

It was all very decorous. The City compensated him for the improvements that he had made at his own expense to the official residence in Aldermanbury Street, and also paid the sum of £200 which they had voted him the year before.

Jeffreys had broken his last official connection with the Whigs. From now on he was, openly and without qualification, the King's man. He was in good company. Pepys, that honest civil servant, who had narrowly beaten off an attempt to implicate him in the Popish Plot, wrote in November 'though the integrity and faithfulness wherewith his Majesty and the public have for so many years been served by us may not at present protect us from malicious reports, yet I am satisfied that God Almighty, who is always just will make it up to us some other way to the shame of those who now triumph over us. . . .'

When Charles heard that the brash young Welshman had received his comeuppance along with Scroggs and the rest, he smiled. He was, he said, interested to find that even Jeffreys 'was not Parliament-proof'. The Commons had just petitioned him to remove all his ministers. The King put the petition in his pocket and ambled off without a word. In private, though, he told Sir John Reresby, a Tory M.P., 'I will stick by you and my old friends, for if I do not, I shall have nobody to stick by me.'

Charles, as usual, was speaking sound political sense.

While they were engaged in this attack on the King's ministers the Commons were at the same time going ahead with their second Exclusion Bill. Its terms were more extreme than those of the first. Lord William Russell—who, incidentally, had claimed that Jeffreys was involved in the Popish Plot—moved '. . . that the Crown shall descend to such person, during the life of the Duke of York, as should inherit the same, in case the Duke were dead.' The Bill went on to declare James guilty of high treason if he should return to England (he was in Scotland at the time)—this of the man who was the legitimate heir and had, at that time, done nothing to forfeit his right to the throne except to declare himself a Catholic. The fact of the matter was that the Whigs were using

James's religion as an excuse to establish a limited—almost an elective—monarchy. Their argument was, as John Trenchard expressed it, that '. . . when a thing is *pro bono publico* we ever step over private rights.' Whether the succession could be considered a private right is another matter.

The second Exclusion Bill passed the Commons and was taken to the Lords with great ceremony by Russell, accompanied by the Whig Mayor and Aldermen of the City of London. In the Upper House Shaftesbury was much weaker, he could normally count on the support of about twenty peers out of a total of just under a hundred. Charles went down to hear the debate; as he stood warming his hands at the fire he remarked that it was as good as a play. Thanks partly perhaps to his presence, partly to the resolute opposition of Halifax which stiffened the waverers, the Bill was rejected by 63 votes to 30. The Earl of Yarmouth expressed the opinion of the majority, when he declared that there was 'no law strong enough to fence out an indisputable title'.

Frustrated, the Whigs looked for revenge, and took it in an unpleasant manner. Lord Stafford, 'old, repulsive, and personally insignificant', one of the five Catholic lords still in the Tower, was impeached. There is no doubt that he was not involved in any Popish Plot, but after a nine days' trial, he was convicted, on the perjured evidence of Oates and the other informers. When the King reduced the sentence to one of beheading, Russell spoke passionately in the Commons for the maximum punishment of hanging, drawing and quartering, but in this matter at least the King's will prevailed. It is instructive to note that Macaulay, who was so shocked by the Tory Jeffreys, does not record the Whig Russell's demand for the full horror. Later, Russell was himself to benefit from the King's mercy.

The Commons made it clear that they would vote no money until the Exclusion Bill was passed and so, in January, 1681, Charles dissolved Parliament. The King had always worked on the principle that if only he could give the Whigs sufficient rope, they would hang themselves. Now, he judged, was the time to launch the royal counter-attack. It was just forty years since events had begun to move swiftly, unexpectedly, and inexorably, to Civil War. It seemed to moderate men that the pattern was in danger of being repeated, the Commons were showing themselves as intractable as the Long Parliament. People were alarmed at the prospect of a repetition of the events of the forties. Dr. John

Peachell, Master of Magdalene, wrote to his old friend, Samuel
Pepys:

> Although it be counted even Popery, yet I cannot but pray God to
> preserve us from the tumults, confusions and rebellions of 1641 and
> '42, which seem to threaten us on one hand as much as Popery on
> the other; I fear God hath a controversy still with the land.

This fear was Charles' strongest card.

Having dissolved Parliament, Charles dismissed all those of his
Ministers who had voted for the Exclusion Bill, and issued writs
for a new Parliament, to meet in Royalist Oxford, away from the
pressures of the City mob and Shaftesbury's 'brisk boys' of
Wapping.

The Whigs brought to Oxford what force they could. Besides
the politicians there were the later Rye House conspirators, the
Duke of Monmouth, Lord Grey of Warke, and Sir Thomas
Armstrong, together with many of the lesser fry from the City—
men such as Stephen College, 'the Protestant joiner', who had
supplied his companions with his 'Protestant flails' and had also
for good measure written a ballad about them:

> Listen awhile and I'll tell you a tale
> Of a new device of a Protestant Flail,
> With a thump, thump, thump a' thump,
>   Thump a' thump thump!
> This flail it was made of the finest wood,
> Well lined with lead and notable good
> For splitting of brains and shedding of blood
> With a . . . etc.

Charles showed himself flexible, and tough. Flexible, for he
offered his opponents 'the expedient'—a compromise suggestion.
He would not put aside his brother, but he would agree to the
setting-up of a regency after his death, to be vested in James's
Protestant daughter Mary, or in her husband, William of Orange.
It was in the circumstances an extraordinarily reasonable gesture.

The Whig-controlled Commons disregarded the suggestion
and immediately set to work on a third Exclusion Bill, coupled
with a demand for annual sessions, 'Parliaments meeting in due
Distance of Time from each other, . . .'

Flexible, but tough; further than the expedient Charles would
not go.

> Let there be no delusion. I will not yield, nor will I be bullied.

Men usually become more timid as they become older; it is the opposite with me, and for what may remain of my life I am determined that nothing will tarnish my reputation. I have law and reason and all right-thinking men on my side. . . .

Having demonstrated to the country the unreasonableness of the Whigs, having allowed people to look over the edge at the danger of civil war, and having, most important of all, secured sufficient money from Louis XIV to make himself independent of parliamentary grants—having achieved all this Charles walked down to the Lords, his state robes following in a sedan chair, and dissolved the Oxford Parliament after only one week. He never called another.

Would the Whigs stand and fight? It was too late. Support was slipping away. Shaftesbury noted 'the damned city flags and falls off', and the Oxford mob cried 'Let the King live and the devil hang the Roundheads.' Everyone was anxious to leave Oxford. Roger North wrote, 'it is not to be expressed what clutter there was in town about getting off. The price of coaches mounted cent. for cent. in a quarter of an hour.'

Charles had saved his brother James. He had saved, too, all the lesser men whose careers, and perhaps whose lives also, were bound up with the royal cause. Among these was Sir George Jeffreys. Now he would play his part in the Royalist counter-attack.

4

The Royalist Counter-Attack
(1681-3)

Tories now took the place of Whigs in the key positions. The arena in which the struggle was being fought out moved from Parliament to the courts of justice and the City Council. A period of state trials opened in which the methods used by the Whigs during the Popish Plot were now turned against their authors on better evidence and with more justice. In July, 1681, the great Earl of Shaftesbury himself was committed to the Tower on a charge of high treason.

By the spring of 1681 Jeffreys' career was once more on the move. He was commissioned in the City of London militia in April and in the following month he and Sir John Chapman were gazetted lieutenants in place of the Whig magnates Sir Patience Ward and Sir Robert Clayton. Jeffreys was also appointed Chairman of the Middlesex Sessions. The jurisdiction of Middlesex extended over all London except for the seven hundred acres of the City, but the Grand Juries were still impanelled by the Whig Sheriffs, and it was the Grand Juries who decided whether or not a case should proceed for trial at the Old Bailey.

The first of the new political trials in which Jeffreys was involved was that of Stephen College on a charge of treason. The 'Protestant joiner' had arrived in Oxford equipped with pistol, carbine, breastplate and headpiece. Besides the flails he had brought with him a stock of green ribbons, the Whig colours, and of anti-royalist broadsheets and cartoons. Punched on the nose by an irate Tory, he had grandly declared: 'I have lost the first blood in the cause, but it will not be the last.' He had also written a number of pamphlets, any one of which would be sufficient to convict him. Nevertheless a Whig Grand Jury endorsed his bill of indictment *Ignoramus*, proof once more of the Whig theory that '. . . the two great pillars of our government are Parliament and Juries. It is these that give the title of freeborn Englishmen.'

College was removed to Oxford. There a Tory Grand Jury found a true bill against him. The writer Narcissus Luttrell drew the obvious conclusion—'if anything of Whig or Tory comes in question, it is ruled according to the interest of party.' The trial was to take place before Chief Justice North and before it opened he received an anonymous letter—'You are the rogue the Court relies on for drawing the first innocent blood.' College was not innocent, and the reactions and counter-reactions to his trial well illustrate the attitude of Whig, of Tory, and of *l'homme moyen sensuel*, to the long series of political trials that extend from 1678 to 1688.

Serjeant Jeffreys, together with the Attorney-General and Serjeant Holloway, were Counsel for the Crown. The trial lasted seventeen hours. It had its moments. When it was shown that College had pistols on him Jeffreys drily remarked, 'I think a chisel might have been more proper for a joiner.' Later, one of the prosecution witnesses, an Irishman named Haynes, swore that College had said he would seize the King 'and bring him to the block as we did the loggerhead [blockhead] his father.' Jeffreys invited College to question Haynes:

COLLEGE (indignantly): Is it probable I should talk to an Irishman that does not understand sense?
HAYNES (with even greater indignation): It is better to be an honest Irishman than an English rogue.
JEFFREYS (very calmly): He does it but to put you in a heat. Do not be passionate with him.

When College called his own witnesses a fellow-lodger deposed that he had heard Haynes say to his landlady: 'God damn me. I care not what I swear, nor who I swear against; for it is my trade to get money by swearing.'

College called Oates to testify against the Crown witnesses. Oates was thus in the interesting position of attacking the characters of some of the very men who a year earlier had supported his own allegations—a point which the Crown lawyers were not slow to seize upon:

ATTORNEY-GENERAL: Mr. Oates is a thorough-paced witness against all the King's Evidence.
JEFFREYS: And yet Dr. Oates had been alone in some matters, had it not been for some of these witnesses.
OATES: I had been alone perhaps, and perhaps not; but yet, Mr.

Serjeant, I had always a better reputation than to need theirs to strengthen it.

Later in the trial there was a second clash between Jeffreys and Oates. Part of the case against College was that he had spoken treasonable words at a dinner given by Alderman Wilcox. Oates gave his version of the affair:

When we came to the Crown Tavern we did, to divert ourselves till Dinner came up, enter into a Philosophical Discourse, ... it was concerning the existence of God, whether that could be proved by natural demonstration, and whether or no the Soul was immortal. ... (One of the Crown witnesses) speaks to Mr. Wilcox to be a Man that contributed Money to buy Arms, Powder, and Shot; I think Sir George Jeffreys knows Alderman Wilcox to be a man of another Employment.

JEFFREYS: Sir George Jeffreys does not intend to be an Evidence I assure you.

OATES: I do not desire Sir George Jeffreys to be an Evidence for me. I had credit in Parliaments, and Sir George had disgrace in one of them.

JEFFREYS: Your servant, Doctor, you are a witty man, *and a Philosopher.*

One can almost hear the light tap of foils, engaging and disengaging. Jeffreys summed up. He made play with College's trade:

This gentleman, whose proper business it had been to manage his employment at London for a joiner, is best seen in his proper place, using the proper tools of his trade. I think it had been much more proper for him, and I believe you will think so too, than to come with pistols, and those accoutrements about him, to be regulating the Government; what have such people to do with the business of Government? God be thanked, we have a wise Prince, and God be thanked he hath wise counsellors about him, and he and they know well enough how to do their own business, and not to need the advice of a joiner, though he calls himself 'the Protestant joiner'.

College was found guilty, and executed the following day. On the scaffold he continued to maintain that he knew of no plot except the Popish Plot, but admitted 'he might in heat have uttered some word of indecency concerning the king and council'.

One month before College's execution the last of the Popish Plot victims had died, so closely did the Tory political trials follow those of the Whigs. But the Plot witnesses had discredited themselves. 'Narrative' Bedloe was already dead 'of a fever occasioned by drinking cider while he was very hot, having rid post'. Dugdale had contracted syphilis and was to die in the following year. Turberville became a Catholic and drank himself to death in a long fit of remorse. Oates, the arch-informer, remained, but there were clear signs that his influence was at an end. His pension was reduced from £1,200 to £104 and he was expelled from his lodgings in Whitehall. (When he left, an official was wisely stationed at the door to ensure 'that none of His Majesty's Goods should be imbezelled'.)

But if the Whigs had lost their influence over the judicial machine, they were still able to deny that influence to the Tories, at least in London, by the endorsement *Ignoramus*, that 'monster engendered in the filth of faction'. In November a Middlesex Grand Jury endorsed Shaftesbury's bill *Ignoramus*, 'upon which the people fell a-hollowing and shouting', and the Earl was released in the following January. 'It is a hard case,' Charles mildly remarked when he heard the news, 'that I am the last man to have law and justice in the whole nation.'

The Grand Jury in Shaftesbury's case included four men who had been Whig members of the Exclusion Parliament, including the foreman Sir Samuel Barnardiston; Thomas Papillon, the London merchant; and Michael Godfrey, brother of the murdered Sir Edmund. The King's secretary, Sir Leoline Jenkins, commented on the Grand Jury panels that they were 'the most strange that ever were; on a panel of fifty, scarce four that went at any time to church. They are so obscure, most of 'em, as never to have been in the freeholder's book, so that the King cannot hope to have justice from them in his own Courts.' It was clear that the future of the struggle must turn on the election of the Lord Mayor and Sheriffs, who chose the juries.

Meanwhile the King was in reality well enough defended against Shaftesbury. The Earl's papers had been confiscated. They contained lists of 'worthy men' and 'men worthy' (to be hanged) and much other material that could be used one day against him. And about the time of the Earl's release, Dryden's *Absalom and Achitophel* was published. The great satire on Shaftesbury has left a smear at least as permanent and undeserved as that which the Whig writers later laid on Jeffreys:

> A Name to all succeeding Ages curst.
> For close Designs and crooked Counsels fit;
> Sagacious, Bold, and Turbulent of wit;
> Restless, unfixt in Principles and Place;
> In Pow'r unpleas'd, impatient of Disgrace.
> A fiery Soul, which working out its way,
> Fretted the Pigmy-Body to decay:
> And o'r inform'd the Tenement of Clay.
> In Friendship false, implacable in Hate:
> Resolv'd to Ruine or to Rule the State.

A week before the *Ignoramus* endorsement, on 17th November, there had been the usual Protestant carnival—Godfrey, the Pope, Devils and Cardinals, Jesuits, an anonymous gentleman on a traitor's sledge (was it Louis XIV, James Duke of York, or merely Roger L'Estrange the Tory editor of the *Observator*? No one seemed to know.) There followed 'some ordinary persons with Halters, as I took it, about their necks.' There was no mistaking the significance of these men, for they were accompanied by an attendant

> who, with a Stentorophonic Tube, sounded Abhorrers, Abhorrers, most infernally . . . these stately Figures were planted in a Demilune about an huge Fire that shined upon them; and the Balconies of the Club were ready to crack with their factious Load, till the good People were satiated with the fine Shew; . . . It might be asked what was the End or Intention of all this Pains and Expence? It is easy to answer it was not for meer Sport; that's too Boyish for such a noble Society, and their Drivers in secret, to design and execute with so much Application. . . .
>
> The Faction had always, upon the Tip of their Tongues, the People, and all their Routs were the People; and now they intended, by this Leviathan Mob, to shew the People in good Earnest. And then the King, if he had not known better, might perhaps have mistaken this Assembly for the People whom he was to satisfy, and whom nothing would pacify but the Exclusion. . . .

Meanwhile the original Abhorrer, Sir George Jeffreys, was created a baronet, with the title 'of Bulstrode in Hedgerley, Co. Buckingham'.

At the very close of 1681 the brilliant, dissipated lawyer, Sir Edmund Saunders, suggested a legal riposte to the problem of the *Ignoramus* juries. The City authorities could be served with a writ of *Quo Warranto*. This would order them to show *by what authority* they had undertaken every detail of their administration.

In the day-to-day control of the greatest city in Europe it was inevitable that they should have committed some unauthorized acts. The powerful City of London, with its trainbands and treasury, its elective Lord Mayor and Sheriffs, its wide franchise, was almost a republic, an English Amsterdam. Besides its own M.P.s it controlled at least eight members from the provinces. This power house of political energy would, if it lost its charter, be reduced to the status of a village. The King might then grant a new charter and appoint the Mayor and Sheriffs which would place the government of the City firmly in Tory hands.

Saunders' plan was neat, ingenious, and practical. It had one disadvantage—it was slow. Legal procedure must be carefully observed. In the event, the original writ was served in December, 1681, and the final verdict was not given until June, 1683.

Pending the destruction of the City's powers, there were perhaps other ways by which the Whigs might be prevented from packing Grand Juries. Although they seemed permanently in control, their majority was not large—in 1681 the Council was composed of about 91 Whigs and 77 Tories. A swing of ten per cent would be amply sufficient to put the Tories in power.

During 1682 a fierce election campaign was waged from May to September. The Tory candidates for the post of Sheriff were Dudley North, a brother of the Lord Chief Justice, and Peter Rich, while John Dubois and Thomas Papillon (the same who had sat on Shaftesbury's *Ignoramus* jury) were the Whig candidates. The campaign was the fiercest the City had ever known. Pressure was brought to bear on the electors in many ways—for instance, the keepers of all ale and coffee-houses in the City were warned that they would lose their licences unless they voted Tory. Roger North wrote:

> Midsummer work indeed, extremely hot and dusty, and the partisans strangely disordered every way with crowding, bawling, sweating and dust; all full of anger, zeal and filth on their faces, they ran about up and down stairs, so that anyone not better informed would have thought the place rather a huge Bedlam than a meeting for civil business. And yet, under such an awkward face of affairs as this was, the fate of the English Government and Monarchy depended but too much on the event of so decent an assembly.

Like the other Tory leaders, Jeffreys was involved in the election campaign. He put his London house at the service of the Tory candidates, and played his part in speech-making and canvassing,

6

but he was not in London when the result was announced in
September. His duties as Chief Justice of Chester had taken him
to the provinces. He visited his father at Acton, and then proceeded to the work of the assizes.

The North-west was in something of a turmoil. The Duke of
Monmouth was beginning to move to the forefront of the com-
plex political scene. This year, he had gone to the North-west
Midlands, in imitation of his triumphant progress through the
West Country in 1680, making contact with the Booth family
and riding as far as Liverpool. On his way back to London
Charles had him arrested at Stafford, although he was allowed bail.

At Chester Monmouth had increased his popularity by riding
his own horse to victory in a race worth sixty pounds. From
Acton Jeffreys wrote to Sir Leoline Jenkins, the King's Secretary:

> I doubt not you have had an account of the Duke of Monmouth's
> reception at Chester. The pretence of his honouring these parts was,
> you know, a race. . . . His Grace won the plate to the joy of all true
> Protestants, for which bonfires have been made in Chester and most
> of the honest people's windows broke, and the plate bestowed on
> the Mayor's child, which his Grace has christened Henrietta.
> Applications are daily made to me about these outrages, being now
> at Wrexham within eight miles. I am next Monday at Holywell
> where I expect the continuance of clamour.
>
> But there is an accident that may be useful to his Majesty's service.
> Chester has not the power of trying treasons. There are at present
> three persons in the city gaol for clipping. If a commission of Oyer
> and Terminer (formally empowering to determine indictments on
> treasons) might be expedited presently (I begin my circuit there
> Monday sen-night and continue a week) and directed as was about
> 1663 for treasonable words (the Clerk of the Crown has the prece-
> dent) and name not the Mayor nor any (of) those rascals concerned
> in his pageantry, it may bear up the honest party of the town at
> present dispirited. . . . If this came to me next week before the
> assizes were ended, which is also the fair time, I hope I could manage
> it for my master's service.

Jeffreys got his enlarged commission, and a pat on the back from
the King, who 'is assured you will do your part'. At Chester the
commission was attacked by the City's Recorder, William
Williams, who had been Speaker in the 1680 Exclusion Parliament. Jeffreys was however able to justify it and to obtain a
Grand Jury which returned a majority of true bills.

'I arrived here last Saturday,' Jeffreys wrote to Jenkins, 'and imparted yours to the loyal gentlemen of the county, which was very grateful, and the commission came here in the nick of time. I ordered precepts to the Sheriffs of the City to prepare a Grand Jury against tomorrow and hope to give you a good account per next. I expect some dispute betwixt the mayor, the Recorder, and myself about the extent of the commission, they being very unwilling that any stranger should intermeddle in their late disorders, especially the Mayor and Alderman Streete, who I could have wished had not been in the commission by reason he is a pestilently troublesome fellow. The greater part, I hope, are of our side. The parsons yesterday did their parts, for which I gave them public thanks, which I hear has offended the mayor.'

From Chester he went on to Mold, where the Flintshire assizes were held. There his mother's Nonconformist friend, Philip Henry, a man who had known Jeffreys when the judge was a little boy, appeared before him, charged with keeping a conventicle. His goods had been distrained and carts had been pressed into service for the purpose. Jeffreys declared the action illegal. He wondered, he said, 'by what new law the gentry pressed carts to remove goods distrained for the offence of going to meeting.' He was able to ensure that no further proceedings were taken against the old man.

His business done Jeffreys returned to London to find that in the City, 'the Chief Refuge of the People, the curb or Bridle to the unjust illegal Ambition of all arbitrary and evil men', as the Whigs had called it, the Tories had won the day. There was now a Tory Mayor and Tory Sheriffs, and the Whigs were once again hoist with their own petard. Just as Whig treason trials had paved the way for Tory treason trials, so now Tory juries would—since Whig juries had refused to return true bills against Whig leaders— be prepared to convict any Whig against whom a reasonably convincing case could be built up.

At the close of 1682 Jeffreys was involved in a case which, though it had its political aspect, was a civil action. He assisted the Attorney-General in the prosecution of Ford, Lord Grey of Warke, on a charge of seducing his sister-in-law, Lady Henrietta Berkeley.

Grey was a leading Whig, a friend of Monmouth and a member of Shaftesbury's Green Ribbon Club, but the charge was not a political smear. The relationship between Lord Grey and Lady

Henrietta had been amusing or scandalizing society for the last four years. During that time Grey had succeeded in keeping his wife in ignorance of what was going on, while Lady Henrietta duped her own family. On one of these occasions Lord Grey had spent two entire days locked in her room, subsisting solely on sweets.

At length the truth came out. The pair separated—for good, they said. Then one Saturday Lady Henrietta fled to London, where Grey kept her hidden. Her infuriated father demanded justice and Grey appeared before the King's Bench judges.

The outcome of the trial was a foregone conclusion. Even the defence could find nothing better to say than that they 'could not justify in strictness *everything* that my lord Grey had done'— which must have ranked as the leading understatement of the year. Lady Henrietta insisted on giving evidence, though Lord Grey's counsel had done all he could to keep her quiet. She proceeded to perjure herself cheerfully and continuously. At length the Lord Chief Justice could contain himself no longer.

'You have,' said Sir Francis Pemberton, 'injured your own reputation and prostituted both your body and your honour, and are not to be believed.'

Her father requested that his daughter be handed over to her proper guardian, himself. Lady Henrietta retorted that she was married—to a mysterious Mr. Turner, who was now suddenly produced in court.

'What are you?' asked the amazed Chief Justice.

'I am a gentleman,' Mr. Turner loftily replied.

'Where do you live?'

'Sometimes in town, sometimes in the country.'

'Where do you live when you are in the country?'

'Sometimes in Somersetshire.'

It begins to sound like a passage from *The Importance of Being Earnest*.

Jeffreys offered some rather more precise information:

'We all know Mr. Turner well enough; we shall prove that he was married to another person before that is now alive and has children by him.'

But Mr. Turner remained unruffled.

'Ay, do, Sir George,' he replied imperturbably, 'if you can; for there never was any such thing.'

'Pray sir,' Jeffreys insisted, 'did you not live at Bromley with a woman as man and wife, and had divers children; and, living so intimately, were you not questioned for it, and you and she owned yourself to be man and wife?'

Mr. Turner declined to be shaken. Whoever he might have lived with, he was now married to Lady Henrietta Berkeley and had witnesses to prove it.

'I will go with my husband!' cried the Lady.

'Hussy! You shall go with me home,' retorted her father.

'I will go with my husband!'

'Hussy, you shall go with me, I say!'

The court broke up in some disorder and, once beyond the doors, swords were out. However no one was hurt, and soon Lady Henrietta Berkeley—or should one say Mrs. Turner—was safe in the King's Bench prison. Grey was allowed bail and judgement was never pronounced.

Lady Henrietta was released before long and when next year Lord Grey fled to Holland after the discovery of the Rye House Plot in which he was involved, Lady Henrietta went with him. So, too, did the egregious Mr. Turner. The Presbyterians among the Rye House exiles were very shocked.

It was not by any means the end of Lord Grey's career. In 1685 he accompanied Monmouth and was in charge of the cavalry, which he grossly mishandled, at the battle of Sedgemoor. After the battle he was captured, but James II spared his life as a reward for turning King's evidence, and Lord Grey proceeded to betray his former associates. After the final Whig triumph of 1688 this treacherous, disreputable man was created Earl of Tankerville.

The trial of Lord Grey must have appealed to Jeffreys' somewhat sardonic sense of humour—a brief interlude, for on the following day he was once more involved in the more serious business of political trials. The Duke of York was claiming £100,000 damages from Thomas Pilkington, one of the Whig ex-sheriffs of London and a close friend of Shaftesbury, 'an honest but indiscreet man that gave himself great liberties in discourse' (Burnet). It was indeed this indiscretion that led to the trial. Earlier in the year when the City Court of Alderman had met to congratulate the Duke on his return from Scotland, Pilkington had dissented from the message of congratulation, bursting out that the Duke had 'twice burned this city, and was now come to cut the inhabitants' throats'. Such accusations were common form at the Green Ribbon Club, but not in the City Council.

Pilkington, who knew something of packed juries, asked that he might be tried before a jury drawn from some other county than Middlesex. The Crown allowed him to choose his county, and he selected Hertfordshire. Nevertheless he was found guilty. Jeffreys' task was easy. There were too many witnesses to the remark— even though one of those for the defence, Sir Patience Ward, was prepared to perjure himself, declaring that Pilkington was not in the room at the time. 'Your invention,' Jeffreys drily commented, 'is better than your memory.'

The damages were impossibly large and, since he would have to stay in prison until they were paid, Pilkington received what amounted to a sentence of life imprisonment. (He was released after the Revolution of 1688.) A consequence of Pilkington's trial was that in the spring Sir Patience Ward was charged with perjury. Jeffreys prosecuted and William Williams defended. Ward was found guilty, but he fled to the Netherlands before sentence could be pronounced, and remained there until 1688. The case has an additional special interest by virtue of the fact that it was the first at which a shorthand report was accepted as evidence.

An unusual case, part political, part social, in which Jeffreys prosecuted was that of William Dockwra who had organized a Penny Post for the City of London in 1681. The scheme was ambitious and efficient. There was a head office in Lime Street, seven sorting offices, and over four hundred 'receiving-houses'. The postage was a penny, parcels up to one pound in weight were accepted as letters, and there was an automatic insurance against losses of up to ten pounds in value—though the public were warned that the company would take no responsibility for 'Breaking, Damage of Choice and Curious Things; nor Glasses or Liquid Matter sent by them, it being altogether unreasonable . . .' Another broadsheet listed the advantages of the new service to all classes including the fact that

> Parents may Converse with their absent Children at Boarding-Schools, &c.

and ending

> . . . we shall leave all the Ingenious to find out Wherein our Invention may be serviceable to them, and refer all people to be convinced by Time and Experience.

THE TRUE TOUCHSTONE OF ALL DESIGNS

There were two reasons why the Court looked askance at this remarkable service. The legal objection was that it infringed the monopoly of the General Post Office which had been granted to the Duke of York. There was also a private political objection. The scheme was a Whig one and could be used to provide information for Shaftesbury and to spread his propaganda.

The Duke of York had brought one action already, which had failed in the days when the Whigs controlled the juries. Perhaps, now that the Tories were in control, he would fare better. Dockwra's defence was, briefly, that where the official Postmaster 'Had not settled an office ... any man might.' He argued that there was nothing to prevent an individual hiring a porter to carry a letter for him. Why then should one not hire many porters, which was what he had in effect done? Jeffreys contended that if a postal service operated in an area, then the monopoly had been established there. Official messengers already existed in London, therefore Dockwra had contravened the law which secured the revenues from the postal service to the Duke of York. The jury found Dockwra guilty, and he was ordered to pay £100 damages.

In December 1682 the great Lord Chancellor Nottingham died and there was a general reshuffle of judicial appointments. Jeffreys himself was not immediately affected, but the way to the top became a little shorter. Nottingham was succeeded by Roger North's brother, Francis, who was given the inferior title of Lord Keeper, and created Baron Guildford. As Charles handed him the Great Seal he said, 'Here, my lord, take it, you will find it heavy.' As usual, the King's judgement of character was exact. North was a nervous little man who within three years had literally worried himself to death—upon which Jeffreys became Chancellor. Meanwhile Sir Francis Pemberton was transferred from King's Bench to North's place in Common Pleas and *his* place in King's Bench went to Edmund Saunders, the man who had originally suggested the method by which the City of London might be brought to heel—the *Quo Warranto* proceedings. In King's Bench Saunders would thus be able to preside at the hearing of the very case that his suggestion had created. Saunders was a cheerful, unconventional person, a great drinker who had grown very fat, and was in fact at this time a dying man. Roger North wrote of him:

He was a very Silenus to the boys, as in this place I may term the students of the law, to make them merry whenever they had a mind to it. He had nothing of rigid or austere about him. If any near him at the bar grumbled at his stench, he ever converted the complaint into content and laughing with the abundance of his wit. As to his ordinary dealing, he was as honest as the driven snow was white; and why not, having no regard for money or desire to be rich? And for good-nature and condescension there was not his fellow. I have seen him for hours and half-hours together before the court sat stand at the bar with an audience of students over against him putting of cases and debating so as suited their capacities and encouraged their industry. And so in the Temple he seldom moved without a parcel of youths hanging about him, and he merry and jesting with them.

Saunders was universally popular. Some year earlier he and Jeffreys had both been engaged in a case brought by the Commissioners of Excise against certain distillers of brandy who, it was claimed, were paying a tax on raw liquor when they should have been paying the higher rate of duty on refined spirits. Samples of the different grades involved were produced as part of the evidence, and were handed round. 'The judges tasted, the jury tasted, and Saunders, seeing the phials moving, took one and set it to his mouth, and drank it all off.' A great cheer went up. The Chief Justice at the time, who had not seen what had happened, ordered Jeffreys to get on with his case.

'My lord,' answered Jeffreys demurely, 'we are at a full stop, and can go no further.'

'What's the matter?'

'Mr. Saunders has drunk up all our evidence.'

And the court dissolved in laughter.

This was the man, pleasant to meet among so many self-seekers, who now presided over the temporary destruction of the Whig power in the City of London.

Before that case came off, however, the Whigs had suffered an even more serious blow in the death of Shaftesbury. The Earl had been released from the Tower in February, 1682, but physically he was exhausted—he was dying of a duodenal ulcer—and politically his judgement told him this was a time to lie low. When Monmouth was taken into custody after his northern 'progress' a warrant was issued for Shaftesbury's re-arrest, but he went underground at Wapping. In November, fresh warrants were taken out and he fled to Holland, where he died in January, 1683.

With his death the Whig party seemed to become more desperate, less prepared to weigh up the political pros and cons. One feels that neither the Whig Rye House Plot of 1683 nor Monmouth's Rebellion of 1685 would have taken quite the form they did if Shaftesbury had been alive. A great judge of what was politically expedient, he only under-rated one of his opponents, the King. Of him he had said, 'His brother, his Minister and his Mistress play the game into one another's hands, and ___ly govern all matters.' And he contemptuously ____ Charles as a man who, had he 'been so ___ as to have been born a Private Gentleman, had ___ for a man of good parts, excellent breeding and ___-natured.' It was the usual contempt of the professional for the amateur, but in this case it was a disastrous misappraisal.

The Whig party, held together by Shaftesbury, now showed signs of dissolving into its component elements. The Tories followed up their advantage. In May, 1683, Saunders presided at the trials of the ex-sheriffs Pilkington, Shute, Cornish and Bethel, together with other prominent Whigs, on charges of rioting during those hard-fought City elections the previous summer. Jeffreys opened for the Crown, described the proceedings and told how the new Tory Lord Mayor had been rabbled:

> When my Lord Mayor came off the hustings, they came upon him, and had him down upon his knees and his hat off, and if some gentlemen had not come in they had trod him under feet. Such an indignity was then done to the Lord Mayor of London, who, I think I may say, deserved as well from the government of this city as any gentleman that ever presided in that office.

The defence was conducted by Jeffreys' usual antagonist, William Williams. He attempted to show that the Lord Mayor had taken off his hat of his own accord.

'My Lord Mayor, I find,' Jeffreys retorted, 'was so extraordinary civil that to this rabble he must not only pull off his hat, but fling his hat on the ground to them.' Jeffreys then called as witness Cartwright, a man who said he had tried to protect the Mayor and who claimed that he sprained his back in the struggle and spat blood for a week afterwards.

JEFFREYS: Hark you, Mr. Cartwright, ever since that time have you found any indisposition?
CARTWRIGHT: I have not been my own man since.
WILLIAMS: He took a surfeit. [Sickness from too much to eat or drink.]
JEFFREYS: He took a surfeit of ill company, I am sure.

One of the defence witnesses, called to show that if there had
been rioting it was certainly not all on one side, provided an
atmospheric picture of the proceedings.

> I was in Cheapside, and I heard a great noise of huzzaing and a
> terrible noise indeed; and I met with a fellow running, my lord, and
> I stopt the fellow, 'What is the matter?' 'Nothing,' said he 'but an
> old fellow riding skimmington and skeleton'; and in the street I saw
> a matter of a hundred with their hats upon sticks, crying, 'Damn
> the Whigs!' Said I, 'Gentlemen, what's the matter?' Said they,
> 'The work is done to stop the poll'; and that is all.

Eventually the jury brought in a verdict of guilty and the
defendants were fined amounts varying from 500 marks to £500.

The conclusion to this phase of the royal counter-attack was
the verdict in the *Quo Warranto* proceedings, which had been
dragging on in King's Bench for eighteen months. On 12th June
the dying Saunders gave his verdict in writing 'that the liberties
and franchises of the said city be delivered into the King's hands'.
The great City, which had behaved almost as a self-governing
republic, had fallen to the King. Evelyn, a moderate Whig,
recorded in his diary:

> Eight of the richest and chief Aldermen were removed, and all the
> rest made only justices of the peace, and no more wearing of gowns
> or chains of gold. The Lord Mayor and two Sheriffs holding their
> places by new grants as Custodes at the King's pleasure. The pomp
> and grandeur of the most august city in the world thus changed
> face in a moment, which gave great occasion of discourse and
> thoughts of heart what all this would end in.

Jeffreys contentedly remarked, 'The King of England is at last
King of London.'

The extreme wing of the Whig party was in a perpetual state of
largely theoretical conspiracy. In 1682 Shaftesbury had been the
co-ordinating mind behind plans for an armed uprising to be led
by Argyll in Scotland and by such men as Essex, Russell, Lord
Grey and Sir Thomas Armstrong in England. Monmouth's 'pro-
gresses' in the west and north had been designed to prepare the
ground for this, to sound out local Whig gentry—though it was
by no means certain that Monmouth himself would benefit.
Shaftesbury was a practical politician, and an astute one; he came
to the conclusion that 1682 was by no means the right year to rise,
and the plans remained at the drawing-board stage.

On Shaftesbury's death control of a possible rising passed to less practical men, the so-called Council of Six: the Duke of Monmouth; John Hampden; the Earl of Essex; Lord William Russell; Lord Howard of Escrick; and Algernon Sidney. They were not so cautious as Shaftesbury. They were enchanted by the mystique of conspiracy—Charles and James were always referred to as 'the Blackbird and the Goldfinch'—and too many people were approached, too much was said.

Meanwhile another plot was also in preparation. Within a fortnight of the *Quo Warranto* decision the Crown offensive received fresh ammunition from the discovery of the Rye House Plot. This was a desperate affair of old Republicans, 'Oliverians', men wedded to the Good Old Cause. Leading figures in this group were the one-eyed former Cromwellian colonel, 'Hannibal' Rumbold, and 'Parson' Robert Ferguson, a Scotsman full of a wild enthusiasm.

The plotters knew that the King always visited Newmarket in April and left again as soon as the racing there was over. You could set a clock by his movements. They arranged to ambush the royal coach as it passed the Rye House, a farm at Hoddesdon in Hertfordshire, leased by Rumbold. In the narrow lane a hail of shot would kill Charles II, the Duke of York, and some of the leading Royalists. The Plot was almost foolproof—but a serious fire at Newmarket put an end to all racing there, and Charles returned to London a week early. Rumbold watched with frustration as Charles passed his house 'very slenderly guarded, only with five or six persons, and those tired and ill-appointed'.

News of the Plot began to leak out. A Scotsman was arrested at Newcastle, his correspondence alerted the government. A fortnight later one of the lesser fry in London took fright and made a statement to Sir Leoline Jenkins. Finally the full Plot was blown by a barrister of the Middle Temple, Robert West. He approached Jeffreys, who sent him at once to Hampton Court, where the Council was in session.

At this point the story of the two plots comes together. The government now had enough information on which to act and they saw that they might use the real Rye House Plot to destroy also the theoretical plotters of the Council of Six, for there had been contact between the two groups of conspirators. The Rye House plotters were persuaded to inform against the aristocratic Council of Six. A fortnight later Lord Howard of Escrick was hauled out of his own chimney at his house in Kensington. He promptly told all, in return for his life. Orders went out to arrest twenty-one of the conspirators. Evelyn wrote:

> The public was now in great consternation, his Majesty very melancholy and not stirring without double guards, all the avenues and private doors about Whitehall and the Park shut up, few admitted to walk in it. The Papists in the meanwhile very jocund and indeed with reason seeing their own plot turned to ridicule, and now a conspiracy of Protestants, as they called them.

Of the Six only one, Howard, escaped scot-free. Monmouth crawled for his father's pardon: 'Nothing under Heaven has struck me so to the Heart, as to be put into a Proclamation of Murdering of you, Sir, . . . though I was not conscious of any design against your Majesty's life, yet I lament having had so great a share in the other part of the said conspiracy. . . .' By the end of the year he was in the Netherlands in semi-official exile. Essex cut his throat while in the Tower awaiting trial; Russell and Sidney were found guilty and executed; Armstrong fled to Holland but was caught and executed a little later. Against Hampden there was insufficient evidence for a charge of treason, but he was found guilty of misdemeanour, fined and imprisoned.

On 13th July, about 9 a.m., the trial began of Lord William Russell, before Chief Justice Pemberton. The Crown was represented by the Attorney-General, the Solicitor-General, Roger North and Sir George Jeffreys. Russell had been vehement in the Popish Plot prosecutions, notably that of the old Viscount Stafford, and had marshalled the Whig M.P.s in the Exclusion Bill debates. Since Shaftesbury's death he had been the leader of the party.

Rumsey, one of the Rye House plotters, gave evidence that Russell had been present at a meeting held the previous November in the house of a wine-merchant called Shepherd. He said that there had also been present Monmouth, Grey, Ferguson, Sir Thomas Armstrong, and Rumsey himself. They had discussed the fact that John Trenchard, 'the movement man of the west', was not able to arrange an insurrection with 1,000 foot and 500 horse, based on Taunton, as he had hoped to do, and had then considered the possibility of overpowering the King's guards and seizing Charles.

Russell admitted that he *had* been at Shepherd's house that night, but went on to say that he had only gone there to taste the sherry.

When pressed, he stoutly maintained that there was a big difference between planning in theory to levy war and plotting in fact to kill the King—in short, he admitted discussing rebellion, but denied that such discussion constituted treason, adding—'Tis hard that a man must lose his life on hear-say.'

Lord Howard of Escrick then spoke, giving his evidence in a low voice. The Chief Justice, Pemberton, told him to speak up, and Howard explained 'there is an unhappy accident happened that hath sunk my voice: I was but just now acquainted with the fate of my lord of Essex.' The news that one of the other leading conspirators had killed himself that morning was bound to weigh heavily with the jury and in his peroration Jeffreys, like the astute lawyer that he was, used the fact that Essex' fate had been mentioned by a witness, to hammer home its implications into the jurors' minds.

> Who would think that my lord of Essex, who had been advanced so much in his estate and honour, should be guilty of such desperate things! Which had he not been conscious of, he would scarcely have brought himself to that untimely end, to avoid the methods of public justice.

This was quite improper, but there was no reason why Jeffreys should not continue until the Judges stopped him—which they did not do.

There is a full record of Jeffreys' speech and, as usual, different writers draw quite different conclusions from it. North, who was himself involved, wrote of the Rye House trials—'... if ever trials in England were fair both in the private and public conduct of them, these were.' Yet the Whig Bishop Burnet described Jeffreys' concluding speech as 'an insolent declamation, such as all his were, full of irony and indecent invectives', while the Tory Dean Swift stigmatized Burnet's own account as 'Incorrect, disagreeable, viciously copious.' Three hundred years after the event, can one hope to judge between such diametrically opposed views? One can do what the critics of Jeffreys have so seldom done; look at what he really said, and draw one's own conclusions.

After the reference to Essex' suicide, Jeffreys examined the evidence. He commented on the witnesses Russell had called to testify to his character:

> Gentlemen, I must confess this noble lord hath given an account of several honourable persons of his conversation, which is a very easy

matter. Do you think, if any man had a design to raise a rebellion against the Crown, that he would talk of it to the reverend divines and the noble lords that are known to be of integrity to the Crown? Do you think the gentleman at the bar would have so little concern for his own life to make this discourse his ordinary conversation? No, it must be a particular consult of six, that must be concerned in this; they must be persons of their own complexion and humour; for men will apply themselves to proper instruments . . .

He concluded:

Gentlemen, I would not labour in this case, for far be it from any man to endeavour to take away the life of the innocent. And whereas the noble Lord says he hath a virtuous good lady, he hath many children, he hath virtue and honour he puts into the scale; gentlemen, I must tell you, on the other side, you have consciences, religion; you have a Prince, and a merciful one too; consider the life of your Prince, the life of his posterity, the consequences that would have attended if this villainy had taken effect. What would have become of your lives and religion? What would have become of that religion we have been so fond of preserving? Gentlemen, I must put these things upon your consciences. I know you will remember the horrid murder of the most pious Prince, the Martyr King Charles the First. How far the practices of those persons have influenced the several punishments since is too great a secret for me to examine. But now I say, you have the life of a merciful King, you have a religion that every honest man ought to stand by, and I am sure every loyal man will venture his life and fortune for. You have *your* wives and children. Let not the greatness of any man corrupt you, but discharge your consciences both to God and the King, and to your posterity.

Reading this, it is hard to see to what Bishop Burnet was referring. For a prosecuting counsel in a treason trial the expressions seem mild in tone. The point is important, since Burnet is the source for many of the accounts of Jeffreys' general behaviour.

Russell was found guilty. The King commuted his sentence from that of hanging, drawing and quartering to one of beheading, quietly remarking, 'Lord Russell shall find I am possessed of that prerogative, which in the case of Lord Stafford he thought proper to deny me.' Nor was Russell's estate confiscated. A week later he was executed in Lincoln's Inn Fields when, Luttrell wrote, 'Ketch the executioner severed his head from his body at three strokes, very barbarously.'

5

'From God the King, from the King the Law'
(1683-5)

The trial of Russell was the last important one in which Jeffreys appeared as an advocate. In August he was at Chester for the second assizes of the year, returning to London in September. Since the death of Saunders in July the post of Lord Chief Justice of the King's Bench had remained vacant; Jeffreys was now appointed, and a week later was sworn a member of the Privy Council.

Thirty-eight years old, Jeffreys now held the second highest judicial post. He owed his advancement partly to the support of Sunderland, partly to the part he had played in the exposure of the Rye House Plot, largely to his success as a Crown Counsel. Sunderland, typically, liked to claim that he had had difficulty in persuading the King, who had been 'very much unresolved and full of objections against him, as that all the judges would be unsatisfied if he were so advanced, and that he had not law enough'. By the time this had passed through Oates' propaganda machine after the Revolution it had become 'he has neither learning, law, nor good manners, but more impudence than ten carted whores'. The Whigs were naturally not over-pleased. Jeffreys, Evelyn wrote, is 'of an assured and undaunted spirit, and has served the Court interest on all the hardiest occasions; is of nature cruel and a slave to the Court'.

On 7th November, 1683, about ten in the morning, Jeffreys presided as Lord Chief Justice at his first state trial, that of Algernon Sidney, the second of the Council of Six.

Sidney was a man of sixty. He had fought in the Civil War against the King, and had been named one of the judges at the trial of Charles I, though he had not attended the proceedings. Nevertheless, he had felt it prudent to go abroad at the time of the Restoration and had spent seventeen years on the Continent. He had returned to England six years before, in 1677, having been granted a pardon. At once he had been drawn back into politics and had quickly become the leading political theorist of the Whigs. He was known to be a rigid republican. Burnet (who did not much care for him) wrote: 'He was stiff to all republican principles, and such an enemy to every thing that looked like monarchy, that he set himself in a high opposition against Cromwell when he was made protector.'

The indictment charged Sidney with plotting rebellion in the Council of Six; with sending a messenger to Scotland to the Earl of Argyll to organize a rebellion there; and with expressing treasonable opinions in papers found in his study. Two witnesses were required to prove a charge of treason. One was Lord Howard, the man who had turned King's evidence. Sidney objected that Howard, being himself involved in the Plot, was buying his pardon by giving evidence and was therefore biassed. Here Jeffreys interposed, with reasonable irony: 'Would you have the King's counsel to call none but men that were *not* concerned in this Plot, to prove that they were plotting?'

The Crown was hard put to it to find a second witness. For this purpose it in the end produced the writings found in manuscript in Sidney's study—the draft of a book arguing that in some circumstances rebellion and the removal of a ruler were justifiable actions, concluding 'we may therefore change or take away kings'. The use of these papers was the weak link in the Crown's case and Sidney attacked it intelligently.

How could they be sure, he first asked, that the manuscript was his? Three witnesses were then called by the Crown to identify the writing as Sidney's.

The book, *Discourses Concerning Government*, had been written as a reply to the work of Tory political philosophy, Filmer's *Patriarcha*, and Sidney next claimed that the arguments in the *Discourses* were purely theoretical ones, designed to refute Filmer. He had, he admitted, written: 'What can be thought of that damnable conclusion, which has been made by fools and knaves, that the multitude may not, if need be, correct or depose their own magistrates?'—but this was not a call to revolution, it was merely abstract reasoning. Jeffreys maintained that the cause of the writing was irrelevant:

> I don't know what the book was in answer to. We are not to speak of any book that Sir Robert Filmer wrote, but you are to make your defence touching a book that was found in your study. . . .

Sidney now fell back on his third line of defence: ˑ

> Then, my Lord, I think 'tis a right of mankind, and 'tis exercised
> by all studious men, that they write in their closets what they
> please for their own memory, and no man can be answerable for it,
> *unless they publish it.*
>
> JEFFREYS: Pray don't go away with that right of mankind, that it is
> lawful for me to write what I will in my own closet unless I
> publish it; I have been told, 'Curse not the King, not in thy
> thoughts, not in thy bedchamber, the birds of the air will
> carry it.' I took it to be the duty of mankind to observe that.
>
> SIDNEY: I have lived under the Inquisition—
>
> JEFFREYS: God be thanked we are governed by law.
>
> SIDNEY: I have lived under the Inquisition, and there is no man in
> Spain can be tried for heresy—
>
> MR. JUSTICE WYTHENS: Draw no precedents from the Inquisition
> here, I beseech you, sir.
>
> JEFFREYS: We must not endure men to talk that by the right of
> nature every man may contrive mischief in his own chamber,
> and he is not punished till he thinks fit to be called to it to be.

Sidney then tried another tack, protesting that isolated passages
might be used to prove anything.

> My lord, if you will take Scripture by pieces you will make
> all the penmen of the Scripture blasphemous; you may accuse
> David of saying there is no God, and accuse the Evangelists of
> saying Christ was a blasphemer and a seducer, and the Apostles
> that they were drunk.
>
> JEFFREYS: Look you, Mr. Sidney, if there be any part of it that
> explains the sense of it, you shall have it read; indeed we are
> trifled with a little. 'Tis true, in Scripture, 'tis said there is no
> God; and you must not take that alone, but you must say, 'the
> fool hath said in his heart there is no God'. Now here is a
> thing imputed to you in the libel; if you can say there is any
> part that is in excuse of it, call for it.

Sidney called his own witnesses, including a rival expert on
handwriting, Mr. Wharton, who explained that, if he were shown
Sidney's papers, he would quickly imitate the writing so accurately
that 'you shan't know which is which'. In his charge to the jury
Jeffreys glanced at this, commenting that Mr. Wharton 'says he
could counterfeit any hand in half an hour. It is an ugly tempta-
tion, but I hope he has more honour than to make use of that art
he so much glories in.'

Jeffreys summed up fairly enough though, as might be ex-

7

pected, on the whole against Sidney. He commented on the Whig theory of limited monarchy: 'It fixes the whole power in Parliament and the people ... the King is but their trustee ... the bringing of the late blessed King to the scaffold was first begun with such kind of principles.' In the matter of the evidence of Sidney's treason derived from his manuscript, he referred to Coke's judgement, given early in the century, *scribere est agere*— to write is to act, therefore to write treason is to commit treason. To modern eyes the use made of Sidney's private manuscripts must seem unjust, but in the nineteenth century Sir James Stephen, in his *History of the Criminal Law*, concluded 'I do not think that the illegality of permitting the jury to treat the possession of the pamphlet as an overt act of treason was as clear as it would be at present.' The matter was clarified in 1696 when an act was passed which established that no person should be convicted for treason except upon the evidence of at least two persons for each separate act of treason.

Jeffreys then reminded the jury of the frequent connection between religious dissent and political rebellion. Sidney, he said, based some of his conclusions on religious arguments

> and quotes Scriptures for it too; and you know how far that went in the late times; how we were for binding our King in chains and our nobles in fetters of iron! ... It is a cause of great concernment, and it is far from the thoughts of the King or any of his judges here, to be instrumental to take away the life of any man that by law his life ought not to be taken away. For I had rather many guilty men should escape than one innocent man should suffer. ... So that on the one side God forbid but we should be careful of men's lives, so on the other side God forbid that flourishes and varnish should come to endanger the life of the King and the destruction of the government.

With this balanced summing-up before one's eyes, one may consider Bishop Burnet's charge that Jeffreys was at this time 'scandalously vicious and was drunk every day'.

The jury retired and returned again within half an hour, about 6 p.m., bringing a verdict of guilty. Five days later Sidney returned to court to hear sentence passed. He protested, and an illuminating exchange took place between himself and Jeffreys.

> JEFFREYS: Don't think that we overrule in your case that we would not overrule in all men's cases in your condition. The treason is sufficiently laid.

Sidney repeated his former defence, admitting the facts, but contending that they did not support a charge of high treason.

MR. JUSTICE WYTHENS: I believe you don't believe it treason.

JEFFREYS: That is the worst part of your case. When men are riveted in the opinion that Kings may be deposed, that they are accountable to their people, that a general insurrection is no rebellion, and justify it, 'tis high time, upon my word, to call them to account.

This was the heart of the matter. There was no common ground between the rival political philosophies of a High Tory and a Republican Whig.

SIDNEY: I must appeal to God and the world. I am not heard.

JEFFREYS: Appeal to whom you will. I could wish with all my heart, instead of appealing to the world, as though you had received something extreme hard in your case, that you would appeal to the great God of Heaven, and consider the guilt you have contracted by the great offence you have committed. I wish with all my heart you would consider your condition; but if your own ingenuity will not provoke you, nothing I can say will prevail with you to do it. If the King's general pardon, in which you had so great a share of the King's mercy, will not, I could wish that, as a gentleman and as a Christian, you would consider under what particular obligations you lie to that gracious King that hath done so much for you. I should have thought it would have wrought in you such a temper of mind as to have turned the rest of your life into a generous acknowledgement of his bounty and mercy, and not into a state of constant combining and writing not only to destroy him, but to subvert the government; and I am sorry to see you so earnest in the justification of the book, in which there is scarce a line but what contains the rankest treason, such as deposing the King. It not only encourages but justifies all rebellion. Mr. Sidney, you are a gentleman of quality, and need no counsel from me. If I could give you any, my charity to your immortal soul would provoke me to it. I pray God season this affliction to you.

Jeffreys then pronounced sentence. It is always difficult to catch the possible intonation of the spoken word in a written account, but Jeffreys' peroration seems reasonable and dignified. Immediately after sentence had been passed, Sidney broke out:

Then, O God! O God! I beseech Thee to sanctify these sufferings unto me, and impute not my blood to the country, nor the city through which I am to be drawn. Let no inquisition be made for it; but if any, and the shedding of blood that is innocent must be revenged, let the weight of it fall only upon those that maliciously persecute me for righteousness sake.

The assumption that the Almighty was necessarily on the side of Algernon Sidney enraged Jeffreys:

I pray God work in you a temper fit to go unto the other world, for I see you are not fit for this.

Sidney retorted:

My lord, feel my pulse and see if I am disordered; I bless God I never was in a better temper than I am now.

And so the two men parted.

The trial of Sidney had played out in public the political conflict that divided the country.

Sidney was beheaded on 7th December, the King having once again reduced the sentence from that of hanging, drawing and quartering. True to his principles of philosophic detachment, he died quietly. 'He had,' wrote Narcissus Luttrell, 'no minister with him nor any of his relations, nor did he seem in the least concerned, and made no speech on the scaffold, but gave a paper to the Sheriff.'

Christmas interrupted the course of justice. This was the winter of the Great Frost, which lasted for six weeks. Jeffreys almost certainly went from his house in the City to the Courts at Westminster by ice, for Luttrell specifically noted:

All this term persons have gone by foot and coach to Westminster, above fifty coaches plying on the Thames; I myself went in one. There were whole streets of booths built in several places, but the most against the Temple Stairs, and most sorts of trades shops there; nay, below the bridge were several booths, and persons went through some of the arches of London bridge on the ice. Carts went commonly on; there were three or four printing houses; a whole ox was roasted on the ice before Whitehall, and a fox trailed along with dogs after the same day; there were multitudes of persons passing on it, and infinite sorts of sports and diversions used daily thereon. This frost was so severe that the harbours of several places were frozen up that no ship could go out or come in; no packet boats went out: the sea was frozen some miles out from the shore; vast flakes of ice of several miles were seen floating in the sea; nay, divers ships were so beset with ice that they could not sail backward or forward, but driven to great distress.

The thaw that followed coincided with the resumption of the Rye House trials. John Hampden, grandson of the John Hampden who had refused to pay Ship Money in Charles I's reign and the last of the Council of Six to be in custody, appeared to face a charge of sedition. He was not charged with treason as only one witness was available—the inevitable Lord Howard. Since he was facing a lesser charge Hampden was entitled to be represented by counsel. He chose Jeffreys' William Williams, and—surprisingly —Jeffreys' cousin 'Squinting Jack' Trevor.

The defence concentrated on the question of the credibility of Lord Howard's evidence:

WILLIAMS: By being a witness against the defendant and others he has procured his own pardon.
JEFFREYS: That is a little harsh expression.
WILLIAMS: I explain myself thus—
JEFFREYS: It is a harsh word and too roundly expressed. You had need to explain yourself. It is a little too rank, as though the King's pardon were to be procured by blood.

As Lord Chief Justice, Jeffreys was bound to protest, but Williams tried again. Essex, he said, had distrusted Lord Howard. This was hearsay, and Jeffreys pointed out that it could not be used as evidence.

WILLIAMS: It is a sort of evidence.
JEFFREYS: Ay, it is a sort of evidence, but it is not to be allowed. If you will prove Mr. Hampden's opinion you may, but you must not for him bring proof of what my Lord of Essex, a third person, thought of my Lord Howard.

Jeffreys added, 'you have offered two or more things today that I know you do at the same time know is not evidence. . . .' Hampden's lawyers disagreed as to whether or not they should address the jury at the close of the trial. One of them, Mr. Wallop, was determined to have his say. Jeffreys watched them with neutral affability, as they argued: 'Go on then, Mr. Wallop, and say what you will,' he observed. Williams intervened, 'My lord, we will leave it here, I think.' Jeffreys answered, 'Take your own course; do not say we hinder you of saying what you will for your client. . . . I'll sit still; make speeches every one of you, as long as you will.' There is irony here, but no hint of the Jeffreys of legend, shouting down defending counsel.

In the end, no one spoke further. Hampden was found guilty,

fined £40,000, and committed to prison until the fine was paid. 'No doubt,' said Jeffreys, 'if you give an account of your contrition and sorrow for your great offence, and decently apply yourself to the King, he will think of showing mercy to you.'

When, after Monmouth's rebellion, Lord Grey became available as a second witness, Hampden was found guilty of treason, but pardoned in 1686.

The final episode in the Rye House affair took place on the day after Hampden's trial. Whilst in the Tower awaiting trial there, Essex had, it will be remembered, cut his throat. Inevitably, rumour suggested that he had been murdered. The whisper snowballed and all sorts of circumstantial details were added. It was claimed that two thirteen-year-old children had actually seen a razor thrown from one of the windows of the Tower, and that 'a horrid old woman' had picked it up and hidden it. The Whigs were delighted, while the Crown saw that the story must be checked. Two barristers, Laurence Braddon and Hugh Speke were brought to trial accused of spreading the rumour. Speke was the second son of the strong Whig, Charles Speke, of White Lackington in Somerset. Monmouth had visited the family during his Western 'progress' and later the family were to be heavily involved in his rebellion.

Confident in its case, the Crown itself called the children as witnesses, a daring action as Braddon had obtained a written statement from them. The boy's father was called to say that his son did not always tell the truth, and then the boy himself, Edwards, was lifted on to a table.

> JEFFREYS: If you should tell a lie do you know what will become of you?
>
> EDWARDS: I should go to hell-fire.
>
> JEFFREYS: That is a terrible thing. And therefore, child, if you take an oath be sure you say nothing but what is truth, for no party, nor side, nor anything in the world; for that God that you say will call you to an account and cast you into hell-fire if you tell a lie and witness to a falsehood knows and sees all you do; therefore have a care—the truth you must say, and nothing but the truth.

Edwards then admitted that he had invented the whole story.

> JEFFREYS: What a dust has such a trivial report made in the world! Admit the boy had said any such thing, what an age do we live in that the report of every child shall blow us up after this rate!

It would make a body tremble to think what sort of people we live among; to what an heat does zeal transport some people beyond all reason and sobriety! If such a little boy had said so, 'tis not an half-penny matter; but presently all the Government is to be libelled for a boy, which, whether he speaks true or false, is of no great weight; and he swears 'tis all false.

The girl, Lodeman, was made of sterner stuff, and stuck to her version, but the Crown lawyers were able to show that, if she had been playing where she said, she could not have seen the window from which the razor was supposed to have been flung.

The defence, represented by Mr. Wallop, suggested that Edwards had changed his tale because he had been told that if he did not do so his father would be hanged.

Jeffreys asked Wallop if he believed the tale. The latter replied, 'I ask questions according to my instructions. . . . I do not say or believe any such thing. . . .'

JEFFREYS: Nay, Mr. Wallop, be as angry as you will, you shall not hector the court out of their understandings. We see plainly enough whither that question tends. You that are gentlemen of the robe should carry yourselves with greater respect to the Government, and while you do so the court will carry themselves as becomes them to you.

WALLOP: I refer myself to all that hear me if I attempted any such thing as to hector the court.

JEFFREYS: Refer yourself to all that hear you? Refer yourself to the court. It is a reflection upon the Government, I tell you your question is; and you shall not do any such thing while I sit here, by the grace of God, if I can help it.

WALLOP: I am sorry for that. I never intended any such thing, my lord.

JEFFREYS: Pray behave yourself as you ought, Mr. Wallop. You must not think to huff and swagger here.

There were other witnesses, and twice, perhaps, one can catch the tone of Jeffreys' voice. On the first occasion he was encouraging another boy witness: 'Prithee speak out,' he said, 'as though thou were at play at check-farthing.' On the second occasion he had tried in vain to persuade a woman witness that hearsay was not evidence. In the end he stopped her with the pleasantly exasperated comment: 'Nay, prithee, mistress, be not so full of tattle, so full of clack.'

When he came to sum up, Jeffreys made some observations

which are of importance for the light they throw on his own sincerely-held political philosophy. Of Braddon he said:

> He is a busy man, you see, a great reformer, that does mightily concern himself in the reformation of the government. I never knew Mr. Braddon had any great share in it: he has not such a prodigious estate, I suppose, that for fear of losing his great estate he should be so wondrous busy and active in reforming the Government; but I have always observed it for a rule that your beggarly inconsiderable fellows are the warmest people in the business of reformation, and for defending liberty and property, as they call it; and then they put it under the disguise of religion, when, alas, those that have no religion are generally the greatest pretenders of taking care of it; and those that have no estates nor properties are usually the fullest of noise about liberty and property. But the meaning of it is plain: if they can but exasperate the people into a rebellion, that is the way to get a property; and if they can but have liberty to do what they please that is all the liberty they contend for.

The jury found Braddon and Speke guilty. Jeffreys had made it clear that the evidence showed that Speke had been only an accessory. Braddon was therefore fined £2,000 and Speke £1,000.

Had justice been done? After the Revolution Braddon received a pension, but a committee of inquiry failed to uncover any further evidence and such Whigs as Burnet were prepared to believe that Essex might have killed himself, for he had 'very black fits of the spleen'. Only Braddon himself went on protesting his belief that Essex had been murdered. His protests were clearly sincere, since in the end they cost him his pension, the money being stopped in Queen Anne's reign.

By the close of this trial the thaw was general, and Jeffreys soon left town on his first assize as Lord Chief Justice. He chose as his circuit that of the West; reasonably accessible from London and a centre of Whig disaffection, the area was an obvious choice, but an ironical one in view of Jeffreys' later assize there after Monmouth's rebellion. By contrast this was an uneventful circuit. From Winchester Jeffreys wrote that the roads were still 'very foul'. At Plymouth the corporation, having agreed to surrender their charter (the King was now using the *Quo Warranto* decision to gain control of the leading cities), were now having second thoughts, on the advice of Maynard, the Whig Recorder of the city. Jeffreys was able to persuade them to return to their original decision. At Exeter he presided at the trial of Allice Molland, one of the last women in England to be convicted on a charge of witchcraft, but unfortunately a detailed account of the trial has not survived.

Six weeks later, the assize concluded, Jeffreys was back in London, where the aftermath of the Rye House Plot provided three more political trials. The first was that of Sir Samuel Barnardiston, a man who had been opposed to the Court for forty years ever since the days before the Civil War—indeed, some said he was the original 'roundhead'. He had brought in the articles of impeachment against Danby, the King's minister, in 1675 and more recently he had been foreman of the packed grand jury that had thrown out the charges against Shaftesbury. He was well-known for his outspoken expressions of opinion—a contemporary nicknamed him 'Sir Shamwell Fireandbrimstone' —and the Government were delighted when they were able to bring him to trial for declaring in private letters that the Rye House Plot was a put-up job. The letters had been ruled to be seditious and Jeffreys passed judgement. As usual, he seized the opportunity to attack the Whigs:

> It is high time for all mankind, that have any Christianity, or sense of Heaven or Hell, to bestir themselves, to rid the nation of such caterpillars, such monsters of villainy as these are.

Sir Samuel was fined £10,000. He did not pay and remained in prison until 1688, when he compounded for the sum of £6,000. If he had waited another six months the Whigs would have been in power again and he would have got his liberty for nothing!

Sir Willoughby Aston of Cheshire had an interview with Jeffreys in connection with the part played by Cheshire in anti-Royalist activities. He recorded that Jeffreys said:

> The Grand Jury are the eyes of the Law. We see what a horrid design has been carried on against the Government. . . . We see there was a design on foot, and though the Duke has the King's pardon, we cannot believe but some ill men made use of him to carry on their wicked designs, I hear that there are several worthy gentlemen amongst those that are presented, and I hope it is true. Nothing is infallible. Grand Jurors may be deceived. . . . I think myself very unhappy that at my first coming into the County I should be obliged to do something that may be ungrateful to many persons of quality, but in this case nothing is left to our discretion.

At a later meeting Jeffreys took up this theme again, saying, "'We cannot favour anything." At which he stepped back and leaning in the window muttered to himself, but so I could hear him say, *fiat Justitia, ruat Coelum* (Justice must be done though the heavens fall).'[1]

In April and in June Jeffreys presided at the trials of two more of the Rye House conspirators. James Holloway, a Bristol merchant, had been outlawed, had fled to the West Indies, and had been seized there and sent back to England. Before his trial he had already confessed to the Privy Council. His was an open and shut case, since he was an outlaw, and the sentence of outlawry meant that, unless he surrendered himself within a year, he lost all right to any trial and was liable when captured to be brought before a judge and immediately ordered for execution.

More dramatic was the trial of the second outlaw, Sir Thomas Armstrong. Sir Thomas, that 'debauched atheistical bravo', that gentleman of fortune, had always had a powerful influence for ill over the Duke of Monmouth. After the exposure of the Rye House Plot he had got away to Holland, where he had been taken at Leyden and handed over to the English authorities. Armstrong's hearing took place on 14th June. He maintained that he had, in effect, yielded to the authorities within a year of his outlawry and that therefore he was entitled to a trial. The Attorney-General took the view that he had been taken against his will and Jeffreys, presiding, supported the Attorney.

SIR THOMAS: I desire to be put upon my trial, my lord.
JEFFREYS: We cannot allow any such thing. We have nothing to do upon this record but to award execution. Captain Richardson, what are your usual days of execution?
RICHARDSON: Wednesdays and Fridays, my lord.

At this, Armstrong's daughter, Mrs. Matthews burst out from the body of the court:

My lord, I hope you will not murder my father. This is murdering a man.
JEFFREYS: Who is this woman? Marshall, take her into custody. Why, how now? Because your relation is attainted for high treason must you take upon you to tax the courts of justice for murder when we grant execution according to the law? Take her away.

[1] Sir Willoughby Aston; *Diary*: quoted in G. W. Keeton; *Lord Chancellor Jeffreys and the Stuart Cause* (London, 1965).

MRS. MATTHEWS: God Almighty's judgements light upon you!

JEFFREYS: God Almighty's judgements will light upon those that are guilty of high treason.

MRS. MATTHEWS: Amen, I pray God.

JEFFREYS: So say I, but clamours never prevail upon me at all. I thank God I am clamour-proof and will never fear to do my duty.

Although Mrs. Matthews had been committed for contempt of court, the Verney papers report that Jeffreys 'very honourably released her' the same day. Meanwhile the argument with Armstrong had concluded as follows:

ARMSTRONG: I ought to have the benefit of the law, and I demand no more.

JEFFREYS: That you shall have, by the grace of God. See that execution be done on Friday next, according to the law. You shall have the full benefit of the law.

With the successful conclusion of the Rye House trials, Jeffreys' position as one of the ring of Court officials was assured. Whig pamphleteers renewed their attacks. Tory poetasters rushed to his defence. Each drew monstrous caricatures. Settle—of whose poetry Dryden wrote that it was 'Free from all meaning'—produced a panegyric on Jeffreys' career. During the days of the Popish Plot, when

. . . all men feared they knew not What nor Why.
Jeffreys alone waked their lethargic souls
And from their lips withdrew the Enchanting Bowls.

His destiny was to 'set the course of staggering nature right' and to

. . . bind our world to Charles and Charles's laws,
He the First Mover, Thou the Second Cause.

Ridiculous stuff—as ridiculous as the Whig attacks.

During the Trinity term of 1684 Jeffreys presided at the prosecution of Nottingham Whigs charged with rioting when the elections took place there under the town's new charter in the preceding autumn. They had penned the new Tory Mayor in his house and had taken possession of the Guildhall. The evidence was graphic. Alderman Rippon, a Tory, deposed:

I was fain to secure the charter, and a farrendine [part silk, part wool] waistcoat that I had on was all rubbed to pieces to save the charter, and I had much ado to save it. My brother Parker, he was so afraid he got off the bench. 'Prithee,' said I, 'stay, for certainly they dare not do these things.' Says he, 'I am afraid of my life, and fare you well.' Mr. Mayor and I sat awhile, for we knew not which way to take, but at last we got away through them. But if I touched ground I wish I might never see my wife again.'

The Court was amused. Jeffreys commented: 'Now whether that be a curse that thou layest upon thyself or no I cannot tell.'

Parker continued with his evidence. He described how he got home, drank a glass of wine, and then said, 'If they must be knocked on the head I will go and be knocked on the head with them.' Jeffreys, clearly still tickled by the evidence, said, 'Ay, his courage came to him again when he had a glass of wine.'

In due course all but one of the accused were found guilty, and fined.

Not all Jeffreys' time was taken up with political trials. In one civil case he crossed swords with Maynard, the Whig Recorder of Plymouth whom he had frustrated during his visit to that place in the spring. This time Maynard had the best of it. When told by Jeffreys that he had forgotten all his law, he retorted, 'Yes, my lord, I have forgotten more law than you ever knew.'

Jeffreys presided at the hearing of Lady Ivy's Case, a complex property case, at that time the second longest that had ever taken place at Westminster. Lady Ivy's father, Stepkins, had bought a newly drained area at Wapping but it was claimed that the land belonged to the Dean and Chapter of St. Paul's. Jeffreys outlined the point at issue as follows:

> The question in short is, whether seven acres and a half of land, now built upon to a very great value, as the witnesses say £2,000 a year, lying on the east side of the land, that is called by the name of Fox's Lane, betwixt that and the mill, called Ratcliff Mill, be part of the marsh that formerly belonged to the family of the Stepkins's, or whether or no that be not part of the Dean and Chapter of Paul's inheritance?

Eventually Lady Ivy lost her case. Even Lord Campbell, who so strongly disliked Jeffreys, admitted in his *Lives of the Chancellors* (1845-7) that in this case Jeffreys' summing-up was 'most masterly'.

The second case, which dragged on from 1683 to 1685, was that of the *East India Company* v. *Sandys*. The Company had been founded by Queen Elizabeth in 1600 and had been given a monopoly of trade with all areas east of the Cape. The monopoly was very profitable and during the second half of the seventeenth century the Company suffered much from the activities of unauthorized merchants, known as 'interlopers'. One of these interlopers, Sandys, brought an action to test the legality of the Company's charter. The case had its political aspects, for Tories supported the Company and the use of the royal prerogative in establishing it, while the Whigs opposed it. As usual, William Williams appeared on the Whig side and—also as usual—Jeffreys crossed swords with him. Williams said that Parliament should 'help' the King to regulate trade. At this Jeffreys observed:

> God be praised, it is in the King's power to call and dissolve Parliaments, when and how he pleases; and he is the only judge of these *ardua regni*, that he should think fit to consult with the Parliament about. And Mr. Williams would do well to save himself the trouble of advising the King what things are fit for him to consult with his parliament about, until such time as he is thereunto called.

He added that he could not help noticing that this attack on the royal prerogative had begun at much the same time as the Rye House Plot, and concluded:

> The East India Company have solely run the hazard and been at great expenses in discovering places, erecting forts and keeping forces, settling factories, and making leagues and treaties abroad. It would be against natural justice and equity (which no municipal law can take away) for others to reap the benefit and advantage of all this.

The East India Company won its case, and once again Campbell is forced to admit that Jeffreys knew his law, calling the judgement 'one of the best specimens of Jeffreys' judicial powers'.

Jeffreys had shown himself to be efficient, loyal and—most important—successful. At Whitehall in July the King gave him a diamond ring 'publicly taken from his own finger', but when at the end of the month Jeffreys left London on assize, this time on the Northern Circuit, Lord Keeper North said the gift had only been made 'to blow his fame as favourite before the circuit', for the northern towns had been slow to surrender their charters to the King. Now, Roger North wrote, they fell before Jeffreys like the walls of Jericho.

Berwick, Carlisle, Kendal, Lancaster, York—all gave way, impressed by fear or by the advice 'consider what privileges or advantages belonging to your Town which was either omitted or not sufficiently granted to you by your old Charter, may be supplied by this new one. . . .' There was plenty of social life too. At York Jeffreys met his old Tory friend Sir John Reresby, who wrote in his Memoirs, 'my lord himself came to me incognito one evening, and being a jolly, merry companion when his business was over, stayed with me over a bottle till one o'clock in the morning'.

On his return to London in September, 'laden with surrenders', Jeffreys was admitted to the select group of the King's advisers. He was already a member of the Council, which sat on Thursdays, but it was at the meetings of the inner ring, meeting on Sundays, that questions of high policy were really settled. It was from these meetings of seven or eight men that the Cabinet later developed—'those few great officers and courtiers,' says North, 'whom the King relied upon for the interior dispatch of his affairs.' On Sunday evenings, in the King's private apartments at Whitehall, in the company of such men as Rochester, Halifax, Godolphin, Sunderland and the Duke of York, Jeffreys stood at the very heart of political power. It was only eight years since he had been made Recorder of the City of London. In another five years he would be dead. Meanwhile he was on the heights.

The Duke of York had instructed Jeffreys to obtain, while on the Northern Circuit, lists of all the Catholics there. It was one step along a road that eventually brought disaster to both the Duke and Jeffreys. At the Cabinet meeting Jeffreys rose and spoke:

> Sir, I have a business to lay before your Majesty which I took notice of in the North. . . . It is the case of the numberless numbers of your good subjects that are imprisoned for recusancy [refusal to attend the services of the Church of England]. I have the list of them here, to justify what I say. There are so many that the great gaols cannot hold them without their lying upon one another.

Many, he continued, were 'rotting and stinking in prisons'.

Lord Keeper Guilford asked searchingly whether all the persons mentioned were actually in prison. Jeffreys admitted that they were not 'for all the gaols in England would not hold them', but pointed out that, by virtue of their crime they were liable to imprisonment at any time. The Lord Keeper returned to the attack. In his opinion a general pardon would be dangerous for it would apply not only to loyal Catholics but also to 'sectaries of all kinds and denominations, perhaps as many or more, who are all professed enemies to your Majesty and your Government in Church and State'. No action was taken.

That night Guilford worried—he was a great worrier—over the suggested change of policy: 'What can be the meaning? Are they all stark mad?' It was clear, his brother thought, that 'Jeffreys was brought forward and buoyed up by the adverse party of the Court on purpose to ruffle my Lord Keeper' and have him out of office, to which Jeffreys 'one ready to do all that was required of him, should succeed'.

And there, for the time being, the matter rested.

In November Jeffreys took his place in Westminster Hall to try the well-known Dissenting minister, Mr. Thomas Rosewall, on a charge of high treason. Three women testified that he had preached a sermon at Rotherhithe in which he had compared the King and his father Charles I to Jeroboam ('We have had two wicked kings now together, who have suffered popery to be introduced under their noses, whom I can liken to no one but wicked Jeroboam.'), had declared that Charles II intended to make England Catholic again, and had gone on to say that he must be resisted. The sermon—'frightful stuff', Jeffreys termed it—had lasted from seven in the morning till two in the afternoon.

Rosewall called witnesses to show that he always prayed for the King. Jeffreys commented, 'So there was praying in this Hall, I remember, for his late Majesty, for the doing of him justice. We all know what that meant, and where it ended.' Jeffreys was alluding to the fact that Charles I's trial had taken place in Westminster Hall where they were now sitting. He was less than fair to Rosewall's witnesses, saying, 'We know well enough you snivelling saints can lie.'

Rosewall was found guilty, but he was pardoned by the King—perhaps because he was a scholar and a gentleman and not a poor ranting working-man, or perhaps because one of the defence witnesses had told the King, 'Sire, if your Majesty suffers this man to die, we are none of us safe in our bed from informers.'

Also, policy was moving on to a new plane—that of toleration for Catholics, and—conceivably—for Dissenters also.

About a week before Rosewall's trial Jeffreys had heard an action for false arrest brought by Sir William Pritchard, a former Tory Lord Mayor, against Thomas Papillon, one of the nominees for the post of sheriff in the disputed City elections of 1682. In the course of the trial Jeffreys accused Ward, the defending counsel, of irrelevancy, of delivering 'flourishes, enamel, garniture and oceans of discourse'. The crowd reacted and 'there was a little Hiss begun. . . .' Jeffreys addressed them directly:

> I hope we are now past that time of day that humming and hissing shall be used in courts of justice; but I would fain know that fellow that dare to hum or hiss while I sit here: I'll assure him, be he who he will, I'll lay him by the heels, and make an example of him. Indeed, I knew the time when causes were to be carried according as the Mobile hissed or hummed; and I do not question but they have as good a will to it now. Come, Mr. Ward, let us have none of your fragrancies, and fine rhetorical flowers, to take people with.

Jeffreys was himself not above the use of 'fine rhetorical flowers', in his summing-up he referred to the picking of juries, and drew a vivid picture of the Whig sheriffs choosing

> this facetious fellow out of one corner, and that pragmatical, prick-eared, snivelling rascal out of another corner, to prop up the Cause, which was tried not according to justness but demureness of look. (The whole pack of them were) notorious Dissenters or profligate atheistical villains that herd together. . . . This, gentlemen, is plain English, and necessary to be used upon all occasions.

The jury found Papillon guilty, and Jeffreys congratulated them:

> Gentlemen, you seem to be persons that have some sense upon you and consideration for the Government, and I think have given a good verdict and are to be greatly commended for it.

Papillon was ordered to pay £1,000 damages.

Embedded in Jeffreys' summing-up are two sentences, in 'plain English', that provide the key to the attitude of both Whigs and Tories—and to his own posthumous reputation:

> We live in an age wherein men are apt to believe only on one side. They can believe the greatest lie if it makes for the advantage of their party, but not the greatest truth if it thwarts their interests.

Jeffreys could believe no good of his political opponents, after his death they could believe no good of him. Both were wrong—and human nature has not changed in the succeeding three hundred years.

6

A New King, and a Pillory'd Prophet
(1685)

'The 6th of February (1685), being Friday, his Majesty King Charles the Second died at Whitehall, about three quarter after eleven at noon'—news that, wrote Luttrell, 'put the town in a great consternation, and the gates of Whitehall were shut up and the guards drawn out.' It was the end of an era—the end of an attempt to retain the powers of an absolute monarchy with the machinery of a limited one. For a quarter of a century Charles had, with infinite skill, manœuvred and compromised. Always prepared to give way over inessentials, he had nevertheless succeeded in holding the power which had been restored to him and even in extending it. Since the dissolution of the Oxford Parliament, the rewriting of the borough charters, and the payment of a pension by Louis XIV, the Crown had known greater security than at any other time since 1640. Charles ambled through his last years in a sunset glow of peace and popularity; these were 'good King Charles's golden days'. Given another thirty years of careful, cautious, flexible, unprincipled rule, England might have joined the absolute monarchies of continental Europe. Instead within four years the new King, James II, was an exile and a constitutional monarchy was in process of being established.

The former Duke of York lost his throne because he was inflexible, because he was a Catholic—above all, because he was stupid. All this had been clear to his brother Charles, who had been heard to speak of *la sottise de mon frère*, and to remark, 'I am much afraid that when he comes to wear the crown he will be obliged to travel again.' He was not alone in his fears. His old enemy Shaftesbury had noted that the Duke of York was a man '. . . heady, violent and bloody, who easily believes the rashest and the worst of councils to be the most sincere and hearty'. On James's accession the French envoy wrote to his master Louis

8   113

XIV: 'It is quite certain that this King is neither so self-controlled nor so great a man as has been supposed. He has all the faults of the King his father, but has less sense and he behaves more haughtily in public.' And years later, when he was an exile at the French court, the sensible Madame de Sévigné observed James and wrote, 'When one listens to him one understands why he is here.'

Charles had accepted human nature, had been able to appreciate why people might oppose him: James could only find, in the slightest resistance to his plans, the treachery of the knave, or the short-sightedness of the fool. Jeffreys was now sure of royal favour, and of promotion—but at a price. Given the new King's character, there was nothing that Jeffreys could do to influence his master. Judges held their posts at the King's pleasure, to oppose James would have been to obtain instant dismissal and ruin. Jeffreys had nothing but his own ability to fall back on—no aristocratic background, no well-born connections. His rise had been spectacular, his fall would be sordid. He might easily end as a little Welsh attorney. For the time being his High Tory and High Anglican principles made it easy for him to accept James's conditions of service.

The Englishman who played the greatest part in James's administration was Robert Spencer, Earl of Sunderland. He was in a different position from Jeffreys. If he were dismissed he had his family connections, his patrician milieu. He could easily live in opposition to the Court. He made no attempt to restrain the King and there is some evidence for regarding him as James's evil genius. Sunderland's biographer has said of him: 'He and James were thoroughly bad for each other. James was an old man in a hurry, Sunderland had forgotten the meaning of the word "restraint"; so neither was capable of putting on the brake until it was too late.'[1]

The year 1685 was Jeffreys' climacteric. He became a baron, and Lord Chancellor; he presided at the trial of Titus Oates; he was in charge of the assize of the West, which posthumously blasted his reputation; he began to suffer agonies from the stone. 'By the force of these singular circumstances and by a certain genius for the terrible which Jeffreys possessed in an almost fascinating degree, the year 1685 is to witness the stormy descent of the Lord

[1] Kenyon, J. P.; *Robert Spencer, Earl of Sunderland, 1641–1702* (London, 1958), p. 330.

Chief Justice into the dark realms of the historically accursed . . .'[1] wrote Irving, the first biographer to treat Jeffreys as a human being and not as a political monster.

Jeffreys' disease was acute, it killed him within four years. Stones in the kidneys or bladder were not uncommon in the seventeenth century. Pepys had his cut out successfully, but the operation was usually a failure.

'. . . in the medical books of the time the term "stone" was used to mean stone in the bladder, whereas "stone in the kidneys" was given its full title and treated differently. The references to Jeffreys' affliction mention always "stone", "fit of the stone", or "stone and strangury". Now, a stone in the bladder, while not producing symptoms so acute as to force the patient to bed, can yet cause such persistent discomfort and constant harassing pain as to make his life a thorough misery. The difficulty of micturition, the frequency of the unrelieving calls by day and night, the perpetual sense of weight locally—these symptoms would inevitably have produced, especially in a man of Jeffreys' inclination, such an irritability of mind that it is little wonder that men who came before him, to argue their defence, should have been greeted with short patience.'[2]

'The staring eyes and working features' mentioned by contemporary observers of Jeffreys' behaviour were probably caused by efforts to master the pain when he needed to maintain complete control of his faculties for business. Certainly Jeffreys shortened his life by the long periods he spent on the bench, or jolting along execrable roads in a primitively-sprung coach.

Early in the year Jeffreys went as assize judge on the Eastern Circuit and then to Bulstrode. The election of James II's first and only Parliament was under way and Jeffreys naturally brought the weight of his name on the Tory side. His efforts were not successful. Bedfordshire was a Whig county, and that party's candidates were powerful men; Lord Brackley, son of the Earl of Bridgewater, and the Honourable Thomas Wharton, who had helped to take the Exclusion Bill to the Lords. The latter was very wealthy and on one critical day alone spent £1,000 in bribes. The Tory candidate, on the other hand, was a Mr. Hackett, described as 'an unknown young gentleman from the neighbourhood of Newport Pagnell'. Jeffreys did what he could. At that time polling

[1] H. B. Irving, *The Life of Judge Jeffreys* (London, 1898), p. 232.
[2] J. Kemble, *Idols and Invalids* (London, 1933), pp. 52 e.s.

lasted for a fortnight and when it became clear that the tide was flowing against Hackett, Jeffreys persuaded the sheriff suddenly to shift the poll to Newport Pagnell, fifteen miles away, where the Tories had taken up all the accommodation. The Whigs, it is said, were forced to camp out, but in spite of these desperate measures, the 'unknown young gentleman' was defeated.

After this excursion into county politics, Jeffreys returned to London to attend the coronation of James and his wife, Mary Beatrice of Modena. In the coronation honours list he received his peerage:

> Since our much loved and right faithful counsellor George Jeffreys, Knight and Baronet, hath advanced through the degrees of juris-prudence with such diligence and success as that when we were Duke of York we chose him to be our Solicitor-General and held his fidelity and courage undoubted in all things which touched our person, especially at that time when by the wicked instigation of some factious persons we were torn from our most illustrious brother, our Lord Charles the Second, . . . we of our will, and from that regard which we bear the said George Jeffreys are of the opinion that he should be admitted amongst the peers of this realm.

Jeffreys had bought the Manors of Wem and Loppington in Shropshire from Daniel Wycherley (father of the playwright) on 23rd December, 1684, for £9,000 and he now took the title of Baron Jeffreys of Wem. He was the first Lord Chief Justice to be ennobled while still in office—but then, Burnet wrote, 'He affected to be an original in everything.'

Original or no, Jeffreys' star was in the ascendant. The next and final step in judicial preferment would be to the Lord Chancellor-ship. At the moment there was no Chancellor. Roger North's brother Francis, now Baron Guilford, was still performing the duties with the lesser rank of Lord Keeper. For almost twenty years his career and that of Jeffreys had run parallel, with North, a little older, one step ahead. Dignified, austere, moral, North was completely out of place in Restoration society and the younger courtiers made his life a misery with a succession of practical jokes. Jeffreys and Sunderland in particular took advantage of Lord Guilford's retiring nature and complete lack of humour to tease him. They suggested that a whore might cheer him up, and offered to supply one. The Lord Keeper replied with some spirit 'that if he *were* to entertain a madame, it should be one of his own choos-ing and not one of their stale trumpery'.

Then there was the matter of the rhinoceros. It was the first ever brought to England, and his brother Dudley took him to see the huge beast. Lord Guilford 'came away exceedingly satisfied with the curiosity he had seen'. At once Sunderland and Jeffreys spread the story that he had been seen riding on the animal and was thinking of buying it to use instead of a horse 'than which a more infantine exploit could not have been fastened upon him'. Dudley laughed and would not deny the story—'And so it passed and the noble Earl of Sunderland, with Jeffreys and others of that crew, made merry and never blushed at the lie of their own making, but valued themselves upon it as a very good jest.'

There was, however, more important business to attend to than baiting the Lord Keeper. On 8th May Jeffreys presided at the trial of Titus Oates for perjury. Nemesis had been catching up with the Salamanca doctor for some time. He had been arrested almost exactly a year before (10th May, 1684) and in November a jury had brought in a true bill against him. On 23rd January, 1685, Oates had pleaded not guilty. Now he faced Jeffreys.

The Lord Chief Justice was deceptively mild. Ailesbury, no friend of his, wrote:

Knowing well the Chief Justice's unlimited passion, I expected he would show himself in his true colours; but I was greatly surprised at his good temper, and the more because such impudent and reviling expressions never came from the mouth of a man as Oates uttered.

In essence, Oates faced two charges. The first was that he had, at Ireland's trial, committed perjury by swearing that he had attended the 'consult' of Jesuits at the White Horse Tavern in the Strand on 24th April, 1678, when he was in fact at the Jesuit Seminary at St. Omer during the whole of April and May, 1678. The second charge was that, at the same trial, he had again perjured himself by swearing that he had seen Ireland in London in 1678 on the 8th and 12th August and again on the 1st and 2nd September, when the priest could be proved to have been out of London from early August to mid-September. Oates' defence was that the statements had been true and—irrelevantly—that everyone had believed him at the time.

As a great cross-examiner George Jeffreys saw that, given a little rope, a man like Oates would soon hang himself.

The trial on the first indictment took place on 8th May. The

Crown called witnesses, fellow students of Oates at St. Omer, to
testify that Oates had been there in April and May, 1678. They
could, they said, remember this clearly, since he had made himself ridiculous, '... his conversation and canting stories after
Dinner and Supper and times of Recreation made him so remarkable that nobody could miss him all the time he was there', and 'a
little boy beat him up and down with a fox's tail'. Oates confined
himself to making each witness admit himself a Catholic, then
asking him what reward he had for giving false evidence.

Jeffreys protested: 'Mr. Oates, you must not ask any such
questions. What know I but by asking him the question you make
him obnoxious to some penalty? You must not ask any questions
to ensnare him.' Oates complained: 'My lord, I do find my
defence is under very great prejudice.' Jeffreys: 'Why so? Because we won't let you ask impertinent questions, or such as may
render the witnesses obnoxious to a penalty?' And, after further
debate, 'Behave yourself as you ought, and you shall be heard
with all fairness that can be desired.'

Oates persisted, and when he accused one of the Crown witnesses, Lord Castlemaine, of speaking out of malice, Jeffreys at
last flared up:'Hold your tongue! You are a shame to mankind!'
Oates answered: 'No, my Lord, I am neither a shame to myself
or to mankind. What I have sworn is true, and I will stand by it to
my last breath, and seal it, if occasion be, with my blood.'
Jeffreys retorted ominously: 'It were a pity that it were not done
with thy blood.'

Oates, against Jeffreys' advice, now began to defend himself on
the grounds that any miscarriage of justice was the fault of the
judges and juries at the time of the Popish Plot.

JEFFREYS: A judge's opinion is of value in points of law that arise
upon facts found by juries, but is no evidence of the fact: for
judges only do presume the fact to be true, as it is found by the
jury; and therefore say they, out of that fact so found, the point
of law arising is thus and thus. Then in case, after a jury has
given a verdict of the fact, a judge's opinion of the fact (which
may be perhaps contrary to the verdict) should be an evidence
as to that fact, that would be to overthrow and nullify the jury's
verdict: no, that is not the judge's province.... And by the
same reason as this, a jury of honest gentlemen here, when I
tell them, here is a plain fact either to convict you, or to acquit
you upon this indictment, are not bound to go by what I say in

point of fact, but they are to go according to their own oaths,
and according to the evidence and testimony of the witnesses.
It is not my opinion that is to weigh at all with them. . . . I
must tell you, there is no doubt, but that those juries did every
one believe the evidence you gave, or they would not have
convicted the prisoners. . . . Alackaday! How many times have
we causes here in Westminster Hall wherein we have verdict
against verdict, and yet no imputation to either juries which
might give different verdicts on different grounds . . . In these
cases we give our opinions always according to the present
testimony that is before us.

The Lord Chief Justice repeated his earlier advice—

If you did call two or three witnesses to prove that you were in
town the 22nd, 23rd or 24th of April, it would be the best
defence you could make.

This Oates proceeded to do, but unfortunately for him the witnesses contradicted one another. One of them, Mrs. Mayo,
attempted to strengthen her evidence by adding that she spoke as
in the presence of the Lord. Jeffreys observed sharply, 'We are
all of us in the presence of the Lord always.'

Oates continued to call witnesses to the state of his credit in
1678, but with little success. Lord Huntingdon for instance, said
'I do believe most of the House of Peers have altered their
opinion as to this man's credit, and look upon his evidence as I do
to be very false.'

JEFFREYS: Do you hear him, Mr. Oates?
OATES: No, my lord, I do not very well.
JEFFREYS: Then, my Lord Huntingdon, turn your face to the jury;
and say what you said to us over again.

Oates persisted: 'My lord, I called you in answer to my question as to somewhat that is past, and not to give your judgement
how you are inclined to believe me now. . . . If at that time my
Evidence was true, it must be true still.' But he got no further
along that line of reasoning.

OATES: Well, my lord, I have done with my Lord of Huntingdon.
MR. JUSTICE WYTHENS: And he has done with you, as I perceive.
JEFFREYS: Yes, truly. Methinks ye shake hands and part very fairly.

The Attorney General returned to the attack with evidence
that at least two of Oates' witnesses in 1678 had since admitted
that they had committed perjury. One was William Smith, a
schoolmaster from Islington, arrested in the early days of the Plot.

Oates, Smith said, had required him to swear that they had dined together on the first Monday in May, 1678; '. . . he threatened me, and so did others too, that he would have me hang'd for being in the Plot, if I did not comply with him, and swear this for him.'

Jeffreys refused to accept Smith's damning evidence against Oates, observing '. . . if he did foreswear himself, why should he ever be a witness again?' The Solicitor-General protested, but Jeffreys stood firm:

> Argue the matter as long as you will, Mr. Solicitor, you will never convince me, but he that has once foresworn himself ought not to be a witness after that in any cause whatsoever. If any man tell me otherwise till doomsday, I cannot be convinced of it. [Roger North, one of the junior counsel for the Crown argued, but Jeffreys cut him short:] Look ye, sir, you have our opinion; it was always the practice heretofore that when the Court have delivered their opinion the counsel should sit down and not dispute it further.

As the trial drew to its close, it became clear even to Oates what the verdict was likely to be, and he asked leave to withdraw 'for I am very weak and ill.' Jeffreys let him go, and then summed up. He pointed out that the verdicts during the Popish Plot scare were 'a thing for which the justice of the nation lies under great reproach abroad.' He had himself played a small part in that miscarriage of justice 'and I am sorry to say it.'

> . . . this profligate villain was caressed, was drunk to and saluted by the name of the 'Saviour of the Nation'. . . . The prisoner has said he will venture his blood in confirmation of his impious falsehoods; but to speak truth he makes no great venture in it; for when he had pawned his immortal soul by so perjured a testimony, he may very easily proffer the venturing his vile carcase to maintain it. . . . And sure I am, if you think these witnesses swear true—as I cannot see any colour of objection—there does not remain the least doubt but that Oates is the blackest and most perjured villain that ever appeared upon the face of the earth.

After a retirement of only a quarter of an hour, the jury returned a verdict of 'Guilty'.

Next day Oates stood his trial on the second charge of perjury. The Crown called witnesses to testify that Ireland had been in Hertfordshire and Staffordshire at the time when Oates had sworn he was in London. Oates persisted in his former defence that men had once thought otherwise.

'Ay, Mr. Oates, we know there was a time when there were

ignoramus juries,' Jeffreys replied, 'and things were believed and not believed as the humour went. What can you, Mr. Oates, say to it? I must needs tell you, *prima facie* it is so strong an evidence that if you have any sense in the world you must be concerned at it.'

'Not at all, my lord ...'

'Upon my faith, I have so much charity for you as my fellow-creature as to be concerned for you.'

'It is not two straw matter whether you be or no. I know my own innocency.'

'Thou art the most obstinately hardened wretch that I ever saw.'

Once again Oates retired. Jeffreys summed up, and took the opportunity to speak of the whole Oates affair, describing how

> a sort of ill-minded men had crept in among us, who had blown us up to such a height, that nothing but what complied with their malicious and devilish designs would be believed; ... When the facetious (by cabals and intrigues) had got sheriffs of their own party, and laboured to get all other offices of their own wicked principles, then came all those other mischiefs we so long laboured under. When those fellows that had so great a share in the late Rebellion, were the only fit men to be trusted with the government; and all the while were designing to destroy it, and to bring us into the same miserable condition we formerly were in ... was it ever known, till justice was designed to be corrupted, that there was any labouring to be sheriffs? No, endeavours were always used to be excused, and fines paid to get off from that office; ... 'Popery was a coming in'. When they found they could not overthrow the government by methods of law, they betake themselves to down-right treason (the Rye House Plot). For by this time the eyes of the honest citizens were opened; and they found what interest was driving on; and it was time to have them open, when a cause in Guildhall was always tried according to the character of the client, and not the merits of the cause; when if a man was blasted by the name of Tory he was sure to lose his case; but if a whining rascal was sanctified by the name of Whig, he was sure to have it on his side.

He went on to refer to the fact that he had received two anonymous letters attacking his defence of Papists as witnesses: 'Let the sober party, as they call themselves, make what reflections they please upon it; I value them not, nor their opinion; let them send as many penny-post libels as they have a mind to, two of which I received last night, about yesterday's trial.' He concluded:

> Gentlemen, I have taken up much of your time, and detained you longer in this matter, because I cannot but say with grief of heart,

our nation was too long besotted; and of innocent blood there has been too much spilt; it is high time we ought to have some account of it.... God be blessed, our eyes are opened; and let us have a care for the future, that we be not so suddenly imposed upon by such prejudices and jealousies, as we have reason to fear such villains have too much filled our heads with of late.

In half an hour the jury found Oates guilty on the second charge. A week later he was brought up for judgement.

Titus Oates had sent innocent men to their death. Jeffreys and his fellow judges would have been glad to sentence him to execution, but perjury was no longer a capital offence.

'... crimes of this nature,' said Jeffreys, 'are left to be punished according to the Discretion of this Court, so far as that the Judgement extend not to Life or Member.

'I think it is impossible for this court, as the law now stands, to put a punishment upon him any way proportionable to the offence that has drawn after it so many horrid and dreadful consequences. We do therefore think it fit to inflict an exemplary punishment upon this villainous perjured wretch to terrify others for the future.'

Then Mr. Justice Wythens pronounced sentence:

First, the Court does order for a fine, that you pay 1,000 marks upon each indictment. Secondly, that you be stripped of all your Canonical habits. Thirdly, the Court does award, that you stand upon the Pillory, and in the Pillory, here before Westminster Hall gate, between the hours of 10 and 12; with a paper over your head (which you must first walk with round about to all the courts in Westminster Hall) declaring your crime. And this is upon the first indictment. Fourthly, (on the second indictment), upon Tuesday, you shall stand upon, and in the Pillory, at the Royal Exchange in London, for the space of one hour, between the hours of 12 and 2; with the same inscription. You shall upon the next Wednesday be whipped from Aldgate to Newgate. Upon Friday you shall be whipped from Newgate to Tyburn by the hands of the common hangman.

To commemorate the dates on which he had perjured himself, Oates was also to stand in the pillory at Tyburn for one hour every year on April 24th, at Westminster Hall on 9th August, at Charing Cross on 10th August, at Temple Gate on 11th August, and at the Royal Exchange on 2nd September—'... and all this you are to do every year, during your life, and to be committed close prisoner as long as you live'.

Oates was taken from the court to Westminster Stairs, and from there by water to the King's Bench prison. As he embarked the mob pressed round him, shouting 'Cut off his ears', and 'Hanging's too good for him.' Next week a spate of broadsheets greeted his appearance in the pillory:

> From three prostrate Kingdoms at once to adore me
> And no less than three Parliaments kneeling before me;
> From hanging of Lords with a Word or a Frown,
> And no more than an oath to the shaking a Crown:
>> From all these brave Pranks
>> Now to have no more Thanks,
> Then to look thro' a Hole, thro' two damned oaken Planks.
> Oh! mourn ye poor Whigs with sad lamentation,
> To see the hard Fate of the Saviour o' th' Nation.
>> *The Salamanca Doctor's Farewell*

> At City Exchange next day he appears,
> Where Whining Phanaticks saluted his Ears;
> Their Pillory'd Prophet they boldly defend,
> Who can't save them, nor himself, in the end.
>> His throne they pull'd down,
>> To the City's Renown,
> The Relicks on Shoulders they bore up and down:
> But tyr'd with Procession, 'twas Judg'd for the best,
> In prison these Zealots should take up their Nest.
>> *Perjury Punish'd, or Villainy Lash'd*

On the following Wednesday, Oates was flogged from Aldgate to Newgate by Jack Ketch. The crowd cried 'Enough! Enough!' Oates, with great courage shouted 'Not enough, good people, for the truth, not enough!' But soon afterwards he fainted. Forty-eight hours later the wretched man had to be dragged on a sledge by way of Holborn and Tottenham Court Road to Tyburn, as he was unable to walk. Someone asked Ketch if he had used more force than usual; the hangman replied coldly 'that he did one day as he might do another.'

Oates disappeared into prison but, as will be seen, he later had his revenge on Jeffreys. Meanwhile the first—and last—Parliament of James's reign assembled. Lord Keeper Guilford had prepared the King's speech for the opening, but the King preferred to deliver one of his own composition. The unlucky Keeper became steadily gloomier. He wrote to his brother Roger that 'all was chip' (worthless, dried up); and that 'as he was a person determined to be laid aside, he was not relied upon in anything, but was truly a seal-keeper rather than a Minister of State, and kept on for dispatch of formularies rather than for advice on trust'.

When the new Parliament met on 19th May Jeffreys' cousin, 'Squinting Jack' Trevor, was elected Speaker. The Lords and Commons heard bad news. The outlawed Earl of Argyll had landed in Scotland with the intention of raising a rebellion there, and there was information that the Duke of Monmouth was preparing to sail with three ships from the Texel in the Netherlands. British agents had seen him on board, disguised 'in seaman's apparel and with great whiskers'.

Influenced perhaps by the international situation, the Government proceeded with two political trials, over both of which Jeffreys presided. Thomas Dangerfield and Richard Baxter were each accused of seditious libel, but at that the similarity ends, for there could not have been a greater contrast between the two men if the matter had been deliberately arranged. Dangerfield was a professional, treacherous plotter. Baxter was a learned and well-respected nonconformist preacher. The difference nicely illustrates the confusion of good sense and blind stupidity that characterizes all the actions of James II.

Dangerfield had written of James that, when he was still Duke of York, he 'had hired him to kill the late King Charles'. The trial was straightforward. There could be no doubt that he had uttered the libel, no doubt too that the Government were anxious to have a slippery and troublesome enemy out of the way. Dangerfield was found guilty, and received—with less justification—a sentence almost as severe as that of Oates, two floggings, the pillory, and a fine of £500.

The sentence had a dramatic epilogue. After his second flogging Dangerfield was being taken back to prison by coach when a Catholic lawyer, Robert Francis, stuck his head through the window and 'askt Dangerfield "how he liked his race, and how he did after his heats"; to whome Daingerfield reply'd, "You are the Sonn of a whore." Francis thereupon, haveing a small caine in his hand, thrust at him, which rann into his eye, and he died next day. It may be presumed Francis had noe designe of killinge, for he had a sword by his side, which was a more likely thing to kill him than that little caine, . . .'

Francis was duly convicted of murder and executed.

On the same day that Dangerfield had been tried in the morning, Richard Baxter appeared before Jeffreys in the afternoon. The latter appreciated the difference between the two men, 'I know how to deal with saints as well as sinners' but in his eyes there was little to choose between them. Had not Baxter attacked episcopacy in his *Paraphrase of the New Testament*, writing that the bishops were 'thorns and thistles and military instruments of the devil'? Had he not read the text, 'The Pharisees went forth and straightway took counsel with the Herodians against Him how they might destroy Him' and then commented, 'What else but devils could make ceremonious hypocrites consult with politique *royalists* to destroy the Son of God?' Both Baxter and Dangerfield were threats to the established order—'if Baxter did but stand on the other side of the pillory with him [Oates] I would say two of the greatest rogues and rascals in the kingdom stood there together'.

In the account of Baxter's trial that has survived, Jeffreys' bias for the first time seems to exceed what was natural for the period. The defence had scarcely opened before he referred to Baxter as 'an old rogue, who encouraged all the women and maids to bring their bodkins and thimbles to carry on the war against the King and Government'. When Pollexfen, speaking for the defence, attempted to cite canonical authority for Baxter's long prayers, Jeffreys again interrupted: 'No, no, Mr. Pollexfen, they were long-winded extempore prayers such as they used to say when they appropriated God to themselves'—and, throwing up his hands and droning through his nose in the manner dissenters were supposed to use, Jeffreys continued—'Lord, we are thy people, thy peculiar people, thy dear people.' Pollexfen pointed out that Charles had once offered Baxter a bishopric. 'Ay, we know that,' Jeffreys commented, 'but what ailed the old stockowl, unthankful villain that he could not conform . . . ; I am sure he hath poisoned the world with his linsey-woolsey doctrine.'

When Baxter himself had spoken for a little while, Jeffreys intervened again:

Richard, Richard, dost thou think we will hear thee poison the Court? Richard, thou art an old fellow, an old knave thou hast written books enough to load a cart; every one is as full of sedition (I might say treason) as an egg is full of meat; hadst thou been whipped out of thy writing trade forty years ago, it had been happy. Thou pretendest to be a preacher of the gospel of peace, and thou hast one foot in the grave; it is time for thee to begin to think what account thou intended to give; but I leave thee to thyself, and I see thou wilt go on as thou hast begun; but, by the grace of God, I'll look after thee. I know thou hast a mighty party, and I see a great many of the brotherhood in corners waiting to see what will become of their mighty don; and a Doctor of the party (*looking at Doctor Bates*) at your elbow; but, by the grace of Almighty God, I will crush you all.

Baxter was fined 500 marks, was to be imprisoned until the fine was paid, and was bound over for seven years. The picture of Jeffreys droning through his nose is amusing, but a little disquieting. He had behaved impartially at the trial of Oates, why was he so obviously biased at the trial of Baxter? There are several facts which may account for the difference. First, and perhaps most important, the only records of this trial are those of Baxter and his supporters, no official report has survived and the 1776 edition of the *State Trials* considers that the remaining accounts are of doubtful authenticity.

Assuming that Jeffreys' behaviour has been improved upon, it is still possible that he took a stronger line than at the trial of Oates, simply because the country was in a dangerous situation, with Argyll in, and Monmouth expected to land at any moment. In Jeffreys' eyes there was nothing to choose between the rebels from overseas and the fifth column of 'factious, snivelling Presbyterians' in London, as he made quite clear:

Tis notoriously known there has been a design to ruin the King and the nation; the old game has been renewed, and this has been the main incendiary; he is as modest now as he can be; but time was when no man was so ready at 'Bind your kings in chains, and your nobles in fetters of iron', and 'To your tents, O Israel'. Gentlemen, for God's sake don't let us be gulled twice in an age by the cant of those who preach rebellion by texts.

In this connection it is significant that Baxter was discharged from prison in the following November, as soon as the danger from Argyll and Monmouth was past.

Finally, Baxter was particularly unpopular with Anglicans because, in a Chancery case in 1684, he had sworn that he conformed to the practices of the Church of England, in order to obtain a bequest. Dissenters were beginning to adopt this practice of Occasional Conformity, by which they received the Sacrament once a year, and then attended their own services for the remainder of the time. It seems likely that Jeffreys was referring to this in the words 'he hath poisoned the world with his linsey-woolsey [neither one thing nor the other] doctrine'.

7

'Gaffer Scott's Vagabonds'
(1685)

On Thursday, 11th June, between ten and eleven in the morning, the Duke of Monmouth's force, three ships and eighty-three men, dropped anchor off Lyme Regis. A little after five in the afternoon the men landed to the west of the harbour. The Duke knelt on the beach and prayed while his flag—green, with the non-committal inscription *Fear Nothing But God* embroidered on it—was unfurled. By 4 a.m. on Saturday the news had reached King James, carried to London by two customs officers from Lyme. The train of events that was to lead to the execution of Monmouth and of about 250 of his supporters, and to the transportation of many more, had been set in motion.

The pamphleteers rushed into print:

Monmouth Degraded
or *James Scot*, the little King in
LYME

A Song

To the Tune of Hark, hark, the Thundering Cannons roar, &c.

Come Beat Alarum, Sound a Charge,
As well without as in the Verge,
Let every Sword and Soul be large,
To make our Monarch Shine Boyes;
Let's leave off Whores and Drunken Souls,
And windy words o'er Brimming Bowls;
Let English Hearts exceed the *Poles*,
   'Gainst Perkin, King in *Lyme* Boyes.
Such a Fop-King was Ne'er before
Landed on our *Western* shore,
Which our black Saints do all adore,
Inspir'd by Tub-Divine Boyes.
Let us assume the Souls of *Mars*,

127

And March in Order, Foot and Horse,
Pull down the Standard at the Cross,
Of *Perkin* King in *Lyme* Boyes.

The rebellion had been planned for some time. It was based on the 1683 Plot prepared by the Council of Six. Argyll, a refugee in the Netherlands, was to sail to Scotland, while Monmouth was to land in the West and take advantage of the Whig contacts he had made there during his 'progress' of 1680. The declared aim of the rebels was to be the summoning of free parliaments in England and Scotland, nothing more. The final plans had been co-ordinated in Amsterdam at the house of a Taunton merchant, Thomas Dare.

William of Orange allowed the expeditions to sail from his ports, but gave no other help. As James's son-in-law, he himself hoped one day to succeed that childless King. He was the astutest political operator in Europe, and it did not need great political insight to appreciate the weakness of Argyll and Monmouth. William gave his father-in-law a hint of what was happening, and privately advised the Whig grandees to sit tight. One day he might need their support himself, and meanwhile it would be on the whole more satisfactory if Monmouth did not succeed.

In the north the rebellion never got under way. Argyll hung about in his own part of the Highlands and was taken before he ever moved. He was brought down to London together with Monmouth's liaison officer, the same Rumbold who had been involved in the Rye House Plot. The latter was a brave republican, too good to die for men like Argyll and Monmouth. At his trial he made no bones of the fact that 'he did not believe God had made the greater part of mankind with saddles on their backs, and bridles in their mouths, and some few booted and spurred to ride the rest'.

Meanwhile in the West Monmouth had set out from Lyme on Monday the fifteenth having recruited about two thousand men. Before leaving the port he had been persuaded by Argyll's liaison officer, Ferguson 'the Plotter', to issue a *Declaration* repeating all the old slanders against James—that he had started the Fire of London, been a prime mover in the Popish Plot, ordered the murder of Sir Edmund Berry Godfrey, and so on—and warning the King's supporters that they might expect no mercy, 'we would have none that appear under his banner to flatter themselves with the expectation of forgiveness'.

Certificate for the transportation of two rebels from Topsham to Virginia

Transcript:

Memo   Oct 1685
Shipt on board the Ship the Exchange of Topsam (Topsham)
Christopher Haycroft comander for York river in Virginia, John
Edwards and Edward Lloyd, to be delivered there according to
recognizances entered into by Sir William Booth in that behalf:
                                    John Baker of Hamwood in Summerset

James, Duke of Monmouth

Lord Chancellor Jeffreys

At first there was no opposition. At Axminster the local militia melted before him as 'The Lord sent a hornet of fear among them.' By midday on Thursday Monmouth was in Taunton, having encountered no real opposition. Men were arriving in encouragingly large numbers. True, the great gentry were curiously silent, but he had received £500 and the contents of his stables from Ford Abbey, the home of Edmund Prideaux. No doubt others would soon follow suit. It was going to be all right.

Next day forty schoolgirls, led by their teachers, Mistress Susanna Musgrave and Mistress Mary Blake, the latter carrying a Bible and a drawn sword, presented him with twenty-seven flags which they had embroidered for their hero. Each was rewarded with a kiss.

It seemed safe to take the next step. The real aim of the rebellion was revealed when, on Saturday in the Taunton market-place, Monmouth assumed the title of King. The proclamation explained that, to make matters legal,

... we have therefore suffered ourselves to be prevailed upon, and have complied with the earnest importunities and necessities of our people, giving way to our being proclaimed king on the 20th day of this instant June at our town of Taunton aforesaid ...

There was no going back now.

Monmouth had been over-persuaded by his reception in Taunton, for success in the West was no guarantee of success anywhere else. The area was ripe for revolt. The ground had been prepared by years of Whig propaganda, and by his own 'progress' five years before. The region had suffered from economic depression for some years. Monmouth's forces were being built from the yeomen and labourers who had endured a series of bad harvests, and from the weavers and other cloth-workers whose industry was losing business to that of Yorkshire. In one Taunton parish alone, out of 273 rebels later presented for trial, 141 were connected with the cloth trade. In 1681 it had been reported that there were five hundred unemployed, a great figure for those days, in Taunton and 'other adjacent fanatic places of trade'. Thomas Venn of Thurloxton added that the men were 'flocking up and down ... with insolent and peremptory resolves that they are ready to break out on their neighbour's rights, before they would starve.'

To economic discontent was added religious enthusiasm.

9

Taunton possessed one of the largest Nonconformist chapels in the West Country, Paul's Meeting House, and there were other, smaller, conventicles. The townspeople had long before declared 'they'll see bloody noses ere they'll desert conventicles'. In 1683 there had been rioting. They had celebrated the fortieth anniversary of the raising of the Royalist siege, 11th May, with a bonfire in the High Street. 'About six in the morning the Mayor having notice of a great company met in the High Street went and ordered them to depart. Most laughed and scoffed, some hollowed and threw up their hats, and the rabble was presently about 1500.' A dozen men were imprisoned, but the bonfire blazed on till one o'clock in the morning.

A fortnight later Stephen Timewell, the Mayor, took his revenge. On 29th May, the anniversary of the Restoration, he organized a rival celebration. He had all the woodwork pulled out of Paul's and out of a Baptist meeting-house, and the ten cartloads of fittings were burnt in the High Street. 'I think,' Timewell said, 'I have broken the neck of the Meeting in Taunton; if not, it shall be done.'

On the contrary, the atmosphere remained explosive. Roger North wrote that many towns 'were become the ordinary asylums of all sorts of rogues that fled from the justice of the sessions, and particularly those that were tumultuous and seditious, and there found protection. And particularly, the town of Poole in Dorsetshire was of this order, and, if I mistake not, Taunton Dean another.' For years the government had been receiving reports to the effect that the West was 'the nursery of rebellions', that it was 'very thin of loyal men', and that Somerset in particular was 'The sink of all the rebellion in the west.' After it was all over the Rector of Chedzoy, Andrew Paschall, wrote 'there is reason to believe that we may impute it to Taunton that the Rebellion did break out in these parts'.

In the light of all this evidence it is hardly surprising that the town had declared for Monmouth even before he reached it. On the sixteenth, when he was still two days' march away, the townsmen had seized control, led by a 'Scandalous Nonconformist Minister' named Vincent, and were busy distributing arms, opening the gaol, and forcing two members of the Corporation to hear the reading of Monmouth's Declaration in the market-place 'or else they would run swords through their guts'.

If Monmouth had not received support in Taunton, he would

have received it nowhere. Unduly encouraged by his reception he
had allowed himself to be proclaimed King. Next he moved north
to Bridgwater and from there advanced on Bristol. But the city
did not open its gates, and Monmouth failed to attack. Attempting to cross the Avon he marched east to Bath. There the Mayor
had already strengthened the defences—the labourers employed
on the job were given two shillings beer money—and Monmouth
was refused a passage across the river. That same evening the
royalist army under Churchill and Feversham entered the city.
Monmouth turned back the way he had come. When rebels
retreat, they are doomed. Soon royalist forces were in contact
with the enemy at Norton St. Philip and at Frome, driving them
back into the West as a sheepdog drives sheep, following so hard
on their heels that on one occasion the troops entering a rebel
lodging found the table 'decently laid' for supper and fifteen pairs
of boots beneath a bed.

On 1st July Monmouth's forces re-entered Wells. Disappointed
and bitter, their dissenting prejudices now showed themselves
clearly. The lower rows of statues on the great west front were
peppered with shot—the marks can still be seen—the horses were
stabled in the nave, and Lord Grey was forced to use his sword to
defend the altar itself from sacrilege.

Next day the retreat continued and on 3rd July the men were
back in Bridgwater. It was exactly a fortnight since they had last
been there. The royal army closed in and two days later made
camp at Westonzoyland about three miles to the east. Monmouth
decided to try a night attack. His army left Bridgwater an hour or
so before midnight and moved quietly across Sedgemoor, the
watery surface of which was threaded by the ditches known
locally as rhines. About 1 a.m. they stumbled on a single trooper,
one of a hundred and fifty patrols out on the moor. Putting spurs
to his horse he got away and roused the royalist foot: 'Beat the
drums, the enemy is come, for the Lord's sake, beat the drums.'
The element of surprise had been lost and with it the chance of
victory.

The rebel cavalry under Lord Grey were mishandled, and
though the infantry fought bravely their ammunition was exhausted by dawn, about four in the morning. The Duke of Monmouth fled, leaving the men he had called from their homes to
their fate.

Of perhaps three thousand five hundred men who were with

Monmouth in Bridgwater, a little under fifteen hundred were killed in the battle and in the slaughter that normally followed a defeat. The Westonzoyland parish register records:

> ... their was killed of the rebels upon the spot aboute three hundred; hanged with us twenty-two, of which four weare hanged in Gemmasses [chains]. About five hundred prisoners brought into our church; of which their was seventy-nine wounded, and five of them died of their wounds in our church.

Adam Wheeler, drummer with the Wiltshire militia, described one man's fate, which may stand for all:

> He was very remarkable and to be admired, for being shot through the shoulder, and wounded in the Belly, He lay on his Backe in the sun stript naked, for the space of 10 or 11 howers, in that scorching hot day to the Admiration of all the Spectatours; and as he lay, a great Crowde of souldiers came about him, and reproached him, calling him "Thou Monmouth Dog How long have you been with youre Kinge Monmouth?" His answer was that if he had Breath, he would tell them: Afterwards he was pittyed, and they opened round about him, and gave him more liberty of the Aire, and there was one souldier that gave him a pair of Drawers to cover his Nakednesse: Afterwards having a long stick in his hand he walked feably to Weston church, where he died that night, and two wounded men more.

It was the end of the last popular rising in England.

About half of Monmouth's supporters were taken prisoner. The Duke himself was found hiding in a beanfield a few miles from Poole. He was carried to London and executed on 15th July. It was five weeks since he had landed at Lyme. Lord Grey was captured a little nearer the coast and, typically, saved his skin by turning King's evidence.

Back in Somerset Colonel Kirke was left in charge of the area. He made Taunton his headquarters and began the summary examination and execution of his prisoners. Kirke had been Governor of Tangier, where he had been able to give free rein to his taste for brutalities, shocking Samuel Pepys—'it is a place of the world I would last send a young man to, but Hell'.

It was the normal procedure for a military commander to execute a proportion of his prisoners, proved traitors by the fact that they had been taken with arms in their hands in rebellion

against their king. Kirke had hardly begun work when to his surprise he received urgent orders from Whitehall to halt the proceedings. King James had decided that the rebels should be made
an example of at the next assize. It was a decision that would not
greatly affect their fate, though it is arguable that the people of the
West probably suffered less at the assize than they would have
done if left to Kirke's tender mercies—but it has affected the
reputation of Jeffreys from that day to this.

The normal assize in the West had been prevented by the rebellion. James now issued a Special Commission to hold this assize
and at the same time try the rebels. The idea was typical of James's
neat, rigid, completely unimaginative mind. In the vast majority
of cases the prisoners' guilt was in no doubt. Punishment was a
question of political expediency not judicial enquiry—a matter of
decimation better left to the licentious soldiery. A wiser king
than James would have kept clear of the whole business. Setting
aside all this, it was a practical impossibility to conduct even the
formal trial of such a large number of prisoners, should they
choose to plead not guilty, in the five weeks or so allotted to the
assize.

James saw none of this. These were problems that the judges
must solve as best they could. No solution could combine the
strict claims of justice and of government.

Five judges were named in the Special Commission. Lord Chief
Justice Jeffreys was to be assisted by Chief Baron Montagu, Baron
Wright of the Exchequer, Justice Wythens of the King's Bench,
and Justice Levinz of the Common Pleas. Montagu and Levinz
were middle-of-the-way men, Wythens, Wright and Jeffreys
were Tories. To these was soon added the name of Sir Henry
Pollexfen, a Whig, to undertake the prosecution.

A second Commission gave Jeffreys the temporary rank of
Lieutenant-General and the command of an accompanying body-
guard. The unsettled state of the West made something of the
sort necessary, but James, in his usual heavy-handed manner, spoke
of a 'campaign'—an ill-judged remark.

On 20th August Jeffreys returned from Tunbridge Wells,
where he had been for the preceding month, taking treatment for
the stone. From London the Commission set out for the West
Country, spending the night of Tuesday the twenty-fourth at
Farnham. Next day the assize opened at Winchester. Routine
cases were dealt with first and then, on Thursday, the judges

heard the only case of treason in Hampshire, but that a most important one.

Alice Lisle was charged with concealing one of Monmouth's followers, John Hicks, a Dissenting minister. The case is significant on several counts: the accused was a well-known lady and hers was the first of the treason trials—hence a conviction was desirable; she had not been directly involved in the rebellion—there was therefore something to argue about, the trial was not a mere formality; it is the only one of the assize trials of which an official —though very suspect—account has survived; and, finally, it has provided the most powerful ammunition for attacks on Jeffreys' conduct.

The accused was a widow of about seventy. Her former husband, John Lisle, had played a prominent part in the trial of Charles I and had, later, presided over a Commonwealth High Court that had condemned several royalists for treason, including Doctor Hewet, a London clergyman who had refused to plead and had been sentenced to death without a hearing. At the Restoration John Lisle had fled abroad and had been assassinated by royalists at Lausanne in 1664. All this was ancient history, but it had made Alice Lisle an obvious suspect and it must have been in the minds of all who thronged the great hall of Winchester Castle. Nevertheless, Alice Lisle had for twenty years lived a retired life at her house of Moyle's Court, near Ringwood, well-respected in the neighbourhood, though known to sympathize with Dissenters.

After the battle John Hicks, together with Richard Nelthorpe who had been outlawed for his part in the Rye House Plot, fled east and lay up at the house of James Dunne, a Warminster baker. From there Hicks wrote to Alice Lisle, asking if she would shelter them. Dunne agreed to deliver the letter, but unfortunately he got lost and at Sutton Mandeville persuaded a labourer, John Barter, to show him the way to Moyle's Court. Dunne saw Alice Lisle and then returned to Warminster. On the following Tuesday Hicks, Nelthorpe and Dunne left Warminster early and reached Moyle's Court the same evening, having travelled twenty-five miles across country. Next morning Colonel Penruddock, a Tory magistrate from Compton Chamberlayne, was hammering at the door. It was half an hour before he was admitted. Alice Lisle protested that there were no refugees in the house, but the buildings were searched. Hicks and Dunne were found in the malt-house, Nelthorpe in a hiding-place by one of the chimneys. Penruddock arrested the three men and Alice Lisle.

What had gone wrong? It was very simple. Barter, after acting as Dunne's guide again on the second journey, had gone straight to Penruddock and told the magistrate that he believed Alice Lisle was hiding two rebels.

So much for the facts. The trial opened in the late afternoon. Alice Lisle was old and deaf and she was therefore allowed to sit down, a man standing at her elbow to repeat the evidence to her. Pollexfen, who was prosecuting, called a number of those who had been captured by Monmouth's force and they testified that Hicks had tried to persuade them to join the rebels. Hicks' position in the rebellion was thus established. There was certainly no doubt that he had been found at Moyle's Court. The only question—but a vital one—was: did Alice Lisle hide the men, *knowing them to be rebels*?

The baker, Dunne, was next called. Pollexfen explained that he was an unwilling witness and asked that he be examined 'a little more strictly'—equivalent to the modern practice of treating a person as a 'hostile witness'. Jeffreys therefore spoke to him as follows:

> Hark you, friend, I would take notice of something to you by the way, and you would do well to mind what I say to you. . . . I would not by any means in the world fright you into anything or any ways tempt you to tell an untruth, but provoke you to tell the truth, and nothing but the truth, that is the business we come about here . . . Know, friend, there is no religion that any man can pretend to can give countenance to lying, or can dispense with telling the truth. . . . For I tell thee God is not to be mocked, and thou canst not deceive Him, though thou mayest us. But I assure you if I catch you prevaricating in any the least tittle (and perhaps I know more than you think I do) [Jeffreys had examined Nelthorpe before leaving London] no, none of your saints can save your soul, nor shall they save your body neither, I will be sure to punish every variation from the truth you may be guilty of.

The unfortunate Dunne was anxious to tell a tale that would clear himself, without convicting anyone else. He therefore claimed that he knew nothing about Hicks and Nelthorpe, having never seen them before, and that he had only done what they had asked him to do. This was clearly improbable and Jeffreys asked him what he had got out of it.

'Nothing but a month's imprisonment, my lord.'

'Thou seemest to be a man of a great deal of kindness and good nature,' Jeffreys commented drily. He then repeated Dunne's story, concluding, 'and all to carry a message from a man thou never knewest in thy life, to a woman thou never sawest in thy life neither. . . .'

Dunne was soon hopelessly confused over the details he had invented, but he refused to go further than 'I cannot tell'. Jeffreys ordered him to stand aside for the moment. Barter then gave his evidence, describing how Dunne had carried a letter to Alice Lisle and had talked with her in the kitchen. Later he asked Dunne what they had been laughing about. Dunne told him that Alice Lisle had asked if Barter knew anything of the 'concern'.

At this Jeffreys recalled Dunne: 'Let my honest man, Mr. Dunne, stand forward a little. . . . Did you not tell him [Barter] that you told my lady when she asked whether he was acquainted with this *concern*, that he knew nothing of the business?'

It was late in the day and besides Dunne was, as he later said, 'quite cluttered out of his senses'; it seemed a little thing to admit that Barter was telling the truth.

'Yes, my lord, I did tell him so.'

It was fatal.

'Did you so? Then you and I must have a little further discourse: Come now and tell us *what business was that?* . . .'

Too late Dunne saw his mistake; earlier he had said on oath that he knew of no business. He must give himself time to think. 'Does your lordship ask what that business was?' he repeated.

'Yes, it is a plain question: what was that business that my lady asked thee whether the other man knew; and then you answered her that he did know nothing of it?'

For a quarter of an hour Jeffreys persisted, while Dunne failed to think of a plausible answer. Then at last he had an idea. The 'business' was that Hicks was a Nonconformist. It was a hopelessly weak explanation but Dunne clung desperately to it.

The room was getting dark.

'Hold a candle to his face that we may see his brazen face,' ordered Jeffreys. As twilight came Dunne stuck to his tale. 'That is all nonsense,' exclaimed the exasperated Jeffreys, 'dost thou imagine any man hereabouts is so weak as to believe thee?'

Once more Dunne stood aside, while Barter completed his evidence. Next Colonel Penruddock described how he had

searched the house and found the men after Alice Lisle had denied
that they were there. At this point Mistress Lisle spoke.

'My lord, I hope I shall not be condemned without being heard.'

'No, God forbid, Mistress Lisle,' said Jeffreys. 'That was a sort
of practice in your husband's time; you know very well what I
mean. But God be thanked it is not so now. The King's courts
never condemn without a hearing.'

It was an improper reference to Dr. Hewet's condemnation by
John Lisle. As soon as he had spoken Jeffreys realized this and in
his summing-up took care to remind the jury that nothing her
husband might have done was relevant to this case.

Mistress Lisle said she had not known that Hicks had been in
Monmouth's army, she had only believed he was a Presbyterian
in danger for preaching. The word enraged Jeffreys and he broke
in, '. . . there is not one of those snivelling, lying, canting Presbyterian rascals but, one way or other, had a hand in the late horrid
conspiracy and rebellion . . . Presbytery has all manner of villainy
in it; nothing but Presbytery could lead that fellow Dunne to
tell so many lies as he has told here; for show me a Presbyterian
and I will show you a lying knave.' Alice Lisle then continued and
made the point that she had only come down to Moyle's Court
from London after the rebellion was over.

Jeffreys summed up, in general, unfavourably. He considered it
impossible that the defendant should not have realized that the
two men were runaway rebels, and that was the matter at issue.
If she knew, then, 'neither her age nor her sex are to move you
who have nothing else to consider but the fact you are to try. I
charge you therefore, as you will answer at the bar of the last
Judgement, where you and we must all appear, deliver your
verdict according to conscience and truth.'

The jury raised a point of law. Hicks had not yet been convicted, he was at Wells still awaiting his trial: 'Pray, my lord,
some of us desire to know of your lordship in point of law
whether it be the same thing, and equally treason, in receiving
him before he was convicted of treason as it had been after?'

Jeffreys informed them: 'It is all the same, that certainly can be
no doubt, for if in case this Hicks had been wounded in the rebels'
army, and had come to her house and there been entertained, but
had died there of his wounds, and so could never have been convicted, she had been nevertheless a traitor.'

Was this good law? After the Revolution Alice Lisle's attainder was reversed on the ground that it was not, but in the nineteenth century Sir James Stephen, though no friend to Jeffreys, concluded in his *History of the Criminal Law*, '. . . I think this is another of the numerous instances in which there really was no law at all. . . .' and in fact Jeffreys' interpretation was adopted also by judges after the 1745 rebellion.

Half an hour later the jury returned to say they were not satisfied that the defendant knew Hicks to be a rebel. Jeffreys repeated Dunne's evidence to them: '. . . did she not enquire of Dunne whether Hicks had been in the army? And when he told her he did not know, she did not say she would refuse him if he had been there, but ordered him to come by night, by which it is evident she suspected it.' The jury once more retired and, after a quarter of an hour, brought in a verdict of guilty. It was midnight.

Next morning the sentence of burning was pronounced. This was the customary punishment for women convicted of high treason, intended to be equivalent in terror to the hanging, drawing and quartering of men. Jeffreys added that the sentence would normally have taken place that afternoon, 'But withal I give you, prisoner, this intimation: we that are the judges shall stay in town an hour or two; you shall have pen, ink and paper brought to you, and if in the meantime you employ that pen, ink and paper and this hour or two well (you understand what I mean) it may be you may hear further from us deferring the execution.'

Jeffreys could hardly instruct Alice Lisle directly to petition the King for mercy, but all modern biographers agree that this was what he was hinting. She did write and her execution was in consequence postponed until 2nd September, but King James would do no more than commute the sentence to one of beheading, and she was executed in Winchester about four o'clock in the afternoon. A contemporary newsletter recorded '. . . she was old and dozy and died without much concern', a blessing for one who had perhaps got caught up in affairs beyond her understanding.

The account of Alice Lisle's trial was published thirty-four years later and modern authorities consider the text unreliable, but its course seems to have been substantially as described above. Much of the horror it later aroused came naturally from the sentence pronounced, but it must be remembered that the barbarous punishment that Alice Lisle so narrowly avoided—through taking

Jeffreys' advice, it should be noted—had nothing to do with the judges, it was the law. Later that year, in a case in which Jeffreys was not involved, a woman, Elizabeth Gaunt, *was* burnt for harbouring Burton, a Rye House plotter and refugee from Monmouth's army, and the punishment remained on the statute book until 1790.

From Winchester the judges moved on to Salisbury, where there was little to detain them, and then continued to Dorchester. There on Saturday 5th September, in what is now the Oak Room of the Antelope Hotel, they began the trial of about three hundred rebels. In the morning thirty men were brought before them. The evidence was conclusive, they had been caught with weapons in their hands, or wounded. They nevertheless all pleaded not guilty. If this continued, the assize would take, not weeks, but years. Pressure was brought to bear. Lord Ailesbury records that the Deputy Clerk of the Assizes '... by Mr. Pollexfen's orders, went into the prisons and made the poor people believe they had nothing to save their lives but by pleading guilty, on which each strove who should be first'. From then on if a prisoner pleaded not guilty and was nevertheless convicted he was executed immediately, while the majority of those who pleaded guilty were not sentenced to death. The pleas of not guilty were futile, but Pollexfen's message that any prisoners who pleaded not guilty and were nevertheless convicted might expect no commutation of their sentence was, at the very least, on the borders of illegality.

In the afternoon sixty-eight prisoners pleaded guilty. One hundred and three cases were heard on the following Monday and a further sixty-nine on Tuesday. In all, over two hundred and fifty were condemned to death at Dorchester, but only seventy-four were finally executed.

On Saturday night Jeffreys had dictated an account to be sent to the King, to which he added a letter in his own hand to Sunderland:

> I most heartily rejoice (my Dearest Dearest Lord) to learn of your safe return to Windsor. I this day began with the trial of the rebels at Dorchester, and have dispatched ninety-eight; but am at this time so tortured with the stone that I must beg your lordship's intercession to his Majesty for the incoherence of what I have adventured to give his Majesty the trouble of and that I may give myself so much ease by your lordship's favour as to make use of my servant's pen to give a relation of what has happened since I came

here: My Dearest Lord; may I ever be tortured with the stone if I forget to approve myself

Dorchester: 10	My Dearest Lord,
p.m. night 5th	Your most faithful
for god's sake make	and devoted servant
all excuses, and write at	Jeffreys.
leisure a word of comfort	

Three days later, while he was still at Dorchester, Jeffreys learnt that on the day he wrote to Sunderland the Lord Keeper had died in Oxfordshire. Little Lord Guilford had murmured, 'It will not do' and then 'lay down and expired'. His brothers Sir Dudley and Roger rode up to London with the Great Seal, 'that pestiferous lump of metal', wrapped in silk. The King's only reaction was to remark that he had thought Guilford was getting better, and then to enquire what had happened to the official Purse of State, in which the Seal should have been kept.

Jeffreys would be the natural successor to Guilford, perhaps even to the vacant higher title of Lord Chancellor. As soon as the news reached him, he wrote to Sunderland again:

Give me leave (my Dearest Lord) with more importunity than ordinary, to beg your Lordship's patronage and protection; it's that station that (next to his Majesty) I will to Eternity owe to your Lordship's favour, and desire to continue no longer in any condition than whilst I act my gratitude more than I can speak it. I heartily beseech your Lordship to render my most humble duty and thankfulness to his Majesty for his most gracious thoughts of me, and assure him I will to the utmost approve myself his most loyal and faithful servant:
And

My Dearest Lord,
Your Lordship's most entirely devoted
Jeffreys.
Dorchester 7 oclock 8th.

Meanwhile, between the writing of these two letters, the execution of thirteen men had taken place at Dorchester. Jack Ketch, the London executioner, had come down from London for the business, together with his assistant, a butcher known as 'Pascha' Rose. Other executions took place at Lyme (12), Weymouth (12), Sherborne (11), Poole (11), Bridport (10), and Wareham (5).

The judges left Dorchester on Friday, 11th September, and reached Exeter the following day. The rising had only touched south-east Devonshire and of almost five hundred men who had joined Monmouth from that area it was said that about three hundred and fifty were still at large. Forty prisoners were tried and twenty-one sentenced to death, nineteen of whom had pleaded guilty. Twelve were executed and their bodies exhibited in Axminster, Barnstaple, Bideford, Colyton, Crediton, Dartmouth, Exeter, Honiton, Ottery St. Mary, Plymouth, Tiverton, Totnes and Torrington.

On Thursday, 17th September, the assize reached Taunton and there in the Great Hall of the Castle 526 prisoners were tried on Friday and Saturday. Almost all pleaded guilty and 139 were sentenced to death. Three of these were hanged at once and about ninety were executed later.

From Taunton the judges moved north, splitting into two groups, Levinz, Montagu and Wythens journeyed to Wells, while Jeffreys and Wright made their way to Bristol. The city had refused to admit Monmouth and there were no rebels there, but on the twenty-first Jeffreys rated the Mayor and Corporation for another matter. Having dismissed the procession that welcomed him as 'a couple of puffing trumpeters' he reminded his audience that 'rebellion is like the sin of witchcraft' and then turned to another matter—the Bristol habit of kidnapping people for sale in the plantations of America and the West Indies:

> The very magistrates, that should be ministers of justice, fall out with one another to that degree that they will scarce dine with each other; . . . yet I find they can agree for their interests. Or if it be but a kid in the case (for I hear the trade of kidnapping is in much request in this city), they can discharge a felon or a traitor, provided they will go to Mr. Alderman's plantation at the West Indies. . . . Sir, Mr. Mayor, you I mean, kidnapper, and an old Justice of the Peace on the bench, I do not know him, old knave; he goes to the tavern for a pint of sack, he will bind people servants to the Indies in the tavern.

On Tuesday, 22nd September, Jeffreys wrote again to Sunderland: 'I think this city worse than Taunton. . . . Taunton and Bristol and the county of Somerset shall know their duty both to God and their King before I leave them, and in a few days don't despair to perfect the work I was sent about.' This particular vehemence against Bristol remains a little mysterious.

At Wells, where the five judges met again, the prisoners were tried in the Market Hall, the two ends of the open building being shut in by screens. Here there were 542 prisoners of whom only one pleaded not guilty. He was found guilty and executed in the afternoon. Of the remainder, ninety-three were sentenced to death, though not all were in the end executed.

The assize in the West was over. The judges made their way back to London. For most of the prisoners the critical decision of life or death was made later. How many finally suffered? It is only in the last fifty years that the original judges' lists sent in to the Treasury on 12th November, 1685, have been examined and analysed.[1] These can be checked against the names of those known to have been executed during the assize, against Jeffreys' warrant dated 26th September, and against what is known of the actual fate of those sentenced in various towns. The three sets of information do not tally exactly, but they provide the following figures which are probably accurate within five per cent either way:

Total found guilty	1,381	
Executed during the assize	81 ⎫	321
Ordered for execution later	240 ⎭	
Executed later	160/170	
Sentenced to transportation		847
Fined, imprisoned, or whipped	34 ⎫	
In custody, bailed, or discharged	95 ⎬	257
Bound over	128 ⎭	
Pardoned		79

Of those ordered for execution later but not executed, many died of gaol fever (typhus) and smallpox, some had their sentences commuted to ones of transportation, a few escaped.

Since the plantation of colonies in the New World transportation had become a recognized punishment—and remained one until 1866. Every year criminals were sent to work for a period of five years. At the end of that time they were free, but during their servitude they were treated worse than the black slaves, since the latter were their masters' property for life, while the value of a transported man depreciated rapidly as the time approached when he would once again be free. Freedom brought a miserable bounty of five pounds—and then there was the problem of getting home again. In the case of the rebels sentenced to this grim fate, the term was fixed at ten years instead of five. In January, 1690, they were pardoned by William III.

[1] Muddiman, J. G., *The Bloody Assizes* (London, 1929).

On Saturday, 19th September, Jeffreys had written from Taunton to the King:

> I received your Majesty's commands by my Lord Sunderland about the rebels your Majesty designs for transportation, but I beseech your Majesty that I may inform you that each prisoner will be worth £10, if not £15 apiece and that if your Majesty orders them as you have already designed, persons that have not suffered in your service will run away with the booty and I am sure that your Majesty will be continually perplexed with petitions for recompense for sufferers as well as rewards for events.

James paid no attention to this letter. The rebels transported were granted to seven great personages: the Queen, allotted 100; Sir William Stapleton, Governor of the Leeward Islands, who acted as agent for Lieutenant Colonel Charles Pym, 100; Sir Philip Howard, Secretary to the Council, 200; the Queen's Italian secretary, Ieronimo Nipho, 100; Sir William Booth, a merchant dealing with Barbados, 200; Sir Christopher Musgrave, a merchant dealing with Jamaica, 100; and Captain John Price, who owned 40,000 acres in Carolina, 50.

It is impossible to discover how many were actually transported. Some died in prison and perhaps a quarter on the voyage out. Here much depended on the ship. Thus the *Happy Return* from Weymouth brought all her ninety-one rebels safely to Barbados, but the *John* from Bristol, also bound for Barbados with ninety rebels, lost twenty-two on the crossing. A surprisingly large number escaped in England, Sir Philip Howard made a list showing that out of the two hundred 'given' him by the King, thirty-three escaped between Sherborne and Weymouth. When all these facts are taken into account it seems likely that less than three-quarters of those sentenced reached their destination.

Neither Jeffreys nor any of the other judges were 'given' any of the rebels who were transported. They received their customary fees, Jeffreys being paid £1,416 10s. He was also 'given' Edmund Prideaux. An Axminster rebel had turned King's evidence and had testified that Prideaux knew of the money and horses that had been supplied to the rebels from his house of Ford Abbey. Prideaux was not charged but was told that he might strike a bargain with Jeffreys. Eventually he bought his pardon for £14,760. This was the only occasion on which Jeffreys, judged by the standards of his own times, perhaps behaved improperly. Even here one cannot be sure. The mental climate was so different: until the middle of the eighteenth century it was common form for royal officials to be rewarded with what we should today regard as the illegal perquisites of office.

In 1685 Jeffreys was not the blood-stained monster of later legend, but a hero—at least outside the West Country. He and Churchill had, in their different ways, destroyed 'the Dissenting Rebellion', sent 'gaffer Scott's vagabonds' packing, and saved the country from the miseries of another Civil War. Cambridge University, usually Whig, burnt Monmouth's portrait, a Lely. In the Commons Sir Edward Seymour, a West Country Tory, thought that 'this last rebellion has contributed to our future peace, and those engaged in it have sung their penitential psalms and their punishment rejoiced by all good men'. Sir Charles Lyttleton, also from the West, was shocked by the sight of the quartered bodies—'The country looks,' he wrote, 'already like a shambles'—but added, 'Those who suffered here were so far from deserving any pity, at least most of 'em and those of the best fashion . . . that they showed no repentance as if they died in an ill cause, but justified their treason and gloried in it.' Pepys, in many ways a sensitive man, was busy supporting the petition of a sea captain for a grant of rebels, and enquiring in a business-like way '. . . what sort of usage these fellows are to receive, whether to be sold entirely, as blacks are to slavery for their whole lives, or how long. . . .' He was relieved that matters had turned out as they had: 'The dust being now laid which was raised by the late troublesome rebellion, a man may hope to look about again . . .'

Later, when he was in exile, James claimed that Jeffreys had exceeded his orders, but all the contemporary evidence points the other way. It was James who had decided in the first place what should be done and while the assize was in progress a foreign ambassador observed that he was almost obsessed with the rebels' punishment, being able to speak of nothing else at dinner, while Sunderland wrote to Jeffreys, 'His Majesty approves very well of what you have done. . . .'[1]

In the West Country itself, the establishment approved. *Te Deum* was sung at Wells; in Dorset a Church of England minister, Blanchard, complained that the whippings were not sufficiently severe; at Exeter, a month or more after Jeffreys had left, Dr. Lamplugh the Bishop was demanding that justice should continue to be done until the rebels were completely destroyed.

[1] Sunderland Papers, II, p. 284.

Capture of Jeffreys at Wapping, 1688

Oak Room, Dorchester. Used as a court-room in 1685; John Tutchin was sentenced here

St. Mary's Aldermanbury; Jeffreys was eventually buried in the chancel

And the executions did continue well into the winter. The contemporary Muddiman newsletter recorded the punishment of rebels in Minehead and the neighbourhood in December, adding, 'Which is but a seasonable admonition, since some of them of late have taken the boldness to creep out of their holes and commit acts of violence and rapine upon the community.'

Dr. Lamplugh, Bishop of Exeter, and Mr. Henry Muddiman, journalist, were both wrong. The slow retribution, by keeping the horror constantly before people's eyes, played a great part in giving the 'bloody' assize its name. As usual James's marble-hearted methods were psychologically disastrous.

The Sheriff's warrant for the executions at Bath has survived, dated 16th November; it needs no comment:

> I require you immediately on sight hereof to erect a gallows in the most public place of your said city to hang the said traitors on, and that you provide halters to hang them with, a sufficient number of faggots to burn the bowels of four traitors and a furnace or cauldron to boil their head and quarters, and salt to boil therewith, half a bushel to each traitor, and tar to tar them with and a sufficient number of spears and poles to fix and place their heads and quarters, and that you warn the owners of four oxen to be ready with a dray or wain and the said four oxen at the time hereafter mentioned for execution, and yourselves together with a guard of forty able men at the least, to be present on Wednesday morning next by eight of the clock, to be aiding and assisting to me, or my deputy, to see the said rebels executed. . . . You are also to provide an axe and a cleaver for the quartering of the said rebels.

Royal proclamations rubbed salt in the wounds:

> And thus by their rash and unadvisedness they brought themselves to disgrace, who otherwise might have lived peaceably and happy in their Stations and been profitable to their Country.
>
> By this it is to be perceived how much Loyalty and Obedience is to be preferred before Disloyalty and Stubborness, how much a calm and peaceable temper exceeds a restless and unsatisfied Disposition, . . .

8

Lord Chancellor Jeffreys
(1685-8)

On his way back from the West, Jeffreys halted at Windsor to report to the King. There, on 28th September,

> His Majesty, taking into his royal consideration the many eminent and faithful services which the Right Honourable George, Lord Jeffreys of Wem, Lord Chief Justice of England, has rendered the Crown, as well in the reign of the late King of ever-blessed memory as since his Majesty's accession to the throne, was pleased this day to commit to him the Custody of the Great Seal of England with the title of Lord Chancellor.

At the age of forty Jeffreys had become the youngest Lord Chancellor in England's history. He had reached the top of what Disraeli called 'the greasy pole'.

As Lord Chancellor, Jeffreys passed to some extent from public view. As a Judge he now sat in Chancery, hearing cases and making decisions which are perhaps his most important contribution to legal history, but which are by the nature of the Court, comparatively private and comparatively undramatic. As what may be termed a member of the Government, his actions take place in the privacy of the Council Chamber or of the King's closet, and usually one can only guess at what happens there.

By virtue of his new appointment Jeffreys took over the house in Queen Street that had belonged to the late Lord Keeper Guilford. The new tenant was greeted with both flattery and vilification. In one lane a broadsheet described

> An aspect open and a brow that's clear,
> Without the flattering, sly, insidious leer,
> A front that's awful; yet a friend may see
> The truest signs of affability.
> An eye so keen, what villain can have sense
> Pierced by its terror to plead innocence?

Those alarming eyes once more.

In the next street another poem, the work of Joshua Barnes, M.A., praised the recent Assize in the West:

> Well did thy wisely-pruning Hand
> Lop off those Suckers of the Western land,
> That once design'd to draw away
> The vital sap of Britain's Royal Tree,

—an action that had made the Crown secure

> Till Jeffrey's Fame's asleep, and
> Time itself be past.

But in other streets, other opinions were available. There Jeffreys was

> ... a forward fool,
> A bawling, blundering, senseless tool,
> Whose mouthing at Whitechapel first began,
> Who regularly to his greatness ran
> Thro' all the vile degrees of treachery,
> And now usurps the Court of Equity.

Another writer, most probably John Tutchin, went further

> Let a lewd Judge come reeking from a wench
> To vent a wilder lust upon the Bench;
> Bawl out the venom of his rotten heart,
> Swell'd up with envy, over act his part.
> Condemn the innocent by laws ne'er framed,
> And study to be more than doubly damn'd.
>
> (*True Englishman*, 1686)

A quick sketch this for Tutchin's later full-scale caricature. The lines of Tories and Whigs have nothing in common—except perhaps the quality of their verse.

Jeffreys' promotion involved a reshuffle of judicial appointments. The new Lord Chief Justice was Sir Edward Herbert, a respected royalist and one of the few officials to follow James into exile; Mr. Baron Wright became a King's Bench judge—at the Revolution he tried to escape, but was captured and put in Newgate, where he died of gaol fever. Sir Edward Nevill, a run-of-the-mill Tory, took Wright's place in the Exchequer; 'Squinting Jack' became Master of the Rolls, an office in which he would act as Jeffreys' deputy in Chancery, and Roger North got a junior post as Attorney to the Queen.

Wearing his new robes, Jeffreys was in great form. North acidly recorded:

> I had such holy water from him, such elaborate speeches of encouragement as I never hope to, or rather hope never to, hear again. There was no service he could do me but he would lose his sleep and run at all hours to do it. I had, said he, lost a brother, but found a friend.

On the first day of the Michaelmas term the new Lord Chancellor went to King's Bench to swear in the new Chief Justice. Addressing Sir Edward, Jeffreys expounded his own political *credo*:

> Be undaunted and courageous; be sure to execute the law to the utmost of its vengeance upon those that are known—and we have reason to remember them—by the name of Whigs! And you are likewise to remember the snivelling Trimmers! For you know what our Saviour Jesus Christ says in the Gospel, that "they that are not for us are against us". . . . In fine, sir, as the sum of all your duty, fear God and honour the King; but use your utmost authority for the suppression of those that are given to change.

In November, James II's first Parliament was prorogued, and never met again. It had sat for only eleven days. Jeffreys, like other public speakers before and since, apparently found it difficult to adjust his manner to the intimate atmosphere of the best club in Europe, for Burnet (a hostile witness) wrote that when he spoke 'in his rough manner' then 'he was soon taken down'.

In the following January Jeffreys presided over the last case ever heard before the Court of the Lord High Steward. Two peers were involved in Monmouth's plots—Lord Grey, who had of course played a leading part but who had been pardoned by James as his reward for telling all he knew, and Lord Delamere, who was now accused of having gone home to Cheshire to prepare a rising there. Delamere was the former Henry Booth who had in 1680 attacked Jeffreys' conduct at the Chester Assizes.

Peers facing capital charges were entitled to be tried by their peers. When Parliament was prorogued or dissolved this function of the House of Lords was exercised by a court specially set up for the purpose and presided over by the Lord High Steward, who was normally the Lord Chancellor.

As president the Steward would appoint a committee of twelve or more peers to act as a jury—the Lords Triers. At the end of the

trial each would have to return his verdict individually and publicly. A simple majority was sufficient to convict or to acquit.
The trial over, the Steward would snap his white staff to indicate
that his office was at an end.

When the trial opened, twenty-seven peers were present. They
were, not surprisingly, mostly members of the Court party, but
Jeffreys appears to have conducted the trial with impartiality.
Ailesbury wrote that he 'kept himself better than usual in bounds
as to his tongue, however he launched out sometimes.'

The proceedings began with the Clerk of the Crown reading
the commission which authorized the trial. Then the white staff
was brought forward by Garter King-of-Arms and Black Rod.
Having accepted it, Jeffreys handed the staff back to Black Rod
who held it during the proceedings. Then he opened the trial:

My Lord Delamere, the King being acquainted that you stand
accused of high treason, not by common report of hearsay, but by a
Bill of Indictment found against you by gentlemen of great quality
and known integrity within the County Palatine of Chester, the
place of your residence, has thought it necessary in tenderness to you
as well as justice to himself to order you a speedy trial.

My Lord, if you know yourself innocent, in the name of God do
not despond, for you may be assured of a fair and patient hearing
and in your proper time a free liberty to make your full defence; and
I am sure you cannot but be well convinced that my noble lords
that are here your peers to try you will be as desirous and ready to
acquit you if you appear to be innocent as they will to convict you
if you appear to be guilty.

Delamere contended that, since Parliament was only prorogued,
he ought to be tried by the whole House of Lords. Jeffreys, correctly, offered to hear the argument if the prisoner had his
counsel ready. Delamere had not, and Jeffreys then dismissed the
plea as 'frivolous'. Delamere pounced on the adjective:

DELAMERE: My Lord, I hope the privilege of the peers of England is
not frivolous.
JEFFREYS: Pray, good my Lord, do not think I should say any such
thing that the privilege of the peers is frivolous. As I would not
willingly mistake you, so I desire your Lordship would not
misapprehend or misrepresent me. I spoke not at all of the peers'
privilege, but of your plea.
DELAMERE: I hope your grace will be pleased to advise with my Lords
here present, it being upon a point of privilege.

JEFFREYS: Good my Lord, I hope that you that are a prisoner at the
bar, are not to give me direction, who I should advise with or
how I should demean myself.

After this sharp passage of arms, the trial was something of an
anticlimax. The Crown lawyers attempted to show that Delamere
had planned a rising of 10,000 men which had only been abandoned for lack of money. Delamere, cross-examining, was able
to demonstrate that the chief witness, Saxon, was committing
perjury. Jeffreys summed up, briefly and fairly:

Your Lordships are judges: and if you do not believe the testimony
of Saxon, whose testimony has been so positively contradicted by
divers persons of quality, the prisoner ought to be acquitted of this
indictment.

After half an hour the Lords Triers returned to the Court. The
Lord High Steward addressed the junior peer, Lord Churchill,
the future Duke of Marlborough: 'How say you, my lord Churchill, is Henry, Baron of Delamere, guilty of high treason whereof
he stands indicted and hath been arraigned, or not guilty?'

Churchill, as the rules prescribed, stood up, laid his hand on his
heart, and gave his verdict: 'Not guilty, upon my honour.'

One by one the other Triers followed. Delamere was acquitted.

The verdict bore out James's statement before the trial 'that he
had named persons that would not find a man guilty, right or
wrong.' Three years later Delamere, who had on this occasion
said on oath, 'I pray God bless his Majesty, and long may he reign',
behaved as he had been accused of plotting to do. He raised
Cheshire on behalf of William of Orange—and was rewarded
with an Earldom.

Receiving back the white staff, Jeffreys held it above his head
and snapped it, thus dissolving the Court. It was the last meeting
of the Lord High Steward's Court, which had endured in that
form since at least the year 1400. It was also the last criminal trial
at which Jeffreys was ever to preside.

At this time Jeffreys was drinking and entertaining on a grand
scale. In the early part of 1686 he had suffered a bad attack of the
stone, and it was generally held that plenty of liquid would dis-
solve the obstruction, or at least relieve the pressure. Jeffreys'
guests included most of the great names of Court and City. There
were the Ministers of State; Clarendon, Rochester and Sunderland; the High Tory merchants like the 'Great Smoker' and his

nephews; the Lord Mayor, Sir Robert Jeffreys; Alderman Charles Duncombe, reputed to be the richest commoner in England; and 'my most honoured friend' Samuel Pepys, now Secretary of the Navy. Moderate Whigs were part of the same circle, including Sir Robert Clayton, the 'Prince of Citizens', the lawyer Henry Pollexfen who had been on the western assize with Jeffreys—'a very learned, upright and useful man' a colleague called him; and John Evelyn the diarist.

Another friend, Sir William Trumbull, the diplomat, sent luxuries from abroad, bands and ruffles 'with which he is much pleased', and 'a nightdress of *point-de-Paris* for the head of my Lady Jeffreys'. On his way to the Levant Sir William wrote: 'When I arrive at Smyrna I shall endeavour to get some good hawks sent according to your commands. In the meantime my wife sends Lady Jeffreys four of the best orange trees she could procure in these parts.'

Soon after Delamere's acquittal Jeffreys gave a dinner at Great Queen Street, of which Sir John Reresby, Governor of York, and a rather strait-laced Tory, wrote in his diary as follows:

1686: January 18th.
After dinner the Chancellor, having drunk smartly at table (which was his custom), called for one Mountford, a gentleman of his that had been a comedian, an excellent mimic; and to divert the company, as he called it, made him give us a cause—that is, plead before him a feigned action, where he aped all the principal lawyers of the age in their tone of voice and action or gesture of body, and thus ridiculed not only the lawyers but the law itself. . . .
[It was] not so prudent as I thought for so eminent a man in so great a station of the law, since nothing could get a man more enemies than to deride those whom they ought most to support.

This satirical cabaret sounds, when measured by Restoration standards, a very intellectual amusement, but one sees Sir John's point. It enabled, for instance, the cautious Roger North to write of Jeffreys that

His friendship and conversation lay much among good fellows and humorists, and his delights were accordingly drinking, laughing, singing, kissing, and all the extravagances of the bottle. He had a set of banterers for the most part near him, as in old times great men kept fools to make them merry. And these fellows abusing one another and their betters were a regale to him. And no friendship or dearness could be so great in private which he would not use ill, and to an extravagant degree, in public. No one that had any expectations from him was safe from his public contempt and derision which some of his minions at the Bar bitterly felt. Those above or that could hurt or benefit him, and none else, might depend on fair quarter at his hands.

In point of fact, other houses provided heavier drinking. Only a fortnight after the evening described above, Jeffreys enjoyed 'a great debauch of wine' at Alderman Duncombe's and

> . . . he and my Lord Treasurer, with others, drank to that height as 'twas whispered that they stripped into their shirts, and had not an Accident prevented, would have got upon a sign-post to drink the King's health, which gave occasion of derision, not to say more of the matter.

Perhaps it was this escapade on a cold night in winter which brought on an attack of the stone so serious that for a few days it was thought he might die. Sir William Trumbull was told: 'The Lord Chancellor having voided 64 stones in one day is still very ill'—but, Luttrell wrote, 'he is since, by the use of means, pretty well recovered'.

While his town house was overflowing with guests, dependents, and their families, Jeffreys was also engaged in rebuilding Bulstrode, which had been partly destroyed by fire. In February he went down to the new house and spent about a month there recovering from his attack of the stone. The new house '. . . was a long, low building—the south front measured 200 feet. On the East there was a fine hall two storeys high, but with this exception the house had only one storey. The principal rooms are said to have been very handsome, but the bedrooms cannot have been particularly comfortable, as they were all situated in the basement.'[1] Almost a century later Horace Walpole—who preferred Gothic—described it as

> a melancholy monument of Dutch magnificence; however there is a brave gallery of old pictures, and a chapel with two fine windows of painted glass. The ceiling was formerly decorated with the assumption, or rather presumption, of Chancellor Jeffreys, to whom it belonged; but a very judicious fire hurried him somewhere else.

By the end of March Jeffreys was back in London, attempting to cope with his royal master's increasingly impossible demands. The

---

[1] H. M. Hyde, *Judge Jeffreys* (London, 1940), p. 245.

King's prerogative to suspend or dispense with laws had been used in earlier times, but in the seventeenth century it had become one of the main points at issue between King and Parliament and James was determined that the judges should make a clear declaration in favour of the King's dispensing power. 'I am determined to have twelve judges who will be all of my mind in this matter,' the King said. It was reported that Chief Justice Jones of Common Pleas had tartly replied, 'Your Majesty may find twelve judges of your mind, but hardly twelve lawyers.' James proceeded to reconstitute the Bench. Jones, it is hardly necessary to say, was dismissed, together with two others, and the opinion was that 'Our Judges sit very loosely upon their benches.'

As soon as James had secured his pliant Bench, a test case was brought. Godden, a coachman, informed against his master, Sir Edward Hales, a Catholic who held a commission in the army by virtue of the King's dispensing power. In *Godden* v. *Hales* the judges duly found, by 11 to 1, in favour of Hales. The way was now open for the appointment of Catholics to all those positions from which they had formerly been excluded by the Test Act.

By July James's Cabinet of advisers had polarized into two groups—five Catholic Tories led by the Jesuit Father Edward Petre, and three High Anglicans, Rochester, Clarendon and Godolphin. Two men remained unattached. No one knew what Sunderland believed; as late as the autumn of 1687 he was still cannily attending both Catholic and Anglican services. Jeffreys— for the first and last time in his life—attempted to trim between the two factions. At first it seemed that he might move cautiously into opposition. In April he raised certain legal objections to the dispensing power. In May James insisted that a pamphlet, written in France in defence of the Huguenots, should be publicly burned. Again Jeffreys objected. It was, he argued, a matter for the French to deal with—though perhaps, if the King wished, the printers might be prosecuted. James interrupted him: 'I have made up my mind to this; dogs defend each other. . . . I think Kings should do the same.' The paper was duly burned. Sir William Trumbull wrote 'the Chancellor is not so keen for the Catholics, though he . . . is still firm for the Prerogative and on the Penal Laws. . . .' In Dublin the rumour ran that the Chancellor would shortly fall.

Jeffreys was torn between loyalty to his King and loyalty to his Church, but he had really no choice, as even the little matter of the French pamphlet had shown. His career, his livelihood, his very safety depended on his remaining in power. His principles made it impossible for him to join the Whigs, even supposing that they would have him, and there was no place for retirement from the King's service this side of death or disgrace.

There was no place for argument either. To James, as to all the Stuarts except Charles II, loyalty implied absolute agreement with his own views. If a man who had been loyal opposed him that was, for the King, proof that the loyalty had not been genuine.

In the end Jeffreys was able to convince himself that there was no real conflict of loyalties. If he resisted, the King would be advised by a Catholic, who would not even be such a good lawyer. As the only powerful Anglican in the inner council it was therefore his duty to maintain his position and protect the interests of the established Church, while in doing so he would also be protecting the King's real interests.

It was a logical argument, but it was for Jeffreys a fatal one. From now on he worked in isolation. He was not able to influence James's behaviour one iota, but he himself was ruined by the King's fatal rigidity.

In the summer of 1686 Jeffreys was a little involved in family matters. His brother James Jeffreys had entered the Church, and had become a Canon of Canterbury in 1682 and a D.D. in the following July. Now the Lord Chancellor tried to procure for him the See of Chester. Jeffreys failed, the appointment went to Cartwright, a pliant tool of James II. Apparently James Jeffreys was too friendly with the Dean of Canterbury, Doctor Tillotson, who was known to favour Dissenters. The following letter makes the point:

LONDON
3rd Augt 1686

DEAR BROTHER

I received yours at Bulstrode from whence I returned last night; and as for Sydalch I have ordered the Writings to be prepared, so that you may see them executed at your coming to London, and carry 'em with you into Wales in your designed Journey. I desire you to take all care for the payment of the money as I shall order, being very unwilling to alter my established Resolution of giving creditt to any beyond the River Dee.

As to your desire upon the promotion of Dr. Parker, there will be no opportunity offered. As to other Hopes which I guess you are more often saluted with, I hope you will be wise enough to leave that to my management and discretion, and not to be too much corrupted by your own humour, or that that you know I think is worse—that of your Guardian the D[ean], thereby to prevent that advantage that your Friends think you deserve, and I shall always be willing to promote.

My Wife is somewhat better than she had been; my Brother Sir Thomas is now well, tho' he has of late been troubled with my unhappy Distemper. We design next week for Tunbridge where we hope to see you. My service to my Sister.

I am with all Sincereity,
Your most affectionate Brother and Servant
JEFFREYS C.

James Jeffreys remained only a Canon until his death three years later.

The Chancellor was better able to help his brother Thomas, who was now Consul in Alicante. He had the advantage, in the King's eyes, that he had become a Catholic, and when he visited England in 1686 he was knighted at Windsor.

On the return journey Sir Thomas's ship ran into a great storm in the Channel and had to put in to Deal. From 'The Three Kings' there he wrote feelingly, 'it was by God's infinite mercy I did not bust. . . . For God's sake let me have a line from you now and then, which will be the only comfort of my life.' Safely back in Spain, he married a Spanish lady, was made a knight of Alcantara, and was still living in Alicante in 1698.

In July the King established a new Court, the Commission for Ecclesiastical Causes. This was modelled on the earlier Court of High Commission, which had been declared illegal by Charles I's Long Parliament. The old Court had been used to silence attacks on bishops, the new Court was designed to punish attacks upon the Catholic Church. It was to consist of the Lord Chancellor, together with three clergymen and three laymen, of whom the Chancellor and three others would form a quorum, and might take action 'notwithstanding any law to the contrary'. Besides Jeffreys the members were to be Sancroft, Archbishop of Canterbury; Crewe, Bishop of Durham; Sprat, Bishop of Rochester; Chief Justice Herbert; Sunderland; and Rochester. Sancroft did not attend, pleading ill-health and old age, begging that he might be excused 'to the end he may the better mind those things which belong to his peculiar care'. James had no alternative but to agree, adding sourly that if Sancroft was too ill to sit on the Commission he had better not come to Council meetings either.

The new Commission, sitting at Whitehall, heard its first case in August when the Bishop of London, Compton, appeared before it. Dr. John Sharp, a clergyman in his diocese, had preached against Catholicism and Compton had refused to suspend him.

Jeffreys opened the proceedings, asking 'What was the reason you did not suspend Dr. Sharp when the King commanded . . . ?' Compton answered that he had intended no offence to the King, but considered that Sharp ought first to be summoned before the usual Ecclesiastical Court. Jeffreys replied: 'You ought to have known the law, and it was a wonder you did not. The King is to be obeyed, and if you have any reason to show in this particular we are ready to hear you.'

'I knew not what would be laid to my charge,' Compton answered, 'and therefore was not provided to make such a defence as I might have done. But if your Lordships will give me a copy of the indictment, I will endeavour to give your Lordships satisfaction.'

'My Lord, I would not misinterpret your words,' Jeffreys said, 'but shall desire you to explain their meaning. If by desiring a copy of our commission you design to quarrel with the jurisdiction and legality of the court I have another answer for you. But till I know your meaning here my answer is that no copy of the commission can be granted, and it is unreasonable to desire it. It is upon record; all the coffee-houses have it for a penny apiece, and I doubt not but your Lordship has seen it.'

Compton objected that he did not go to coffee-houses—they had a slightly suspect reputation, and were identified in the popular mind with Whig schemers. He then continued that he still wished to see a copy of the commission 'a thing altogether new to this generation'. Jeffreys consulted his colleagues and, after a recess of a quarter of an hour, told the Bishop that his request could not be granted, for otherwise everyone that appeared before them might challenge the commission and then 'all our times will be spent in reading, and we have something else to do . . . it is a short question I ask, Why did you not obey the King?'

'It is a short question, but requires more words to answer it,' Compton retorted. He asked for an adjournment until the beginning of the next legal term, and was granted a week.

When the Commission reassembled Compton announced that he had only got hold of a copy of the commission the previous evening, and that he had not been able to obtain a legal opinion on it, since counsel were all out of town on circuit. 'If your lord-ship doubts the truth of this, I have the person ready to make oath here of it.'

'My lord,' Jeffreys protested blandly, 'you are a person of honour, and we will not question the truth of what you say; there needs no oath. But, my lord, I must tell you we will not admit of any quarrelling with our commission. We are well assured of the legality of it; otherwise we would not be such fools as to sit here.'

Compton now asked for a further adjournment. 'I hope a fort-night will not be unreasonable.'

'Agreed. You shall have until tomorrow fortnight in the morning.' Then Jeffreys suavely reintroduced the coffee-house theme. 'My lord, when I told you our commission was to be seen in every coffee-house, I did not speak with any design to reflect on your lordship, as if you were a haunter of coffee-houses. I abhorred the thoughts of it, and intended no more by it but that it was common in the town.'

A fortnight later the Bishop's legal experts raised technical objections. While they were doing so, Compton noticed that the Crown advocate, Dr. Pinfold, was taking notes.

'My lord, I desire that care may be taken concerning the minutes . . . that I may not be misrepresented to the King by the mistake of the penman.'

'You need not fear it. I hope you have a better opinion of us,' said Jeffreys. 'There shall be no advantage taken by them or us.' But a fortnight later, when the Commissioners announced their judgement, Jeffreys got his own back; 'to prevent mistake,' he told Compton, 'we have ordered it to be put in writing.'

The Bishop was suspended from his office. The legal instrument carried the seal of the new Commission, a *C* on one side and *J* 2 on the other, with the inscription *Sigillum Commissionariorum Regiae Majestatis ad Causas Ecclesiasticas*. This was essentially the same as the seal of the old Court of High Commission, and it is significant that none of the Commissioners chose to sign the instrument.

The Ecclesiastical Commission was a novelty. The Lord Chan-cellor's traditional sphere of activity was the Court of Chancery. Three days a week in term time Jeffreys presided in Westminster Hall or in the 'cause room' attached to the house in Duke Street to which he later moved.

Chancery existed to afford redress when it could not be obtained in the common-law courts—for instance, to ensure performance of a contract, to set aside a transaction carried through by fraud, to make a trustee discharge his obligations. There were few fixed rules, much depended on each Chancellor, 'the Keeper of the King's Conscience'. A common lawyer, John Selden, had said of the vagueness of interpretation: "Tis all one as if they should make the standard for the measure we call a foot, a Chancellor's foot; what an uncertain measure would this be!'

This scope for individual decision suited Jeffreys, and he is seen at his best in Chancery, dealing with private cases in which there was no question of politics or prejudice, and where he could use his acute mind and his ability to cut through verbiage to the heart of the matter. He intended, he said, 'to make decrees according to his own conscience, and every case was to stand on its own bottom.'

The Chancery administration was shaken up. Defendants were to receive their full costs, and not a nominal 20s. as heretofore. Half a dozen Chancery officials were suspended for suspected corruption. One man complained indignantly, 'I made him', claiming that he had employed Jeffreys in the latter's early days. 'Well then,' the Chancellor said grimly when he heard this, 'I will lay my maker by the heels.' And off to gaol the attorney went—but first Jeffreys had him to dinner.

To the layman the Chancery cases are of limited interest. They lack the drama of the political trials, and they are concerned with technicalities. This is unfortunate, since lawyers are agreed that Jeffreys was a very able Chancellor. Lord Birkenhead wrote that what has survived is

> sufficient to justify the contention that, both at law and in equity, his conclusions do not differ markedly from those of judges against whose legal knowledge no criticism has been urged. They do not show a grasp of principle such as enabled judges like Coke, Hale, Holt, Mansfield and others to determine the broad road of legal principle. They are rather decisions on the facts of the case, and prove that he was unusually competent to see the real point and to decide it properly and fairly.[1]

Professor Keeton, in his magisterial study of Jeffreys' legal career, concludes that

> During his three years of office there was some development of major equitable principles. There was sound application of others,

[1] Birkenhead, Lord, *Fourteen English Judges* (1926), p. 96.

and there was a real and considerable attempt to grapple with the shortcomings of Chancery administration... Those who have considered Jeffreys' decisions have been impressed by them, and it is significant that although many of them were challenged after the Revolution, very few of them were disturbed.[1]

The cases do not in general lend themselves to brief description, but one (*Firebrasse* v. *Brett*) may be mentioned for the light it throws on seventeenth-century society. Brett and Sir William Russell, starting with eight guineas, won £900 from Sir Basil Firebrasse in one day after dinner at his house. Then Sir Basil, 'being somewhat inflamed with wine', went upstairs and came down again with a bag containing about £1,000 in guineas, and Brett won that money also. Firebrasse, not unnaturally suspecting that he had been cheated, called the servants, seized the money, and prosecuted Brett for playing with loaded dice. Brett was acquitted and in his turn sued Firebrasse for his winnings. Firebrasse went to Chancery, repeating that Brett had cheated and had made him drunk. There Jeffreys said that he thought it 'a very exorbitant sum to be lost at play at one sitting between persons of their rank, and that he would discourage as much as in him lay extravagant gaming'. He referred to a case in King's Bench in which Chief Justice Hale had commented that 'great wagers proceeded from avarice and were founded in corruption'. In the end the two parties agreed to keep what they already held.

In one of the cases that came before him in Chancery, *The Earl of Pembroke's Creditors* v. *Lady Charlotte Herbert*, Jeffreys was himself indirectly involved, since his son John was engaged to Lady Charlotte. The question at issue was whether or not certain of her father's debts were recoverable by his creditors. Jeffreys took the precaution of consulting two other judges before deciding that about two-thirds of the total debts were not recoverable. Popular opinion drew the obvious conclusion

> Old Tyburn must groan,
> For Jeffreys is known
> To have perjured his conscience to marry his son.

Nevertheless, popular opinion was wrong, for the judgement was upheld by the Lords after the Revolution, when Jeffreys himself was dead and disgraced.

[1] Keeton, Professor G. W., *Lord Chancellor Jeffreys and the Stuart Cause* (London, 1965), pp. 395, 494. The Chancery decisions are examined in detail in Chapter 13.

It was said that one Chancery case later helped, indirectly, to destroy Jeffreys. Burnham, a scrivener from Wapping, was the defendant. The plaintiff's counsel, hoping to play on the Chancellor's well-known prejudices, said of Burnham that 'it was thought he was a trimmer'. The remark had the desired effect.

'A trimmer!' Jeffreys exploded. 'I have heard much of that monster, but never saw one. Come forth, Mr. Trimmer; turn you round and let us see your shape.'

And the unfortunate Burnham was exposed to a Jeffreys' lecture. Nevertheless the Lord Chancellor dismissed the case against him. Outside, his friends were waiting to ask Burnham how he came off.

'Came off? I am escaped from the terrors of that man's face which I would scarce undergo again to save my life; and I shall certainly have the frightful impression of it as long as I live.'

The sequel will be seen later.

In 1687 Jeffreys, by virtue of his position as Lord Chancellor, found himself called upon to arbitrate on a matter very different from those that usually concerned him—a matter of aesthetic judgement. The Temple Church, recently restored by Wren, required a new organ. Two instruments were constructed, one by a French builder, Renatus Harris, and one by Father Bernard Schmidt, a German who had recently made an organ for Westminster Abbey. The Inner Temple liked Harris's organ, the Middle Temple preferred Schmidt's.

A series of contests followed. Both organs were erected, Harris's to the south of the altar, Schmidt's in the north transept. Blow and Purcell played Schmidt's organ, the Queen's organist demonstrated Harris's instrument. But the two Inns could not agree. Harris suggested to Schmidt that they should each construct additional stops, including a vox humana, cremorne, and double bassoon. This they each did. Still no decision could be reached.

At this stage the two Societies called in Jeffreys. After hearing the instruments Jeffreys chose Schmidt's, suggesting that Harris (whose organ he found 'discernibly low and weak') should receive £100 as a consolation prize. Schmidt's organ was duly bought for £1,000 and remained in the Temple Church until the Blitz in the Second World War.

In April of the same year Jeffreys moved from his house in

Queen Street to a new one in Duke Street, Westminster, over-
looking the park. The house had been built by Moses Pitt, a
speculative builder, 'just against the birdcages in St. James's Park,
... I let it to the Lord Chancellor Jeffreys, with stables and coach
houses to it, for £300 per annum'. Jeffreys came to look over the
house with his friend Alderman Duncombe, the great banker.
Between the house and the Park they noticed a vacant piece of
ground and Jeffreys instructed Pitt to build him a cause room
there in which he might transact Chancery business. In due course
a 'court room, vault and other conveniences' were built, including
a flight of steps from the house to the park which survived until
1910. Later, there were difficulties. The piece of ground belonged
to the King and Jeffreys had assumed he would be able to get hold
of it. Unfortunately for Pitt, the King had given it to Sir Edward
Hales and later Pitt found himself in the awkward position of
having built part of a house on someone else's land.

During 1687 Jeffreys had less congenial occupations than those
of music critic and man of property. The political situation had
worsened considerably. In January his friend Rochester had been
dismissed from his post as Lord Treasurer and in the following
December his patron Sunderland at last took the plunge and declared himself a Catholic, leaving Jeffreys and a nonentity, the
Earl of Mulgrave, as the only Anglicans in the Inner Cabinet.

Anti-Catholic feeling was meanwhile growing in strength.
When a Catholic chapel was opened in the City the Lord Mayor,
fearing a riot, ordered its doors to be locked. The chapel was soon
reopened, guarded by the militia. During Mass an apprentice
strolled around inside 'laughing and staring. An officer bade him
go out since he appeared not by his behaviour to be of that religion. He said he would not go out, and if they said much to him,
he would break their crosses and juggling-boxes down, where-
upon a riot seemed to form'. This was not the only incident of its
kind.

In April James had carried his own plans a stage further. On the
fourth he issued his first Declaration of Indulgence, suspending
the penal laws against Catholics and Nonconformists alike, and
establishing complete religious toleration. The Declaration was
signed by Sunderland and two Bishops, but not, significantly, by
Jeffreys. Evelyn wrote in his Diary: 'What this will end in, God
Almighty only knows; but it looks like confusion, which I pray
God avert.' In the counties the work of moulding public opinion

in favour of the new policy, of seeing that suitably inclined persons were J.P.s, and of preparing the ground for the summoning of a new Parliament, was in the hands of the Lord-Lieutenants. Jeffreys was appointed for two counties where he held property, Shropshire and Buckinghamshire, but like the other Lieutenants he was unsuccessful in his efforts.

While all this was going on, James was also putting pressure on the universities. In February Cambridge had refused to admit a Benedictine monk, Alban Francis, to the degree of Master of Arts without administering the statutory oaths and on 27th April a delegation headed by the Vice-Chancellor and Master of Magdalene, Dr. John Peachell—'whose red nose,' Pepys wrote, 'makes me ashamed to be seen with him, though otherwise a good-natured man'—appeared before the Ecclesiastical Commission.

The following dialogue then took place between Jeffreys and Peachell:

Now, Mr. Vice-Chancellor, why did you not obey his Majesty's command in behalf of the gentleman mentioned here?
My lord, you inquire of me why I did not admit Mr. Francis according to the King's letter?
Yes, that's the question I ask.
Is this the only question your lordship is pleased to ask me?
Nay, Mr. Vice-Chancellor, we will not capitulate in the very beginning. Pray answer first, and then you shall know what we have to say more.
My lord, I beg time to answer you. I am a plain man, not used to appear before such an honourable assembly, and if I should answer hastily it may be I might speak something indecent or unsafe, which I should be afterwards sorry for; therefore I beg leave, my lords, to have time allowed us for giving such an answer, as may be both for our safety, and your lordships' honour.
Mr. Vice-Chancellor, as for your own safety, my lords are willing that you should take all the care you can; but for what concerns our honour, do not trouble yourself; we are able to consult that without any interposition of yours.

There was a little more verbal fencing, and in the end Peachell's request was granted. When the matter was resumed in May he was in a great state. Jeffreys asked him the words of the oath he had taken as Vice-Chancellor, but he found he could not remember them. Other members of the delegation began to prompt him.

Jeffreys quickly stopped this. 'Nay, good Doctor,' he said to Dr. Cook of Jesus, 'how came you, who never were Vice-Chancellor and so never took this oath, to know it better than one that is Vice-Chancellor and hath taken it?'

Peachell's fears were justified. He was deprived of his Vice-Chancellorship and of his Master's office, while his colleagues received an ironical rebuke from Jeffreys: 'Therefore I shall say to you what the Scripture says, and rather because most of you are divines—go your way and sin no more, lest a worse thing come unto you.'

Peachell wrote sadly to his friend Pepys, 'The Laws of the Land and the oaths we lie under are the fences of God's Church and religion, and I cannot suffer myself to be made an instrument to pull down those fences.' For many High Tories 1687 was the parting of the ways. But James pushed on. The case against Cambridge was scarcely at an end before the Commissioners were involved with Oxford. The President of Magdalen had died in March. The Fellows received a royal order to elect in his place Anthony Farmer, a Catholic convert. It was, to say the least, an odd choice. Farmer had been expelled from Trinity, Cambridge, had run an amateur brothel in Oxford, and, after he had been nominated by the King, had gone to Abingdon to celebrate, had got drunk, and had thrown the stocks into the nearest pond—charges, the Bishop of Chester wrote in his diary, 'that any modest man would blush to hear.' Quite apart from his character, Farmer was disqualified by the College statutes, being under thirty and not a fellow of Magdalen or New College.

The Fellows proceeded to elect a Dr. John Hough. In June they were summoned to appear before the Commissioners and obtained the usual postponement to prepare their case, Jeffreys commenting sourly to the Vice-President, 'That is like a man of your coat, first to do an ill thing, and then to advise with counsel how to defend it.' The Fellows submitted their case in writing, expressing regret, but pointing out that they were bound by their statutes. Jeffreys noticed that one of their number, Dr. Fairfax, had not signed the document. Jeffreys turned to him.

'This looks like a man of sense and a good subject, let's hear what he will say.'

Fairfax replied that he had not signed because he refused to recognize the Court. By what commission, he asked, did they sit?

Jeffreys was naturally indignant. 'Pray,' he said, 'what com-

mission have *you* to be so impudent in court? This man ought to
be kept in a dark room. Pray let the officers seize him.'

The incident provides another opportunity to check the in-
accuracy of Macaulay's account. He wrote that Fairfax 'hinted
some doubts' and that Jeffreys 'roared at him like a wild beast'.
Perhaps Jeffreys did, but there is no evidence. On the contrary,
while contemporary accounts make no comment on the Chancellor's behaviour, one authority (Luttrell) writes that Fairfax was
'very bold there', and another (Verney) describes him as 'arguing
with very great heat'.

In the end the Fellows were forced to accept a Catholic as
President, James himself addressing them: 'Get you gone, know
I am your King. I will be obeyed, and I command you to be gone.'
However, the new President was *not* Farmer. Jeffreys had seen
to that, telling him 'that the Court looked on him as a very bad
man.'

While the university cases were being decided, the King was
proceeding with his plans for religious toleration. Historians remain divided on the question of James's sincerity, but they are
united on two points: that this was not a new idea of the King's,
and that it was a disastrous one.

Ten years earlier, in 1676, James had said that he thought
'Presbyterians should be made use of in order to divide the two
Houses'. *Made use of*—that was what his enemies had always
suspected. Yet at much the same time it was reported 'that the
Duke was very much troubled that any persons should be
troubled for serving God that was within their conscience they
thought they ought to do'. After his accession he told the Dutch
and Spanish ambassadors that '. . . although he wished to see his
own religion embraced, he thought it contrary to the precepts of
Holy Writ to force conscience; . . .' and when 1,600 Quakers
were released from gaol, they testified 'it doth the less surprise us
since it is what some of us have known to be the declared principle
of the King, so well long before as since he came to the throne'.

Sincerity, or political expediency? The evidence can be read
either way. What is clear is that, whatever James might feel,
Jeffreys was disturbed. He was a sincere Anglican; he had no love
for Catholics, and none for Dissenters either. His feelings may be
imagined when, among the names of the new Aldermen
appointed in the City, he found not only Whigs, but a Baptist and
even an Anabaptist. Before the year was out he had even greater

shock—his old Whig antagonist William Williams had suddenly announced his conversion to Catholicism and had received his reward, the post of Solicitor-General and a knighthood. 'There are people,' the French ambassador Barillon commented, 'who think it is not a thing to be proud of.' Sir John Bramston was less diplomatic: 'This is he that was Speaker of the House of Commons, and that without the King's [Charles II's] approbation; this is he that was so great a stickler for the Bill of Exclusion; this is he that was fined £10,000 and payd eight of it.'

The King's policy of religious toleration was an ill-considered gamble. James was losing the support of the only considerable group pledged to uphold him, the middle-of-the-way Tories. Bishop Burnet, wise after the event, wrote in his *History*, 'The King threw off his old party in too outrageous a manner ever to return to them again.' A Tory, on his way to the Lord Mayor's banquet, was heard to mutter that 'all the jolly genteel citizens are turned out, and all the sneaking fanatics put in their places'. When James visited Chester the Bishop preached in the Cathedral, the King attended a Catholic service in the Shire Hall, and Mr. Penn the Quaker 'held forth in the tennis court'. It was all very disturbing. Barillon, the French ambassador, wrote to his master Louis XIV, 'It is difficult to see what will happen.'

The Tory gentry were beginning to withdraw their support by the middle of 1687. They were not prepared to resist the King, but they were not prepared to help him either. They sat quiet in their country houses. For Jeffreys such a course of action was not possible. He was a professional lawyer with no broad acres to support him, and meanwhile he had to resist the growing pressure from either side of Whigs and Catholics—plenty of people would be glad to see him down, if only to take his place. If William Williams by attending Mass could become Solicitor-General, then at any moment Jeffreys might find himself called upon to surrender the Great Seal to one of the 'sneaking fanatics'.

Throughout the autumn the City buzzed with rumours that the Chancellor's fall was imminent. There was, for instance, the story of the Queen's bed. Jeffreys had accompanied James on a tour of the West and it was said

> At Marlborough the Lord Chancellor took down the Queen's bed and set up his own in its place; she dissembled her resentment till she came to Bath, and then showed it so openly and fully that the King sent for Lord Dover to discharge him [Jeffreys] from his office

and the Court.... Some think Lord Castlemain, others Lord
Dover, will succeed him.

Court tittle-tattle, for Lord Dover was a very unlikely candidate,
but it showed which way the wind of favour was blowing.
Meanwhile a French observer saw in Jeffreys the one stable factor:
'The Chancellor, a very violent man, *is the only one who is not
involved in intrigue*'.

In October Jeffreys' eldest daughter Margaret was married from
Bulstrode to William Stringer, the son of the barrister, Sir Thomas
Stringer. From Spain Jeffreys' brother, Sir Thomas, sent his con-
gratulations, adding

> Now there is only wanting that poor Sally be accommodated, which
> I hope you will assist in, for she is a mighty modest pretty girl, and I
> dare say will make a good wife; and if this were effected, I should be
> much at ease, and so would my lord, I am sure. For the rest [the
> children of Jeffreys' second marriage], I hope the mother will take
> good care of them and thereby lessen ours.

Jeffreys now suffered the severest attack of the stone that he had
yet had. He fell ill just before Christmas, was thought to be dying,
and was not able to get about again until March. Lord Clarendon
called on him one February afternoon and was told that Jeffreys
'was asleep and not to be spoken with. He had been in the Chancery in the morning for a little while; but he is much indisposed
in health.' While he was out of action someone stole the Chancellor's mace and the official purse in which the Great Seal was
carried. The insignia were recovered, but the thief got away.

James now decided that the time had come to call a Parliament
to endorse his religious policy. The Lord-Lieutenants were instructed to sound local opinion. Jeffreys was not well enough—or
perhaps he was too disillusioned—to make the long journey to
Shropshire himself and instead he wrote to Mr. Edward Kynaston,
one of the former members:

From my house
in Duke Street, Westminster
24th March, 1688

Sir,
   His Majesty having been pleased to do me the honour to make me
his Lieutenant of the County of Salop, but his service requiring my
attendance upon him here, whereby I am prevented from the
happiness I proposed myself of waiting upon you in person in the

county, therefore I am commanded to give you the trouble of this by my servant, whom I have ordered to attend upon you for that purpose.

I doubt not, sir, but that you have perused and well considered his Majesty's late gracious Declaration for Liberty of Conscience, and thereby are fully convinced of his Majesty's real intentions to use his uttermost endeavours to have the same established into a law. For that purpose he does very suddenly design to call a Parliament to have the same effected. Wherein he doubts not to have the concurrence of his Houses of Parliament in the carrying on of so good a work which is of public advantage to all his kingdoms; and in order thereunto has commanded me and the rest of his Lieutenants to propose to Deputy Lieutenants and Justices of the Peace within our respective Lieutenancies the questions following,

[would he, if elected, vote for the repeal of the penal laws; would he support candidates willing to do so; would he live at peace with those of all religious persuasions].

Mr. Kynaston's reply was unaccommodating. He could not 'in conscience' accept the King's proposals. However, he continued, 'I shall always continue my allegiance to my King and live peaceably with my neighbours'. The majority of the country gentlemen made much the same reply. The Lord-Lieutenant of Cornwall added that if the King got rid of these men 'their successors would give exactly the same answer'.

9

'A Very Hard Game to Play'
(1688-9)

James II moved forward with firm, blind steps towards disaster. Since it was clearly no use calling Parliament he decided in April to issue a second Declaration of Indulgence, based on the royal dispensing power. The Declaration was to be read in church on two successive Sundays. There was nothing new in this method of announcement, Charles II had used it to make his views known to the country in 1681, and in the Exclusion Bills it had been proposed that James's own fate should be made known in just this way. The pulpits were the broadcasting stations of the time.

What was new was the content of the message the Church was being asked to announce. The clergy were committed to non-resistance, to the doctrine that to resist a king was a crime against God, but there was no reason why they should actively assist in their own destruction. To read the Declaration would, many believed, be the end of the Church of England. Seven Bishops, including the Archbishop of Canterbury, petitioned James. The Declaration, they said, was 'founded upon such a dispensing power as hath been often declared illegal in Parliament. . . . Your petitioners therefore most humbly and earnestly beseech your Majesty that you will be most graciously pleased not to insist upon the distributing and reading your Majesty's said declaration.' James, who had relied on the Anglican doctrine of non-resistance, was astounded: 'This is a great surprise to me; here are strange words. I did not expect this from you. This is a standard of rebellion.'

The petition was printed and, in consequence, the seven were ordered to appear before the Council. Jeffreys was thoroughly alarmed at the turn events had taken. He told Clarendon privately how much he disapproved, that at one time the King had been prepared to take no action; 'that he was grieved to find he had changed his mind; that he knew not how it come to pass, but said there was no remedy; some men would hurry the King to his destruction.'

When the Bishops appeared before the Council, Jeffreys was responsible for their examination. 'Is this,' he asked Archbishop Sancroft, 'the petition that was written and signed by your Grace . . . ?'

> SANCROFT: Sir, I am called hither as a criminal, which I never was before in my life, and little thought I ever should be, especially before your Majesty; but, since it is my unhappiness to be so at this time, I hope your Majesty will not be offended that I am cautious of answering questions. No man is obliged to answer questions that may tend to the accusing of himself.
>
> JAMES II: This is mere chicanery. I hope your Grace will not do so ill a thing as to deny your own hand.
>
> SANCROFT: . . . if your Majesty positively commands me to answer I will do so in confidence that a just and generous prince will not suffer what I say in obedience to his orders to be brought in evidence against me.
>
> JEFFREYS: You must not capitulate with your sovereign.
>
> JAMES II: If you choose to deny your own hands I have nothing more to say to you.

At this the Bishops withdrew for a quarter of an hour's private discussion. When they returned Jeffreys asked them again if the petition contained their signatures.

> JAMES II: I command you to answer the question.
>
> SANCROFT: I own that I wrote this petition and that this is my hand.

After the rest of the Bishops had made similar confessions, they were addressed by Jeffreys:

> It is his Majesty's pleasure to have you proceeded against for this petition, but it shall be with all fairness in Westminster Hall. There will be an information against you, which you are to answer; and in order to that, you are to enter into a recognizance.

But the Bishops refused to give bail—a shrewd tactical move, since the Council were now reluctantly compelled to imprison them in the Tower. Their journey down the Thames from Whitehall became a triumphal procession as crowds cheered from the banks, or waded out through the mud for the Bishops' blessing.

Clarendon wrote that Jeffreys 'was much troubled at their prosecution and made many professions of service for them which he desired me to let them know.' The Chancellor had good reason to be alarmed, both as a loyal Anglican and as an astute lawyer—not to mention an exasperated royalist. He knew that the charge might not stick. He knew, too, that it would be just as well if the Ecclesiastical Commission had nothing to do with the case. In consequence the Bishops were tried in King's Bench, where the egregious William Williams failed to obtain a conviction 'upon which there were shoutings, so long continued,' wrote Burnet, 'and as it were echoed into the City, that all people were struck with it. Every man seemed transported with joy. Bonfires were made all about the streets. And the news going over the nation, produced the like rejoicings and bonfires all over England.'

Jeffreys, sitting in Chancery across the Hall from King's Bench, was seen to smile at the cheering and then hide his expression in the posy that he held, though whether with joy for his Church or pleasure at Williams' discomfiture, no one knew. Once again his legal instincts had been correct. He told Clarendon that he hoped the King might now be persuaded to take more moderate counsels, and he 'called the judges a thousand fools and knaves'.

If James had suffered a serious political defeat in the acquittal of the Seven Bishops, he appeared to have won a victory in a more personal field. There was now a male heir to the throne. On 10th June, a Sunday, about ten in the morning, Mary of Modena was brought to bed of a son. The succession was secure. Or so it appeared to James. In fact, the event hastened his downfall. James's opponents might put up with an old and childless king, they could not tolerate the possibility of an indefinite line of Stuart Catholic sovereigns. The royal birth made the Revolution inevitable.

The Whigs quickly claimed that the child was suppositious, smuggled into the Queen's bedroom in a warming-pan. The tale will not stand up to scrutiny. For one thing—largely to scotch such stories—it had long been the rule that the Queen of England gave birth in public, the room thronged with spectators, a custom that was not abandoned until Queen Victoria's reign. There is evidence that Mary of Modena found the custom embarrassing, as well she might. Her daughter, Princess Anne, described how of the bed curtains 'the two sides were open. When she was in great pain, the King called in haste for my Lord Chancellor, who came up to the bed side to shew he was there; upon which the rest of the privy counsellors did the same thing. Then the Queen desired the king to hide her face with his head and periwig, which he did; for she said she could not be brought to bed, and have so many men look on her; for all the council stood close at the bed's feet, and my Lord Chancellor upon the step.' (Godolphin, cautious as usual, stood by the fireplace, where he could hear everything and see nothing.)

With such a cloud of witnesses, deception was practically impossible. Later, depositions were taken. Jeffreys deposed as follows:

> That he being sent for to St. James's on the tenth of June last, by a messenger that left word the queen was in labour, soon after this the deponent came to St. James's, and was sent for into the Queen's bed-chamber; and to the best of his, the deponent's apprehension, the Queen was in labour, and had a pain or two to the best of the deponent's remembrance before the rest of the lords were called in. The deponent stood all the time at the Queen's bedside, and heard her cry out several times as women in travail use to do, and at length after a long pain, it was by some of the women on the other side of the bed said the child was born. The deponent heard the Queen say she did not hear it cry. The deponent immediately asked the Lord President [Sunderland] what it was, he whispered that it was a boy, which the deponent understood he had hinted to him by the Lady Sunderland. Immediately the deponent saw a gentle-woman, who he hath since heard her name to be Mrs. Labadie, carry the child into another room whither the deponent followed, and saw the child when she first opened it, and saw it was black and reeking, so that it plainly seemed to this deponent to have been newly come from the womb. The deponent doth therefore depose, he doth steadfastly believe the Queen was delivered of that child that morning.

> JEFFREYS. C.

Nevertheless inspired rumours continued to circulate that Mary had either never been pregnant or alternatively that her child had been stillborn. Some of the stories were very circumstantial—but not more so than, for instance, Oates' false evidence at the time of the Popish Plot. Experts in political propaganda abounded. There were, of course, insuperable physical objections to the warming-pan theory, as a contemporary observed:

> The warming-pan is no feasible project, unless you break the back of the child to put it in; moreover, as this is supposed to be a tender infant, just reeking and wet from its mother's womb, in that tender

state it would either have cried out in the passage, or have been stiff and dead, and in the variety of motions of tossing it up and down, it would have been a perfect jelly.

As usual each side believed what they wished to believe. But when the baby grew up his behaviour as the Old Pretender showed only too clearly that he was James II's offspring.

In the month following the royal birth Jeffreys' son John was married to the daughter of the Catholic—and probably homicidal —Earl of Pembroke. 'Jacky' was now fifteen, 'very low of stature, but a fine scholar', while his bride was thirteen and taller than her husband. Her mother, Henriette de Querouaille was the sister of that Duchess of Portsmouth who had been Charles II's mistress and Jeffreys' patron. She had lived long in England but her command of the language was still shaky—'The last letter I received from my dafter put me worth of a gred troble for it was rapported hed her Ingland wois in a gred troble but bay her letter I doe faind it is a fals repord'. The vagaries of seventeenth-century spelling admirably catch her accent.

Since the pair were of different religions there were two marriage services, a Protestant one on 17th July, followed by a Catholic one on the twenty-first. 'The King was pleased to Weare a Wedding favour', he and the Queen dined at Bulstrode, and favours were distributed to all the members of the Privy Council.

A noble marriage and a royal smile can nevertheless have done little to quiet Jeffreys' political apprehensions. James was still pursuing his policy of showing favour to Catholics and Dissenters at the expense of his old supporters, the Anglican Tories and moderate Whigs. On the very day that Jacky Jeffreys was married, John Trenchard, the Whig conspirator from Taunton, kissed hands. Jeffreys might tell Clarendon that 'he had still great hopes the King would moderate when Parliament met', but his own position remained insecure. At a Council meeting a Catholic lawyer complained that the Chancellor was 'a man not wholly for his Majesty's interest', and rumours must have reached Alicante for Sir Thomas Jeffreys wrote anxiously from there to his brother James:

I should be glad that you would let me know how affairs go with my Lord [Jeffreys], for I heard various reports of him, some that he stands as fast as ever, others that he is much declined at Court, and is abundantly uneasy and out of humour. Pray, brother, tell me the whole, and what else you know of his domestic affairs.

In September he wrote again:

> Ever since I left England, I know my Lord hath rubbed through
> many discontents, as well as in his domestic as public affairs, and I
> have heard that our nearest relation [probably Sir John Trevor]
> hath been much wanting in his obligation, so he hath (poor man) a
> very hard game to play, and I believe it will be worse if the Parlia-
> ment meets. I pray God assist him. I wish he would trust less to those
> that so much frequent his table, who are but mere spies and pro-
> moters of debauchery. . . .

At Court opposition mounted, James vacillated, and Jeffreys
was in and out of favour as the wind shifted. The advice he gave
was sound: 'The King should set all things on the foot they were
at his coming to the Crown,' and 'Now honest men, both Lords
and others (though the King has used them hardly) should appear
often at Court; I am sure it would do good.' But it was not taken.
'Honest men', more shrewd—or less loyal—than Jeffreys, stayed
at home, or got in touch with William of Orange.

For William, with a double claim to the throne, through his
own mother and also through his wife, James's daughter Mary,
was at last preparing to move. For ten years he had waited,
through the Popish Plot and the Rye House Plot, the rebellion in
the West Country and the rebellion in Scotland. He had waited
so long that James did not believe he would ever move, but as
early as 25th August the French envoy had bluntly told the King
'that if his Majesty believed the Prince of Orange had any other
intention than that of making a descent on England, then he was
the only man in Europe of that opinion.'

In September, as the situation worsened, it appeared for a
moment that Jeffreys had succeeded. The King gave him orders
'to restore all the honest old aldermen who had been turned out',
writs were prepared for the calling of a new Parliament, to meet
on 27th November, and a Declaration was drafted in which the
King promised that he would maintain the Church of England
and that no Catholics would be allowed to sit in Parliament.
Although the opposition were already in touch with William
these measures, carried out consistently and completely, might
yet have saved the situation.

Three days later the writs were withdrawn. The King had
listened to other voices. As Jeffreys ruefully observed: 'All was
naught, some rogues had changed the King's mind, that he would
yield in nothing to the bishops, that the Virgin Mary was to do all.'

There was no longer any semblance of consistency in the King's actions. He changed his mind again. The Ecclesiastical Commission was dissolved. Jeffreys himself was sent to the City to restore its old Charter and its old liberties. The crowd cheered his passage from Temple Bar to the Guildhall—but they were cheering the Charter not the Chancellor, for on the way back they hooted at his coach. Seething against Papists and Presbyterians alike, they broke Sir William Williams' windows, and wrote 'reflecting' inscriptions on his door—as well they might!

Matters now moved with increasing acceleration to their climax. In the middle of October William, with his invasion fleet poised to take advantage of the first favourable wind, issued a Declaration to the people of England. A courtier asked Jeffreys if he knew what were its principal heads. The Lord Chancellor smiled thinly, 'I am sure mine is one, whatever the rest are.' Strong measures were taken, a strict censorship was imposed on all coffee-houses and news-letters. On the nineteenth, William put to sea, but his fleet was driven back by a violent storm. James relaxed again, it was the Hand of God.

On 14th October Jeffreys celebrated the King's birthday by giving a small dinner at his house to a group of leading lawyers, Tory and Whig. To one of the Whigs invited 'to eat a piece of mutton' he wrote

> I am morally assured you won't think me fool enough as to be thought so cunning as to endeavour to ensnare you . . . if thereupon you shall think me otherwise than what I hereby intimate, you may for ever publish that I cannot be, sir, a friend to justice, honesty, or to you.

The unbuttoned style was symbolic of a new Jeffreys. During the critical months of October, November and December, he was remarkably calm. He had made his effort to save the King and the kingdom in September and by a hairsbreadth he had failed. Now there was nothing to do but carry out one's legal duties and await the inevitable.

The Lord Chancellor made no attempt to secure his own safety, but he began to prepare, in a careful legal way, for the security of his family. At the end of October he settled his real estate outside London (the baronies of Wem and Loppington, the manors of Dolby, Broughton, Bulstrode and Fulmer) on his wife and son. He settled £3,000 on each of his daughters and made an allowance of £150 a year to his son John. The trustees were his brother

James; his brother-in-law Sir Thomas Bludworth; a London merchant, Thomas Coulson; his old Whig friends Sir Robert Clayton and Henry Pollexfen; the family lawyer Edward Jennings, and the Bishop of Peterborough—one of the Seven Bishops. He sent his wife and family to Leatherhead, to the house of his brother-in-law, where he hoped they might be safe. He himself remained in London.

Meanwhile Jeffreys' old patron, Sunderland, behaved very differently. The Pope's envoy wrote that 'He shows the utmost fear at the perilous position he is in.' Through his wife's lover, Henry Sidney, he was already in touch with William. He carefully 'mislaid' the draft of a treaty with France. On 29th October James dismissed him: 'I hope,' the King said, 'you will be more faithful to your next master than you have been to me,' adding to the French ambassador that 'he would not leave a man who had allowed himself to be overmastered by fear in so important a post.' A month later Sunderland was in Holland.

Now the Channel winds changed. The 'Popish weather' gave place to a 'Protestant wind' and on 5th November William docked at Torbay in Devonshire. On the ninth he entered Exeter and then began to move slowly towards London at the head of an army of 15,000 men. Slowly, since his army was mainly composed of foreign mercenaries and a pitched battle against English troops could easily swing opinion against him. Meanwhile the news was good: Yorkshire, Cheshire and Nottingham had risen and, given time, his father-in-law James could no doubt be relied on to do something foolish.

James was making his will. (Drafted and witnessed by Jeffreys, and with marginal notes in the Chancellor's own hand, it still exists.) That done, the King left to join his army at Salisbury. In the capital Jeffreys and five Privy Councillors carried on the government of the country. Ten days later the King was back, having failed to make contact with the enemy. One of his leading lieutenants, Churchill, had changed sides, his second daughter Anne had deserted him, his nose was bleeding. Once again he had failed to persist in the course of action he had chosen to follow. He should have fought. His army was larger than William's, Churchill had advised it, the struggle would quickly have become one of Englishmen against foreigners and, as a contemporary observed, 'The truth is our countrymen love no cause nor man so well as fighting, even sometimes without any cause at all.'

What was now to be done? On the day after his return James
held a Council at Whitehall. Jeffreys advised the immediate summoning of Parliament; the King agreed and on the following
morning Jeffreys announced the decision in Westminster Hall.
Later that day—it was a Wednesday—the King ordered Jeffreys
to move into the Palace of Whitehall. The Chancellor occupied
the 'little old bedchamber' which had been Father Petre's, for
that purveyor of impractical advice had disappeared and it was
reported that he had 'retired beyond the sea'. One by one James's
counsellors were slipping away. Some, like Clarendon, rode hotly
west to join the invader. Others, like Sunderland, hastened abroad.
At the end of November Jeffreys, too, left London—but only to
visit Leatherhead, where his daughter Ann lay dying. She was
buried on 2nd December—and then Jeffreys calmly went back to
London. On the following Saturday he was dealing with Chancery business in the morning as usual. Throughout these weeks
when his colleagues were fleeing the country or making their
terms with the new order, Jeffreys carried out his duties with
apparent unconcern, sitting in Chancery a fortnight after William
had landed and giving decisions at the rate of three or four a day
on private property claims. (It was on 24th November, in the
case of *Comer* v. *Hollingshed*, that he gave his last official judgement, that the Chancery Masters were not responsible if money
had been invested in securities which later proved to be defective.)

He knew quite well what was happening, though, and continued to put his affairs in order. Before moving into the Palace he
paid all his outstanding debts. On the afternoon of 8th December
he mortgaged his Leicestershire estates to Jeffrey Jeffreys for the sum
of £9,000. That evening James summoned him. The two men
went into the little room which had once been Chiffinch's. There,
where so many dusty secrets had been whispered, Jeffreys handed
over the Great Seal to his sovereign and became once more
a private citizen. Now, at last, he would consider his own
safety.

That was on Saturday. On the following Monday, about 2 a.m.,
the Queen sailed down the river to Gravesend, there to take ship
to France. There was heavy rain and wind. That evening James
told Jeffreys to be sure to attend him next morning. Then, when
the Chancellor had gone, the King burnt the writs summoning a
new Parliament and left Whitehall by coach a little after midnight.
He crossed the Thames at Millbank, throwing the Great Seal over-

board in midstream—but even in this he was unsuccessful, for a fisherman hauled it up again, accidentally, a few months later.

And so, when Jeffreys went to the royal closet on Tuesday morning he found no one there. The Palace was in chaos. There were reports that the mob was out in the City. During the day Catholic chapels were sacked and on Tuesday evening the Spanish ambassador's house was burnt to the ground—'all sober people,' Pepys wrote, 'are extraordinarily concerned at this violation of the law of nations.'

Jeffreys had stayed at his post longer than anyone, not excluding the King. Now it was time to disappear. This he did, so effectively that—although several conflicting accounts survive—it is impossible to be sure where he spent the thirty hours between Tuesday morning and Wednesday afternoon. One thing is fairly certain; he did not go back to his house in Duke Street.

The most circumstantial account of his flight suggests that Jeffreys made his way to the docks at Wapping and there boarded a collier, officially going to Newcastle, but in fact bound for Hamburg. To cover his tracks more effectively, he spent the night on another boat. On Wednesday morning he made up his mind to go ashore again. No reason is given, perhaps they had missed their tide, or perhaps rumours of a search had reached the ship. It was a dangerous move. Wapping was one of the recruiting grounds for the London mob, the home of Shaftesbury's 'brisk boys'.

Jeffreys went by way of King Edward's Stairs up Wapping High Street, east along Queen's Head Alley, and across Green Bank to 'The Red Cow', kept by Mr. Porter, in Anchor and Hope Valley. There he lay down upstairs between a couple of blankets. It was ebb-tide at noon and there would be some hours to wait before he could sail. And there they caught him.

About half-past one a search party knocked at 'The Red Cow'. Having searched the ground floor the party clattered upstairs and found a man, black with coal, his eyebrows shaved, and wearing sailor's slops—fur cap, loose neckerchief, and rusty coat—the late Lord Chancellor of England. It was said that Jeffreys had been betrayed by the collier's mate. Later the legend ran that he was recognized by the very trimming scrivener he had once frightened in Chancery (p. 160)—dramatically neat, but statistically a little unlikely.

Asked if he were the Chancellor, Jeffreys answered wearily, 'I

12

am the man.' Then 'in his blue jacket and with his hat flapped down upon his face' he was taken to the house of a Captain Jones and from there by coach to Grocer's Hall, the residence of Sir John Chapman, the Lord Mayor. By this time the news had got around and the mob was out in strength. A member of the trained bands had to sit on Jeffreys' lap to shield him from the mud and stones flung at the coach. 'There never was such joy;' wrote Sir Edmund King the same evening, 'not a man sorry that we could see. They longed to have him out of the coach had he not had a good guard.' Jeffreys, it was said, cried, 'For God's sake keep them off.' It was hardly surprising, he was not alone in his danger. The Quaker, William Penn, had a narrow escape from the mob, and Evelyn, comparatively safe at Deptford, wrote anxiously to his Tory friend Pepys to enquire after his old friend's safety, for 'this shaking menaces every corner'.

Chapman was horrified, 'struck with the terror of the rude populace and the disgrace of a man who had made all people tremble before him'. He kissed Jeffreys' hand and sat him down to dinner. It was now about three in the afternoon. The Wappingers continued to howl in the street below, so that in the end the Lord Mayor was forced to go out on to his balcony and there 'with his hat in his hand desired the people to go away and keep the peace, and did promise them that he had already sent to the Lords of the Council about the matter and that they should have justice done them'.

At about this point everyone seems to have burst into tears: Sir Robert Jeffreys, the Chancellor's old friend; Jeffreys himself, asking, 'What have I done that people are so violent against me?'; the Lord Mayor, who 'fell a'crying, then into a fit for which he was blooded and put to bed; so, ... being ill, he could not sign any warrant.' One suspects a diplomatic illness—perhaps unjustly, since Chapman died about three months later.

As dinner ended Lord Lucas, Lieutenant of the Tower, reached the Hall. Protected by companies of train-bands Jeffreys was moved to the Tower, where he would at least be safe from lynch law. There he lodged in the house of Bull, one of the warders, until apartments could be made ready for him in the Bloody Tower. The same evening the Council, led by Halifax, signed a warrant for Jeffreys' committal on a charge of high treason.

The Revolution continued. 'That evening,' noted Sir Edmund King, 'the mobile extremely violent and ungovernable.' And, most sinister, 'Dr. Oates, I am told, is dressed in all his doctor's robes again, and expects liberty quickly.' In fact no terror took place. For one thing, both parties had been involved in William's invasion and everyone was anxious to make it appear that nothing extraordinary had happened. Thus when over-enthusiastic Kentish fishermen recognized James—they called him an 'old hatchet-faced Jesuit'—and sent him back to London, the embarrassed revolutionaries had to arrange for him to be allowed to escape all over again, for no one knew what to do with such an embarrassing prisoner. The King safely in France, it was eventually agreed that the throne was vacant. William and his wife Mary, James's daughter, were invited to fill the vacancy. Business could now be resumed as if the rules had never been broken.

Jeffreys, meanwhile, remained in the Tower, virtually the only one of James's ministers who had not fled or changed sides, an inconvenient reminder of what had actually taken place. He was something of a rarity and on Sunday 16th December, there was a much larger congregation than usual at the morning service in the tiny Tower Chapel of St. Peter-ad-Vincula. They hoped to see the former Lord Chancellor—'but he came not out'.

For four months Jeffreys was in the Tower, until his death in the following April. He was already a dying man when he was admitted—a fact that may help to explain his fatalistic attitude when James's Government was collapsing around him. Inflammation from the stone had spread to his kidneys, which were now being rapidly destroyed and in consequence his blood was becoming poisoned. A twentieth-century opinion is that

> ... along with the stone, he would have had, by this time, severe chronic cystitis, or inflammation of the bladder, and, almost certainly, the germs would have caused an ascending infection of the kidneys. This pyelo-nephritis may already have advanced to the stage of pyo-nephrosis, the condition in which the kidneys are to a large extent eaten away, so that impaired renal function, together with grave toxaemia, was bringing him to death's very door.[1]

On 15th December three Lords of the Council (North, Chandos and Ossulston) examined him. They asked four factual questions: what he had done with the Great Seal (he had delivered it to James); if he had sealed all the writs for the summoning of Parliament ('to the best of his remembrance' he had); if he had

[1] J. Kemble, *op. cit.*, p. 63.

sealed patents of office for the coming year (several); if he had a permit to leave the country ('he had several passes to go beyond the sea').

In 1689 a Committee reported to the Convention Parliament that, although the Privy Council had mentioned no crime when committing Jeffreys to the Tower, nevertheless the commitment was justified because of 'the Notoriety of his crimes, known almost to the whole kingdom', which they proceeded to enumerate. These were: the Rye House trials of Russell, Sidney, College and Armstrong; his support for the late King's dispensing power; 'the management of the prosecution in the West for High Treason, after the late Duke of Monmouth's invasion'; the support he gave to the Ecclesiastical Commission, 'intended for the utter subversion of the Protestant religion, and the subject's property and liberty'. To what extent these four groups of charges were justified, the reader must judge for himself. The proportions of the Committee's report are interesting—three-quarters of it deals with the activities of the Ecclesiastical Commission, a comparatively undramatic aspect of Jeffreys' work but legally perhaps the least defensible in a court of law. No further action was taken.

During the months that he lay dying, Jeffreys had a number of visitors, including that Dr. Sharp whom the Bishop of London had refused to suspend; one of the Seven Bishops, White of Peterborough; and Frampton of Gloucester. The last described his visit:

> I found him sitting in a low chair, with a long beard and a small pot of water, weeping with himself; his tears were very great ones. I told him not to weep for hardships, but for past sins, in which case his tears were more precious than diamonds.
>
> 'My lord, all the disgrace I have suffered hitherto I can bear, and by God's grace will submit to whatever shall befall me, since I see so much of the goodness of God in sending you to me; you, that I never in the least deserved anything from—for you to visit me when others who had their all from me desert me. It can be no other than the motion of God's spirit in you. I thank you for your fatherly advice, and desire your prayers that I may be able to follow it; and beg you would add to this another visit, at what time I would receive the Sacrament.'

By the middle of April it was clear that Jeffreys had not long to live. He could not even eat fish, '. . . he has hardly been in a capacity to take anything to sustain nature, unless a little sack to revive it when it has been almost spent. About three weeks since he had a mind to a bit of salmon, which he had, but could not digest it, nor scarce anything, unless a poached egg'—the pamphleteers reported.

On Monday, 18th April, Jeffreys made his will. He had already disposed of most of his property in the previous October. He appointed as executors his wife, his brother James, his son-in-law William Stringer, and the two nephews of Alderman John Jeffreys:

'I, George Lord Jeffreys of Wem, being heartily penitent for my sins and begging forgiveness for the same, give and submit my soul to God who gave it, and my body to the grave to be decently and privately buried.' To his wife he left his personal estate, jewellery, and 'all her dressing plate with the whole furniture formerly in her chamber and closet in Duke Street.' His son's allowance was reduced to not more than eighty pounds. All his servants were to receive any wages due to them and a bonus of two pounds each—one of them, Joseph Gosling, received an annuity of forty pounds. Small grants, varying between ten pounds and two pounds, to buy rings or mourning, were made to his cousin John Trevor, his daughter's father-in-law Sir Thomas Stringer, his two sisters-in-law, Lady Moore and Mrs. Mary Bludworth; to his trustees, Sir Robert Clayton and Henry Pollexfen, Edward Jennings and Thomas Coulson; to the bishops of Gloucester and Peterborough; to Dr. Scott, Dr. Sharp, the Dean of St. Asaph, and Mr. Hesketh of All Hallows.

'And I desire my trustees to take special care of the virtuous education of my children by my former wife and hope my now wife will be careful of hers.'

He asked to be buried in the City church of St. Mary, Aldermanbury, 'as near as may be to my former wife and children, and at about ten of the night without escutcheons and all funeral pomp and show, and with few persons thereto.' The will concluded with Jeffreys' *Apologia*:

I was in hopes, notwithstanding my long indisposition of body, I might by the blessing of Almighty God have recovered so much strength as to be able to have vindicated myself if called to account, and made out that I never deserved to lie under the heavy censures I now do. I am sure I would have excused myself from having betrayed that Church of which I have lived and died a member. I mean the Church of England, which I take to be the best Church in the world; and, in the words of a dying man, I declare I never contrived the Ecclesiastical Commission, and never acted thereon save in order to the service, not overthrow, of that Church. And I do charge all my children, upon the blessing of a dying father, they be steady to the commands I have given them of being firm even to death to the principles of that Holy Church.

Four days later, on Friday 19th April, 'at thirty-five minutes past four in the morning' Jeffreys died. His friend Edward Jennings wrote to the Lord Chancellor's brother James:

He was taken with a looseness on Saturday which continued upon him till yesterday with great violence. And I did not think it was possible for him, when I came to him on Monday, to continue so long. He was very sensible to the last and had his speech till a quarter of an hour of his death, which he was apprehensive on Monday was approaching. . . . I suppose he will be interred privately on Saturday or Sunday night in the Tower, so it will be necessary for you to come up Saturday if possible.

William issued a warrant instructing the governor of the Tower to hand over Jeffreys' body to his relations, but the Chancellor was buried in the Tower Chapel, quite close to the Duke of Monmouth. Three years later a second warrant authorized the removal of the coffin and in November, 1693, the body was reinterred in St. Mary's Aldermanbury, without a monument. In 1810, when the chancel was being repaired the coffin was found 'in its rich clothing of crimson velvet with gilt furniture' and on 3rd November *The Times* reported as follows:

JUDGE JEFFRIES. The workmen employed to repair the church of St. Mary, Aldermanbury, discovered a few days since the remains of the notorious Chancellor JEFFRIES. A large flat stone was removed near the communion-table, and in a vault underneath men found a leaden coffin, containing the body. The coffin did not appear to have suffered much decay. It was closed, and a plate remained on it, inscribed with the name of Chancellor JEFFRIES. His son and daughter are also buried in the same vault. . . . The coffin was not opened; and after public curiosity had been gratified, it was replaced in the vault, and the stone fastened over it.

Towards the end of the nineteenth century a memorial tablet was placed in the church:

IN MEMORY OF GEORGE BARON JEFFREYS (OF WEM)
RECORDER OF LONDON, CHIEF JUSTICE OF THE
KING'S BENCH, AND CHANCELLOR OF ENGLAND, 1685,
FORMERLY A RESIDENT OF THIS PARISH, AND WHOSE
REMAINS ARE BURIED IN THIS CHURCH.

The Lord seeth not as man seeth.
1 Sam. xvi. 7.

That is not quite the end of the story. In the German blitz of December, 1940, the church was severely damaged. In August, 1964, *The Guardian* was reporting as follows:

Dismantling of church
for US starts soon

Another stage was reached yesterday in the task of transporting, stone by stone, the bombed ruin of one of the City of London's Wren churches to an American campus and raising it there in new and restored glory. The co-ordinating architect of this extraordinary project, Mr. Patrick Horsburgh, stood among the willowherb and fern running wild in the frail shell of St. Mary's Aldermanbury yesterday and said that he thought the church would be in daily use as a college chapel at Fulton, Missouri, in three years from the first dismantling of the stones this autumn . . . It will commemorate Sir Winston Churchill's famous speech on the campus on March 5, 1946. This called attention to the 'Iron Curtain' which had 'descended across the Continent' and asked for co-operation among the English-speaking people in achieving 'an overwhelming assurance of Security.'

Office workers may perhaps lunch and stroll over Jeffreys vaulted bones.

10

'The Lies of this Age
will be the History of the Next'

Jeffreys had been something of a legend, and a clear target for the
pamphleteers, when he was alive. It was not to be supposed that
the attacks would end or the legends cease to accumulate now that
he was dead. As a scapegoat for the Tories and a painted devil for
the Whigs he provided an invaluable political convenience. A
hostile climate of opinion was already being created by the
revolutionaries while he was still alive. His capture was celebrated
in verse:

> When Wide-mouth resign'd up the Purse and the Mace,
> Whose impudent Arrogance gain'd him his place:
> When, like Lucifer, thrown from the height of his Pride,
> And the knot of his Villainy's strangely unty'd;
> > From the Chancery bawling
> > He turns a Tarpaulin
> Men will catch at anything when they are falling
> But to hasten his fate, before he could scour, [run]
> He was taken at Wapping, and sent to the Tow'r.
> > *Revolutionary Ballad of* 1688

One pamphlet estimated that one and a half ells of cambric
would be quite sufficient to dry all the tears at his funeral, and half
a pint of burnt claret more than enough for all the mourners likely
to be there. Another suggested that Jeffreys should cut his throat,
and offered any help that might be required, concluding sinisterly,
'I am your lordship's in anything of this nature. From the little
house over against Tyburn, where the people are almost dead with
expectation of you.'

This was run-of-the-mill stuff, but in Axe Yard, an obscure
court near Westminster, the hatchet-men were at work on a more
grandiose—and, as it turned out, less ephemeral—production.

Early in 1689 a little sixteen-page pamphlet appeared anonymously:

The PROTESTANT *Martyrs:*
OR, THE
BLOODY ASSIZES

Giving an Account of the *Lives, Tryals,* and *Dying Speeches,* of all those Eminent *Protestants* that suffered in the *West of England,* by the Sentence of that Bloody and cruel Judge *Jefferies;* being in all 251 Persons, besides what were Hang'd and destroyed in cold Blood.

CONTAINING ALSO

The Life and Death of *James* Duke of *Monmouth;* His Birth and Education; his Actions both at Home and Abroad; his Unfortunate Adventure in the *West;* his Letter to King *James;* his Sentence, Execution and Dying-Words upon the scaffold; With a true Copy of the Paper he left behind him. And many other curious Remarks worth the Reader's Observation.

It sold well, combining in nice proportions sanctimoniousness and horror—always a winning combination—and soon other works followed in quick succession: *The Dying Speeches, letters and prayers of those eminent Protestants who suffered in the West of England; The Second and last Collection of the Dying Speeches; etc.* Then these were collected in an omnibus volume, *The Bloody Assizes, or a complete history of the life of George, Lord Jefferies, etc.,* and finally came *The New Martyrology.* All this in 1689. Demand grew, and the authors continued to expand and rearrange their material, until by 1705 the final version was a good-sized book:

The Western Martyrology or Bloody Assizes containing the Lives, Trials, and Dying-Speeches of all those Eminent Protestants that Suffer'd in the West of England, and Elsewhere From the Year 1678, to this Time Together with the Life and Death of George L. Jeffreys. The Fifth Edition. To which is now added, to make it complete, An Account of the Barbarous Whippings of Several Persons in the West. Also the Trial and Case of Mr. John Tutchin (the Author of the Observator), with the Cruel Sentence pass'd upon him; and his Petition to K. James to be hang'd: Never before Printed. With an Alphabetical Table to the Whole. London Printed for John Marshall at the Bible in Grace-Church-Street. MDCCV.

The contents of these works included a small amount of political theorizing, a vast number of fictitious stories, and some entertain-

ing, slap-dash verse. *The Bloody Assizes* apostrophized Jeffreys at
length, concluding:

> To *Tyburn* thee let carrion Horses draw,
> In jolting Cart, without so much as straw;
> Jaded, may they lye down i' th' road, and tyr'd;
> And (worse than one fair hanging, twice be mir'd)
>
> 'Till thou roar out for Hemp-sake, Drive on Car-man.
> Pelted and curst i' th' road by every one,
> E'ne to be hang'd may'st thou the Gauntlet run.
>
> May the Knot miss the place, and fitted be
> To plague and torture, not deliver thee;
> Be half a day a Dying thus, and then
> Revive like *Savage*, to be Hang'd agen.

The satirical *Merciful Assizes* described the Bloody Assize.

> The many hundreds he hanged in the West, shews he was a stout
> Man, his Entrails Brass, and his Heart Steel; and this was necessary
> in the Post where the King had placed him.—Hang, Draw and
> Quarter, was part of his Loyalty; and yet we may call him a Merciful
> Judge. For he had such respect to the Souls of men, that he scarce
> hanged any but those that were innocent, and of those he has
> sentenced two hundred in a forenoon. If he excelled in one thing
> more than another, 'twas in his Haste to send Whiggs to Heaven:
> For, Hang Men first, and try 'em afterwards (witness Sir Thomas
> Armstrong's death) was his peculiar Talent. And so his having a
> Hand in all the Protestant Blood, from the murder of Godfrey to
> the last that died in the West, shewed him a faithful servant to King
> James; . . .

The *Western Martyrology* recounted the taking of the Lord
Chancellor in

Jeffreys' Elegy:

> Knowing in Villany he'd many Brothers,
> With that betook him to his Heels, and run,
> Thinking by Bribes he could not Ruin shun:
> He took a *Collier's Coat* to Sea to go;
> Was ever Chancellor arrayed so!
> But like to like, He'd needs anticipate,
> Devil Incarnate, *Collier of State.*
> He dealt in Deeds of Darkness, black as Night,
> Such a Black Habit needs must fit him right.
> Brave Sight to see him in a Collier's Skin;
> *Come, Pence a Piece, my Masters, enter in*

My Lord Mayor swooned, and was stricken dumb,
To see his metamorphos'd Lordship come.

The *Mobile* and *Rout* with Clubs and Staves
Swore that his Carcass ne'er should lye in Graves
They'd eat him up alive within an Hour,
Their Teeth should tear his Flesh, and him devour;
Limb him they would, as Boys on *Shrovetide* do,
Some cryed, *I am for a Wing and Arm*; for what are you?
I am for his *Head*, says one; for his Brains, says t'other,
And I am for his *Sowse*; his *Ears*, another;
Oh, cries a third, I am for his *Buttocks* brave,
Nine Pounds of Stakes from them I mean to have;
I know the Rogue is fleshy, says a fourth;
For *Sweet-Breads, Lungs* and *Heart* they're nothing worth;
Yes, quoth another, but not good to eat,
A *Heart of Steel will ne'er prove tender Meat.*
But we must them dispose another Way,
A good *Rich Lawyer* will a round sum pay,
For such a set of Loud and Bellowing *Lungs.*
Enough to save a *Hundred Stentors* Tongues.
We'll sell his Heart th' Pope to make a Show,
A Relique on't, and he'll get money too.
But whilst they were *dividing* him in Thought,
The Lord Mayor order's Soldiers to be brought,
Who rescued him from out the Rabble's Power.
And straight away they took him to the Tower,
With much ado he there was brought at last,
To think on all his Wicked Actions past.

The obscure men of Axe Yard who for sixteen years assiduously
compiled this heap of propaganda were John Dunton, John
Tutchin—and Titus Oates.

In January, 1689, Oates was at large again, he had been seen
walking in St. James's Park 'very fat and trimme'. He had spent
three and a half years in prison and while inside was said to have
married 'a lady Baltinglass, a heap of flesh and brandy'. He now
took up lodgings in Axe Yard. He was free but he did not recover
his former influence. In the summer the Lords reconsidered the
original verdict passed on him and even then, when Catholics and
Stuarts were at a discount, they were not prepared to reverse it.
The voting was 35 to 23 against Oates. Nevertheless the new King,
William III, pardoned Oates in August.

At Axe Yard Oates met John Tutchin, who had already pro-

duced four of the attacks on Jeffreys. Tutchin had been born in
1661. Later he was expelled from school in Stepney for theft. He
took part in Monmouth's rebellion, of which he wrote, a little
obliquely:

> ... when I was seated to the best advantage at the *Black Raven*, in
> Princes Street, London, and was as happy in my marriage as I could
> wish, there came a universal damp on the trade, occasioned by the
> defeat of Monmouth in the West. ...

In 1686 he married Elizabeth Hicks, the daughter of the same
John Hicks who had been executed for his part in the Monmouth
rebellion and whom Alice Lisle had been found guilty of shelter-
ing. Later, in 1704, he was called before the Commons and condemned as a 'daily inventor and publisher of false novelties and of
horrible and false lies' published in his paper, the *Observator*. He
was a born pamphleteer, as he himself recognized: 'I was all over
infected with an itch of printing and I confess I have indulged this
humour to excess.'

John Dunton, the publisher of the later pamphlets, had already
been in trouble for printing obscene books. He had taken part in
the Monmouth rebellion and had got away safely to North
America. He had hurried back to England as soon as he heard of
the Revolution, arriving in the summer of 1689. He has himself
described his meeting with Tutchin and Oates: 'While I lodged in
Axe Yard, I became acquainted with Dr. Oates ... he invited me
to his House to Dinner, and there I met with Mr. John Tutchin.
... They preached up Liberty and Property, and spoke very
despicably of all Kings, not sparing him on the Throne ...'

The final product of the collaboration of these three men was
The Western Martyrology, which contains 'improved' versions of
the earlier works. It begins with two pages of bad verse and then
continues with a history of the Popish Plot and the Rye House
Plot. All this part was written by Oates and the worthlessness of
his account may be judged from the testimonial he gave to
himself and Dangerfield: '... to their eternal Praise, they still
continued firm in their first Testimony, to the Rage and Confusion of their Enemies ...' Of himself he wrote, 'He's open and
frank, and speaks whatever he thinks of any Persons or things ...'
and continued that all future ages would join '... in making
honourable mention of his Name and Services to the Protestant
Religion'.

The next part describes the assize in the West. It begins with some 'General Observations' which suggest, acutely, that what we regard as rebellion depends on our political philosophy:

> . . . if once Principles and Notions are changed, or limited, we shall necessarily have other Thoughts of Things and Persons than we had before; and that Action we called Rebellion, and those Men we thought rebels, while we had a wrong slavish Notion of Obedience; when once that's regulated, and we believe with all the World, and all Ages and Nations, That we are to obey only the lawful Commands of Superiors, and submit only to such unjust ones, as will not much damage the Commonwealth; but resist and defend ourselves, when all we have dear, our Religion, Liberty and Lives, are visibly and undeniably attackt and invaded, either without all Form of Law, or what's worse, the wrested Pretence of it. Then we think truly, that such Men are so far from being Rebels, that they are the worthy true Defenders of their Faith and Country; and such an Action so far from Rebellion, that 'tis highly meritorious and praiseworthy.

This is a very reasonable, clear account of the Whig case for the Revolution of 1688. Soon, however, we are back in the realm of political propaganda: Jeffreys appears on the scene; and the martyrs suffer:

> His dealing with 'em is not to be paralleled by any thing but the new French Dragons dragoons, or the old Cut-throats and Lord Chief Justices of the poor Albigenses . . . Had the Great Turk sent his Janisaries, or the Tartar his Armies among 'em they'd 'scaped better. Humanity could not offend so far to deserve such Punishment as he inflicted. A certain barbarous Joy and Pleasure grinned from his Brutal Soul through his Bloody Eyes, whenever he was sentencing any of the poor Souls to Death and Torment; so much worse than Nero, as when that Monster wisht he had never learnt to write, because forced to set his Name to Warrants for Execution of Malefactors, Jeffreys would have been glad if every Letter he writ had been such a Warrant, and every Word a Sentence of Death. He observed neither Humanity to the Dead, nor Civility to the Living. He made all the West an Aceldama; some places quite depopulated, and nothing to be seen in 'em but forsaken Walls, unlucky Gibbets and Ghostly Carcasses. The Trees were laden almost as thick with Quarters as Leaves. The Houses and Steeples covered as close with Heads as at other Times frequently in that Country with Crows and Ravens. Nothing could be liker Hell than all those Parts, nothing so like the Devil as he. Caldrons hissing, Carcasses boyling, Pitch and Tar

sparkling and glowing, Blood and Limbs boyling, and tearing, and
mangling, and he the great Director of all; and in a Word, dis-
charging his Place who sent him, the best deserving to be the late
King's Chief Justice there, and Chancellor after, of any Man that
breathed since Cain and Judas.

Next follows a detailed description of the trials and executions
of some of those who had suffered in the West, their arguments
with Jeffreys and their last words on the scaffold. The latter may
be true, or based on what observers thought they remembered,
the rest is clearly apocryphal. There was no time during the assize
in the West for the prisoners to engage in extended debate with
their judges. Just as one may check Oates' honesty by his description of his own activities, so one may check John Tutchin's
veracity by his description of his own trial, for he had himself
appeared before Jeffreys at Dorchester, charged with spreading
alarm and despondency with the false news that 'Hampshire was
up in arms for the Duke, that he had seen both horse and foot on
the hills near Christchurch, and that Argyll was in great strength
and on the march within sixty miles of London.' For this he was
sentenced to a fine of five marks or imprisonment, and to be
whipped once. He was imprisoned, but he caught smallpox and
was therefore not whipped at all.

Those are the bare facts of the case. Now consider what
Tutchin made of them.

Jeffreys, Tutchin wrote, had sentenced him to imprisonment
for seven years, to pay a fine of one hundred marks, and to be
whipped through every market town in Dorset each year, which
would amount to a whipping once a fortnight. Here every fact is
untrue, even down to the number of market towns—there were
only eleven in Dorset. Tutchin added further dramatic details.
When the sentence was passed 'the ladies in the Court of which
there were a great many, all burst out a crying'. There was certainly no room for a great many ladies in the Dorchester court-
room. Jeffreys, according to Tutchin, spent some time attacking
this unimportant prisoner, '. . . no Devil incarnate could rage, nor
no Billingsgate Woman could scold worse than this Judge did at
this young Gentleman . . .', but 'Mr. Tutchin smiled in his Face,
and told him, he knew upon what Ground he stood, and when he
was over-match'd.'

The heroic story did not end there. Tutchin described how his
friends had begged him to sue for a pardon, but how instead he

had written direct to King James himself, praying that he might be hanged with his fellow-prisoners! The petition was rejected. Next, he wrote, he tried to get a pardon 'from the People who had Grants of Lives, many of 'em 500, some 1000, more or less,' (it will be remembered that there were in all less than 1,500 rebels brought up for trial). Finally he was 'popt into a Pardon amongst others' for which he had to pay. In actual fact Tutchin had been included in the general pardon issued in March, 1686.

That, false in every detail, is Tutchin's account of the one event during the assize in the West of which he was an eye-witness. It is a reasonable assumption that his description of the other trials, which he had *not* witnessed, is of equal reliability.

There is no need to demonstrate further the fictitious character of *The Western Martyrology* and of the earlier pamphlets on which it was based.

Fictitious—but very successful. The books created a legend from which both Whigs and Tories might benefit—that Jeffreys, who was dead, was responsible for all the ills of the last ten years. It was an age when, according to one's political prejudices, one might believe the best or the worst of a man—like all ages. Especially if he were unable to reply. Jeffreys suffered from the particular disability of being dead. For everyone else, though, that was very satisfactory. James, in France, could blame his servant for everything; Sunderland, in Holland, could shift all responsibility on to his colleague's shoulders; the triumphant Whigs could accept Jeffreys as the scapegoat for the Tories' sins.

While Jeffreys' reputation was destroyed, what happened to those whose lives had been intertwined with his? Of the Axe Yard pamphleteers, Dunton lived till 1733, passing into obscurity after the accession of George I; Tutchin died in 1707, in prison for debt; Oates joined, and was expelled from, yet another congregation—that of the Wapping baptists—in 1701. They described him as 'a disorderly person and a hypocrite'. He died in 1705.

The middle men made their peace with William III. John Trenchard, who had become a courtier in 1688, survived this mistimed shift in allegiance to become in 1692 a secretary of State. William Williams, who had been 'converted' to Catholicism, was very quickly back on the winning side, sitting on the committee that drafted the Bill of Rights in 1689. But he had destroyed his prospects of the highest legal offices and had to be content with the lord-lieutenantship of Merioneth and the post of solicitor-general to the Queen. Even Jeffreys' cousin, 'Squinting Jack', was restored to favour and again became Speaker—though he soon lost the position on a charge of bribery and corruption.

The men who had been responsible for the policies of the reign were the King himself, his Jesuit confessor Father Petre, and above all Sunderland. James died in exile in 1701. In his *Original Memoirs* he demonstrated that ingratitude which was the Stuarts' most constant characteristic, blaming his servants, including Jeffreys, for his own decisions. Father Petre retired from politics and became rector of St. Omer. Sunderland, who more than any other man had been James's evil genius and who has been called 'the craftiest, most rapacious, and most unscrupulous of all the politicians of his age'—Sunderland was back in England within a year, consulted by William, and in high office by 1697.

How did it happen? Sunderland was alive and a member of the establishment, Jeffreys was dead and had been a jumped-up Welsh attorney. Sunderland was connected with the great Whig families, the Sidneys and the Russells, with the Earls of Shaftesbury and of Bristol. As early as May, 1689, one can see the process at work. William Ettrick, in the Commons debates as to who should be exempted from the Act of Indemnity, said 'I hear no mention made of Lord Sunderland, though it is treason to reconcile to the Romish Church.' He was brushed aside or talked down (it is not certain which) and the House discussed instead the iniquities of Jeffreys—who had been buried the previous month. In July there was another attack on Sunderland. 'I am,' said William Harbord, 'for catching the great fishes; . . .' and Sunderland was exempted from the Act of Indemnity. But he sat tight in his great house at Althorp and no one touched him further.

People were at pains to conceal their connections with the scapegoat. In the Domestic State Papers there are no letters to or from Jeffreys after 1685. They are, too, conspicuous by their absence from private collections. It is not only in the twentieth century that history is rewritten to suit new rulers.

Thus the Jeffreys legend was established. Soon Thomas Bruce Lord Ailesbury, who should have known better, was writing that Jeffreys 'swore that all that were guilty should be hanged, and, as I have been told, he passed sentence on eight hundred in one day'. Burnet in his *History*, written some time before 1705, could say 'he was perpetually either drunk or in a rage, liker a fury than the zeal of a judge. . . . He hanged, in several places, about six hundred persons. He ordered a great many to be hanged up immediately, without allowing them a minute's time to say their prayers.'

Nevertheless, it took a little time. In July, 1689, a bargee at Redhill was fined ten pounds for blurting out that it was high time the Whigs there were treated as Jeffreys had treated them in the West Country. Clearly the new interpretation had not reached him. At the other end of the social scale Sir Joseph Jekyll, Master of the Rolls and a very respectable man, said of Jeffreys '. . . he had great parts, and made a great Chancellor in the business of that Court. In more private matters he was thought an able and up-right Judge wherever he sat'. And there is a significant exception to the general chorus of printed denunciation. The anonymous author of *A Caveat against the Whiggs* wrote

But they the Whigs have gone farther yet, and in imitation of their elder brothers, the papists, have furnish'd out a new Martyrology of those Holy Ones who died for rebellion and treason, so that they can not only turn religion into rebellion, but sanctifie rebellion into religion, and by a dash of their pen change a pernicious crew of rebels and traytors into a noble army of Saints and Martyrs. 'Tis a great pity that highwaymen and housebreakers cannot do the like kindness for their poor, suffering, persecuted bretheren!

I have, indeed, sometimes thought, that in Jefferies his Western Circuit, Justice went too far before Mercy was remembered, tho' there was not above a fourth part executed of what were convicted; but when I consider in what manner several of those lives then spared were afterwards spent, as may be instanced in their late scribbler Tutchin, and many others, I cannot but think a little more hemp might have been usefully employed on that occasion.

A strange shift of opinion, what had happened? The answer is very simple: the pamphlet was printed in 1712 when the High Tories were in power for the first, and virtually the last, time since the Revolution. Such opinions would not be expressed again. It is a safe assumption that if the Revolution of 1688 had failed, or had not taken place, or if the Tories had quickly re-established themselves, we should not have grown accustomed to speaking of the 'bloody assize' or of regarding Jeffreys as a drunken roaring brute. It was, however, fifty years before a Tory ministry was again in power and then it inherited nothing but its name from the Tories of the seventeenth century.

By 1725 the monster is complete, horns and all. By then the

13

Revolution was ancient history. In the *Life and Character of the late Chancellor Lord Jeffreys*, the anonymous author wrote:

> He was committed to the Tower, where he died soon after in great Rage and Fury, as well as in great Pain and Agony; and thus he died as miserably as he had lived, angry with every Body, because he had offended every Body, neglected, unfriended, unpitied, and unlamented and his Memory *detested by all Mankind*. . . .
>
> To do him Justice, he had a great deal of Baseness and Cruelty in his Nature, having a particular Delight and Relish in such Things as give Horror to the rest of Mankind. He was in this Case worse than even *Nero* . . .

By the time the pamphlet was reprinted in 1764, even his reputation as a Chancellor had been eroded:

> Upon the Whole, I entirely agree with our common Historians, that the Lord Chancellor *Jefferys* [sic] was a very ill Man: But I must beg Leave to differ when they call him a good Chancellor; . . .

Now it was the turn of the historians. The Whig interpretation of history had triumphed, and it found its classic expression in Macaulay's *History*. In his Fourth Chapter Macaulay painted his portrait of Jeffreys:

'He was a man of quick and vigorous parts, but constitutionally prone to insolence and to the angry passions. . . . Daily conflicts with prostitutes and thieves called out and exercised his powers so effectually that he became the most consummate bully ever known in his profession. All tenderness for the feelings of others, all self respect, all sense of the becoming, were obliterated from his mind. He acquired a boundless command of the rhetoric in which the vulgar express hatred and contempt. The profusion of maledictions and vituperative epithets which composed his vocabulary could hardly have been rivalled in the fishmarket or the beargarden. His countenance and his voice must always have been unamiable. But these natural advantages,—for such he seems to have thought them,—he had improved to such a degree that there were few who, in his paroxysms of rage, could see or hear him without emotion. Impudence and ferocity sate upon his brow. The glare of his eyes had a fascination for the unhappy victim on whom they were fixed. Yet his brow and his eyes were said to be less terrible than the savage lines of his mouth. His yell of fury, as was said by one who had often heard it, sounded like the thunder of the judgement day. . . .

'His enemies could not deny that he possessed some of the qualities of a great judge. His legal knowledge, indeed, was merely such as he had picked up in practice of no very high kind. But he had one of those happily constituted intellects which, across labyrinths of sophistry, and through masses of immaterial facts, go straight to the true point. Of his intellect, however, he seldom had full use. Even in civil causes his malevolent and despotic temper perpetually disordered his judgement. To enter his court was to enter the den of a wild beast, which none could tame, and which was as likely to be roused to rage by caresses as by attacks. . . . Even when he was sober, his violence was sufficiently frightful. But in general his reason was overclouded and his evil passions stimulated by the fumes of intoxication . . . He often came to the judgement seat, having kept the court waiting long, and yet having but half slept off his debauch, his cheeks on fire, his eyes staring like those of a maniac.'

Macaulay gives his sources—the *State Trials*, North's *Life*, and then 'Some touches of minor importance I owe to contemporary pamphlets in verse and prose.' There follow the titles of six of the pamphlets produced by the Axe Yard writers. One wonders if Macaulay knew that Oates had written a great part of these pamphlets, for he wrote of Oates: 'Murder by false testimony is therefore the most aggravated species of murder: and Oates had been guilty of many such murders.' In this case, though, Oates was only destroying a man's character.

Macaulay also refers to 'Lord Campbell's excellent book.' Campbell's *Lives of the Chancellors* had appeared in 1845-7, just before the first volumes of Macaulay's *History*. It was from Campbell that Macaulay appears to have drawn the general conclusion that 'his cruelty and his political profligacy have not been sufficiently exposed or repudiated, and that he was not redeemed from his vices by one single solid virtue.'

Most people will probably admit that Campbell, of whom they have never heard, might be wrong, but—Macaulay? Surely Macaulay was a great historian? Macaulay was a great writer of history—which is not quite the same thing. Historians read him for the picture he paints and not for photographic accuracy. He was not interested in political philosophy—he felt about seventeenth-century Tories as Jeffreys felt about seventeenth-century Whigs, without the excuse of being their contemporary. His approach was unhistorical, he wrote for effect, heightening his antitheses, never seeking to understand or to explain. This is not a modern judgement, but one of nineteenth-century historians. Gardiner said of Macaulay that his judgement of situations was superb, but his assessment of persons was weak. Sir Charles Firth was of the opinion that, in order to display William III, 'he peoples all Europe with pigmies'. Lord Acton concluded, 'He is, I am persuaded, grossly, basely unfair.' All this does not detract from the *History* as a work of art, but it does mean that Macaulay's character-sketch of Jeffreys should not be accepted uncritically.

Unfortunately, this is just what has happened. Ranke, perhaps the greatest historian of the nineteenth century, wrote in 1875 that Macaulay's *History* had permanently deflected the course of English political judgements. Some of the reputations have since been restored. Charles II is now no longer regarded as a flippant political lightweight, and Sir Winston Churchill has rescued the Duke of Marlborough from the charges of treachery and cold-blooded miserliness pressed by Macaulay. But the lesser men have had to look after themselves. It is time to admit that those who lost the political battle in the seventeenth century had their good qualities, as well as those who won.

Meanwhile the seductive brilliance of Macaulay's style and the weight of his reputation combined to influence the ephemeral writers of local history. Their accounts owed nothing to folk memory, and everything to the *Western Martyrology*, to Burnet, and to Macaulay (as the writers themselves very often admit).

Here are four examples, typical of a score of others:

This monster, being found a willing tool of his bigoted master, James II, had been exalted to the post of Lord Chief Justice of England. He was cruel, rapacious, and unscrupulous to the last degree, and was therefore chosen by the King to carry out his plans of repression and revenge.

(*South Petherton in the Olden Times!* 1882)

The cruelty of the King and his advisers was only equalled by their craving for gold ... Among the many places in Somersetshire where the name of Judge Jeffreys is still held in odious memory may be mentioned Ilchester. In the Hall a desk is pointed out where he sat to terrify prisoners with his brutal words and rive them to despair by his even more brutal sentences. The name "Judge Jeffreys' field" is to this day given to a field in Wedmore where many of his victims were hanged.

(*The Story of Somersetshire,* by W. R. Richmond;
no date, but post-1904)

It should be remembered that Jeffreys was never at Ilchester, and that none of the rebels were executed at Wedmore.

> . . . Jeffreys came to hang everybody unless they could pay large sums to be released . . . Every kind of wickedness and tyranny took place at this assize . . . Jeffreys committed every crime that is possible to an unjust judge. . . . He died in prison in time to save himself from the fate to which he had so often sentenced better men.
>
> (*A School History of Somerset*, by W. Raymond; London, 1906)

> Taunton . . . presented him with no fewer than a thousand prisoners. Here he perfectly revelled in his bloody task. The work seemed to have the effect of brandy or champagne upon him. He grew every day more exuberant and riotous. He was in such a state of excitement from morning to night that many thought him drunk the whole time. He laughed like a maniac, bellowed, scolded, cut his filthy jokes on the astounded prisoners, and was more like an exulting demon than a man. There were two hundred and thirty-three prisoners hanged, drawn and quartered in a few days.
>
> (*Bygone Somerset,* ed. C. Walters; London, 1897)

The tide began to turn at the end of the nineteenth century. One can date the moment fairly precisely. The last thoroughly unreliable character-sketch of Jeffreys appeared in Seccombe's *Twelve Bad Men*, published in 1894. Already in 1892, the Somerset historian, A. L. Humphreys, had written in the county's *Archaeological Journal*, that the *Western Martyrology* was '. . . full of errors'. The first full-scale life which attempted to portray a man and not a monster was Irving's *Life of Judge Jeffreys*, which appeared in 1898. It discounts the gossip about Jeffreys' foul language, praises his work as a lawyer, and concludes by examining his portrait: 'It is a face which contradicts the extreme malice of his enemies, but at the same time, by the not altogether pleasant curl of the lip and a certain staring hardness in the eye, affords some reason for the virulence of their hate.'

In the present century three lives have appeared which have reduced the figure of Jeffreys to human proportions, and the assize in the West has also been carefully analysed.[1] The conclusions reached in each book are broadly similar:

> No other judge in the history of England has been faced with such a situation; and no other . . . has been so utterly condemned on the

[1] Schofield, Hyde, Keeton and Muddiman. Full details are given in the note 'Some Books'.

unsupported testimony of his enemies and of the criminals who appeared before him.[1]

. . . he was a great lawyer, a great judge, and a great man . . . He was by no means exempt from the faults of his times, nor was he free from the defects of the judges of his day, but he has chiefly been condemned in modern times for his Western Circuit of 1685, about which the true facts have never hitherto been known. That this condemnation has been unjust, and that the word of the mean scamps of the Axe Yard clique ought never to have been allowed to be the primary source of information about Lord Jeffreys is now clear.[2]

If the picture of Jeffreys, always sober for civil cases and always drunk for political ones, employed in the most complex legal actions though completely ignorant of the law, an unprincipled careerist who was yet the only high official to remain at his post during the Revolution—if this unconvincing picture can now be discarded, what should be put in its place?

One must not fall into the error of replacing a sinner by a saint. Jeffreys was a very able exponent of the law but not a great one. He was a professional whose strength lay in cross-examination, in cutting through the tissue of fiction to the heart of the matter, and in this he was greatly helped by those wide eyes, that powerful voice, that volatile temperament—characteristics that impressed themselves on all those who met him. In his prejudices he was a conventional man, accepting uncritically and adopting enthusiastically the traditional mental attitudes towards monarchy, towards religion, towards crime. In behaviour he was arrogant and impetuous, often irritable or grimly sarcastic, always self-confident. This combination of qualities was an explosive one and there is no doubt that Jeffreys deliberately used it to alarm, when he thought that fear would help him to uncover the truth. Yet even if we accept all that the *State Trials* attribute to him, his vehemence remains in the conventional seventeenth-century tradition: '. . . thou art the greatest Lucifer that ever lived. Thou art a monster . . . a spider of hell!' That could be Jeffreys speaking —but it is not. It is Coke, the greatest lawyer of the seventeenth century and the darling of the Whig historians, prosecuting Sir Walter Raleigh for treason. 'Thou hast the Seven Deadly Sins, for thou art a Whore, a Bawd, a Sorcerer, a Witch, a Papist, a Felon

[1] Schofield, p. 201.
[2] Muddiman, p. 191.

and a Murderer!' That is Coke again, now Lord Chief Justice, addressing the fashionable milliner, Mistress Ann Turner. There was nothing remarkable in Jeffreys' language except the use that his enemies made of it.

One could just as easily compile a list of irreproachable sentiments:

Let not the greatness of any man corrupt you, but discharge your consciences both to God and the King, and to your posterity.

. . . therefore, child, if you take an oath be sure you say nothing but what is truth, for no party, nor side, nor anything in the world.

We live in an age wherein men are apt to believe only on one side. They can believe the greatest lie if it makes for the advantage of their party, but not the greatest truth if it thwarts their interests.

Be undaunted and courageous . . . fear God and honour the King; but use your utmost authority for the suppression of those that are given to change.

Neither the outbursts nor the sentiments should be considered outside the theatrical atmosphere of the law courts in which they were uttered.

When all is said and done, there remains the Bloody Assize. Two hundred and fifty people executed, over eight hundred sentenced to transportation. A vengeance uniquely savage in English history? The astounding fact is that it was no such thing. The punishment inflicted was very much in the line of government action throughout the centuries. Consider the following cases.

One hundred years earlier, in 1569, the northern counties rose in rebellion against Queen Elizabeth I. The total number of men involved was probably under nine thousand. When the rebels had been defeated, between six and eight hundred were executed, care being taken to see that there was at least one victim from each village involved, and the whole of the area was reduced to poverty by fines, confiscations, and the ravages of the army.

In the middle of the seventeenth century, after his victory over the Scots at Dunbar, Cromwell caused about 1,800 Scots to be transported to the New World. Many more had starved to death while imprisoned in Durham Cathedral. In the sixty years that followed Monmouth's Rebellion, Whig governments faced two Jacobite Rebellions. After that of 1715 about 1,000 rebels were transported. Following the Second Jacobite Rebellion of 1745–6

about eighty prisoners were executed. At Carlisle it was decided
'that, while the officers, and others who had distinguished themselves by zeal in the insurrections, should be tried, the great mass
should be permitted to cast lots, one in twenty to be tried, and the
rest to be transported.' About 1,500 rebels were transported.
Meanwhile the Highlands had been harried so that it was 'possible
to travel for days through the depopulated glens without seeing a
chimney smoke, or hearing a cock crow.'

In 1830 the last labourers' revolt took place, a revolt born of
unemployment and starvation. It spread through southern
England from Kent to Gloucester and a good deal of damage was
done to property—machine-smashing and rick-burning—but not
a single person was killed or ruined in fortune by the labourers.
Next year the Whig government set up a special commission to
try the rioters. Pressure was brought to bear on the prisoners to
inform against one another. At Winchester alone, where there
were about 300 prisoners, six were ordered to be executed,
ninety-five to be transported for life, thirty-six to be transported
for shorter periods, sixty-five were imprisoned in England, and
sixty-seven acquitted. *The Times* protested at the sentences of
death, and in the end only two men were executed. One of the
two was Henry Cook, a ploughboy of nineteen, whose wages had
never been more than ten shillings a week and who could neither
read nor write. Throughout the country as a whole, nine men
were executed, 457 transported, and about 400 imprisoned. It
must be remembered that nobody had been killed or seriously
injured by the rioters.

The farm labourers were punished by the party to which
Macaulay belonged, less than eighteen years before he published
the volume of his *History* dealing with the assize in the West.
One's first reaction is to echo Sir Compton Mackenzie's bitter
comment on the treatment of the Jacobites, 'Whiggery has always
been ready to sacrifice honour to respectability.' There may be
something in that, but there is a simpler explanation why one
does not hear more of the Elizabethan executions in the north of
England, or of the aftermath of Culloden, or of the events of 1831.
On each of these occasions the rebels were supporting a lost cause.
They disappeared, and the established order's view prevailed. In
the case of Jeffreys, exactly the opposite happened. The rebels of
1685 triumphed posthumously in the Revolution of 1688 and
became the 'New Martyrs'. This time the lost cause was Stuart

absolutism, which was destroyed together with the reputation of its supporters. Jeffreys had made the mistake of supporting the losing side. As the authors of the *Western Martyrology* had themselves written: 'if once Principles and Notions are changed, or limited, we shall necessarily have other Thoughts of Things and Persons than we had before:' or as Talleyrand later put it, 'Treason is all a matter of timing.'

SOME BOOKS

The history of England in the seventeenth century can be read in the following works:

Kenyon, J. P. *The Stuarts* (London, 1959)
Clark, Sir G. N. *The Later Stuarts* (Oxford, 2nd ed., 1950)
Ogg, D. *England in the Reign of Charles II* (Oxford, 2nd ed., 1955; paperback, 1963), *England in the Reigns of James II and William III* (Oxford, 1955)

Works dealing with the life of Jeffreys include:

The Protestant Martyrs (1689)
The Bloody Assizes (1689)
The New Martyrology (1689)
The Merciful Assizes (1701)
The Western Martyrology (1705)
The Life and Character of the Late Lord Chancellor Jeffreys (1725)
Woolrych, H. R. *Memoirs of the Life of Judge Jeffreys* (1827)
Campbell, Lord. *Lives of the Chancellors* (1845–7)
Macaulay, Lord. *History of England*, Chapters IV and V (1848)
Irving, H. B. *The Life of Judge Jeffreys* (London, 1898)
Schofield, S. *Jeffreys of "The Bloody Assizes"* (London, 1937)
Hyde, H. M. *Judge Jeffreys* (London, 1940)
Keeton, G. W. *Lord Chancellor Jeffreys and the Stuart Cause* (London, 1965)

Contemporary sources include the *State Trials*. The first edition appeared in 1719, but the edition usually available is that of 1840. Pepys' *Diary*, Evelyn's *Diary*, Luttrell's *Brief Historical Relation*, and North's *Examen, Life of Lord Keeper Guilford*, and *Lives of the Norths*, contain interesting background information. Burnet's *History of My own Times*, is useful for the specifically Whig point of view.

Modern monographs which touch on some of the aspects of the period include:

Bryant, Sir A. *Charles II* (London, 1931)
  Samuel Pepys (Cambridge, 1933–8)
Lane, J. *Titus Oates*
Jones, J. R. *The First Whigs* (Oxford, 1916)
Turner, F. C. *James II* (London, 1948)
Kenyon, J. P. *Robert Spencer, Earl of Sunderland* (London, 1958)
Muddiman, J. G. *The Bloody Assizes* (London, 1929)
Little, B. *The Monmouth Episode* (London, 1956)

INDEX

A

Abhorrers, 62, 80
Acton, Lord, on Macaulay, 196
Acton Park, 18, 82
Address and Confession to both Houses of Parliament (1689), 11
Ailesbury, Earl of, 139, 149, 192
Aldermanbury, Jeffreys' house in, 24, 33, 72
  St. Mary's, 33, 181-3
Anne, Princess, 170-1, 175
Argyll, Earl of, 96, 124, 128, 190
Armstrong, Sir Thomas (Rye House plotter), 36, 74, 91-2, 106-7, 186
Arnold, John, 66-7
Aston, Sir Willoughby, 105-6
Axe Yard pamphleteers, 184, 187-91, 195, 198
Axminster, 129, 141

B

Barbados, rebels transported to, 373
Barillon, French ambassador, 165, 173, 175
Barnardiston, Sir Samuel, 79, 105
Barnes, Joshua, 147
Barter, John (trial of Alice Lisle), 134-6
Bath, 131, 145, 165
Baxter, Richard, trial of, 124-6
Bedloe, 'Discoverer' or 'Narrative', 47, 50, 56, 79
Berkeley, Lady Henrietta, 83-5
Berry, Henry, 50
Bethel, Slingsby (sheriff of London), 69, 89-90
Birkenhead, Earl of, on Jeffreys, 158
Blake, Mary, 129
Bloody Assize: special commission issued by James, 133
  trial of Alice Lisle at Winchester, 133-9
  trial of rebels at Dorchester, 139-40
    at Exeter, 141
    at Taunton, 141
    at Wells, 141-2
  assize at Bristol, 141
  numbers involved, 142
  transportation, 142-3
  judges' payment, 143-4
  contemporary reactions, 144
  executions later in the year, 145
  later pamphlets, 185-9
  later descriptions of, 191-8
  compared with repression of other risings, 199-200

Bloody Assizes, The (1689), 185-6, 199-200
Bludworth, Sir Thomas (father-in-law), 24, 34-5
  (brother-in-law), 175
Booth, Henry, *see* Delamere, Lord
  Sir William, 143
Braddon, Laurence, 102-4
Bridgwater, 131
Bristol, 36, 131, 141
Browne, Sir Robert (Clerk of the Council), 27
Bulstrode Park (Jeffreys' house in Buckinghamshire), 29, 32-3, 152, 172, 174
Burnet, Bishop: on Danby, 38
  on Popish Plot, 39, 44, 53
  on origin of Whigs, 56
  on Dangerfield, 64
  on Pilkington, 85
  on Sidney, 96
  on Essex, 104
  on James II, 165
  on acquittal of the Seven Bishops, 170
  on Jeffreys, 93, 98, 116, 148, 192-3
Busby, Dr. Richard, 20

C

Campbell, Lord, on Jeffreys, 49, 108-9, 195
Care, Henry, trial of, 65-6
Cartwright (witness), 89-90
Caveatt against the Whiggs, A (1712), 53
Catherine of Braganza, 40, 44-5, 51, 193
Cellier, Elizabeth, 'the Popish midwife', 64-5
Chancery, 15-16, 157-60, 176
Chapman, Sir John, 76, 178
Charles II, 19, 41, 70, 74-5, 79, 113
Chedzoy, 130
Chiffinch, William (Charles II's secretary), 27, 39, 176
Choqueux (fireworks manufacturer), 43
Churchill, John, 131, 150, 175
Clarendon, second Earl of, 71, 153, 166, 168-70, 172, 176
Clayton, Sir Robert, 23, 59, 70, 151, 175, 181
Coleman, Edward (Duchess of York's secretary), 44, 46-7
College, Stephen, 'the Protestant joiner', 43, 74, 76-8
Comer v. Hollingshed, 176
Commission for Ecclesiastical Causes, 155-157, 170, 174, 180
Compton, Dr. Henry, Bishop of London, 156-7

Cornish, Henry (sheriff of London), 69, 89–90

Court and Country parties, 36–8, 56, see also Whigs and Tories

Coventry, Henry (Secretary of State), 41

Cromleholme, Dr. Samuel, 19

D

Danby, Earl of, 28, 38, 56

Dangerfield, Thomas, 64–5, 124, 188

Dare, Thomas, 64–5, 124, 188

De Saussure, 14

Declaration of Indulgence: first (1687), 161–2; second (1688), 168

Defoe, Daniel, 56

Delamere, Lord (Henry Booth), 70, 82, 148–50

Dispensing power, 168–70, 180

Dockwra, William, 86–7

Dolben, Sir William, 28–9

Dorchester, 139–40, 190

Doughty, 67–8

Dryden, John, 79–80

Dubois, John, 81

Dugdale, 79

Duncombe, Alderman Charles, 151–2, 161

Dunne, James (trial of Alice Lisle), 134–7

Dunton, John, Axe Yard pamphleteer, 184–91

E

Earl of Pembroke's Creditors v. Lady Charlotte Herbert, 159

East India Company v. Sandys (1683–5), 108–9

Edwards, 102–3

Essex, Earl of, Rye House plotter, 91–3, 101–4

Ettrick, William, 192

Evelyn, John: on Quo Warranto proceedings, 90
  on Rye House Plot, 92
  on first Declaration of Indulgence, 161
  on Revolution of 1688, 178
  guest of Jeffreys, 151
  on Jeffreys, 95

Exclusion Bill: first (1679), 57
  second (1680), 72
  third (1681), 74–5

Exeter, 105, 140–1, 144

F

Fairfax, Dr., 163–4

Farmer, Anthony, 163–4

Farnham, 133

Ferguson, Robert (Rye House plotter), 10, 91–2, 128

Feversham, Lord, 55–6, 131

Firebrasse v. Brett, 150

Firth, Sir Charles, on Macaulay, 196

Frampton, Dr. (Bishop of Gloucester), 180–1

Francis, Alban, 162
  Robert, 124

Frome, 131

G

Gaol fever, 13, 142

Gaunt, Elizabeth, 139

Giles, John, 66–7

Godden v. Hales, 152

Godfrey, Sir Edmund Berry, murder of, 41–3, 47, 50, 59, 186

Godolphin, Sidney, 58, 110, 153, 171

Great Frost, the, 100

Green, Robert, 50

Green Ribbon Club, 37, 70, 83, 85

Grey, Lord, 74, 83–5, 92, 102, 131–2

Grove, John, 40, 47

Guardian, The, on St. Mary's Aldermanbury, 183

Guilford, Lord (Francis North), 77, 87, 109–11, 116–17, 123–4, 140

H

Hackett, Mr., 115

Hale, Sir Matthew, 21–3, 159

Hales, Sir Edward, 153, 161

Halifax, Lord, 60, 70, 73, 110, 178

Hampden, John, 91–2, 101–2
  Richard, 57

Harbord, William, 192

Harris, Benjamin, 13, 60–1
  Renatus, 160

Haynes, 77

Henry, Philip, 19, 83

Herbert, Sir Edward, 147, 155

Hewet, Dr., 134, 137

Hicks, John (trial of Alice Lisle), 134–8, 188

Hill, Lawrence, 50

Hipkin, Mary, 30–1

Holloway, James, 106

Hough, Dr. John, 163

Howard of Escrick, Lord (Rye House plotter), 91–3, 96, 101
  Sir Philip, 143

Hyde, Henry, see Clarendon
  Lawrence, see Rochester
  Montgomery, 152

I

Ignoramus, 68–9, 76, 79

Ireland, William, 47–8, 117
  Sir Thomas, 18

Irving, H. B., 63, 114–15

J

Jacobite Rebellion (1715), suppression of, 199
  (1745), 199–200

James II (*as Duke of York*), and the Popish Plot, 44–5, 51
 appoints Jeffreys his Solicitor-General, 55
 and Exclusion, 57, 72–3, 75
 monopoly of General Post Office, 86–7
 defends Catholics, 110
 as King,
 accession, 113
 character, 113–14, 192
 responsibility for the Bloody Assize, 133, 144
 and Jeffreys (1687), 152–4
 policy of toleration, 161–2, 164–5, 168
 and Seven Bishops, 168–70
 birth of a son to, 170–2
 failure and flight of, 175–7, 179
 death of, 192
 on Jeffreys, 191–2
Jeffreys, Ann (second wife), 34–5, 166, 174, 181
 (daughter), 176
Jeffreys, Edward (uncle), 18
 (brother), 18
Jeffreys, George; *early life*
 birth, 18
 education, 19–20
 at Inner Temple (1663–8), 20–1
 first marriage (1667), 21
 career
 called to the Bar (1668), 22
 elected Common Sergeant (1671), 24–9
 knighted (1677), 29
 Recorder of London (1678–80), 29–72
 second marriage (1679), 34–5
 solicitor-general to Duke of York (1679), 55
 abhorrer (1680), 62
 Chief Justice of Chester (1680), 62, 70–1, 82–3
 Sergeant-at-Law (1680), 62
 resigns Recordership (1680), 71–2
 Baronet (1681), 80
 Lord Chief Justice (1683), 95–146
 Baron (1685), 116
 assize in the West (1685), 133–40
 Lord Chancellor (1685–8), 146–76
 disgrace and death
 flight (1688), 177–8
 imprisonment (1688–9), 178–80
 death and burial (1689), 181–2
 reburial (1693), 182–3
 activities
 at trial of Muggleton (1677), 24–6
 at Court, 26–9, 56–9
 at Old Bailey (1678), 30–2
 at Popish Plot trials (1678–9), 46–53
 at trials of Benjamin Harris and 'Elephant' Smith (1679), 60–2

 at trials of Mrs. Cellier, Henry Care, John Giles and 'Elephant' Smith (1680), 64–9
 at trial of Stephen College (1681), 76–8
 at trials of Lord Grey, Pilkington, and Dockwra (1682), 83–7
 at trials of ex-sheriffs of London (1683), 89–90
 at trial of Russell (1683), 92–4
 at trial of Algernon Sidney (1683), 95–100
 at trials of Hampden, Braddon, and Speke (1684), 101–4
 Western circuit (1684), 104–5
 trials of Holloway and Armstrong (1684), 106–7
 trials of Nottingham Whigs (1684), 107–8
 work on civil cases, and on town charters (1684), 108–10
 trials of Rosewall, and Papillon (1684), 111–12
 trial of Titus Oates (1685), 117–22
 trials of Dangerfield and Baxter (1685), 124–6
 assize in the West (1685), 133–44; Winchester—trial of Alice Lisle, 134–8; Dorchester, 138–40; Exeter, 140–1; Taunton, 141; Bristol, 141; Wells, 141–2
 at trial of Lord Delamere (1686), 148–50
 on Commission for Ecclesiastical Causes (1686–8), 155–7, 162–4
 in Chancery (1686–8), 157–60, 176
 and Seven Bishops (1688), 168–70
 at birth of James II's son (1688), 171
 drafts James II's will (1688), 175
 maintains the daily administration (1688), 175–7
 miscellaneous
 friends, and patrons, 22–4, 26–9, 56–8, 150–2
 chambers in King's Bench Walk, 22
 house in Aldermanbury, 24
 house at Temple Bulstrode, 29, 32–3, 152
 private tastes, 33–4
 fire in Pump Court, 55–6
 the stone, 114–15, 133, 150, 152, 166, 179
 house in Queen Street, 146
 family affairs, 154–5, 159, 166, 172–3, 176
 and Temple Church organ, 160
 house in Duke Street, 160–1
 disposes of his property, 174–5
 makes his will, 181
 memorials to, 182–3

Jeffreys, George—*continued*
  character and opinions
    10, 22–3, 26, 28–9, 30–2, 46, 49–50,
    58, 63–5, 94, 98–9, 104–6, 112, 118–
    122, 125–6, 137, 148, 173–4, 181–2,
    191–2, 199
  Contemporaries' estimates of
    22–3, 26, 35, 70, 93–8, 107, 146–8,
    192–3
  the Jeffreys myth
    11–12, 25, 30–1, 49, 68, 70–1, 73, 93,
    108–9, 164, 184–97; reasons for, 184,
    191, 193, 200–1
  modern assessments of,
    158–9, 197–201
Jeffreys, James (brother), 154–55, 172–5,
    181–2
Jeffreys, Jeffrey (City merchant), 23, 181
Jeffreys, John (grandfather), 18
    (father), 18
    (brother), 18
    (son), 33, 159, 172, 174, 181
    (City merchant), 23, 181
    (Alderman), 23, 150, 171
Jeffreys, Margaret (mother), 18
    (daughter), 33, 166
Jeffreys, Sir Robert (City merchant), 23,
    151
Jeffreys, Sarah (first wife), 21, 33, 181
    (daughter), 33, 166
Jeffreys, Sir Thomas (brother), 18, 155, 166,
    172–4
Jeffreys, William (brother), 18
Jenkins, Sir Leoline, 79, 82, 91
Jennings, Edward, 175, 181–2
Jones, Sir William ('Bull-faced'), 46
Justice, aspects of seventeenth century,
    12–17

                    K
Keeton, Professor G. W., 106, 158–9
Kemble, J., 115, 179
Ketch, Jack, 94, 123, 140
Kidnapping, 141
King, Sir Edmund, 178–9
Kirkby, Christopher, 39
Kirke, Colonel Percy, 132–3
Kynaston, Edward, 166–7

                    L
L'Estrange, Roger, 10, 47, 80
Labourers' revolt (1830), 200
La Chaise, Père, 46
Lady Ivy's Case, 34, 108
Lamplugh, Doctor, Bishop of Exeter, 144
Langhorne, Roger, trial of, 50–1
Levinz, Sir Cresswell, 133, 141
*Life and Character of the late Lord Chancellor
    Jeffreys* (1725), 194
Lisle, Alice, trial of, 134–8
Lives of the Chancellors (1845–7), 48, 108–9,
    195

Lodeman, 103
Lord High Steward, Court of the, 148–50
Louis XIV, 44, 75, 113–14, 165
Lucas, Lord, 178
Luttrell, Narcissus, 77, 94, 100, 113, 152
Lyme (Regis), 127–8, 140
Lyttleton, Sir Charles, 144

                    M
Macaulay, Lord, on Jeffreys, 25, 31, 73,
    164, 194–6
Magdalen College, 163–4
Magdalene College, 162–3
Mary, wife of James II, 143, 147, 170–2, 176
Mary II, Queen of England, 143, 170–2,
    176, *see also* William of Orange
Maynard, Sergeant, 104, 108
Meal-Tub Plot (1680), 64–5
Minehead, 145
Molland, Alice, 105
Monmouth, James, Duke of, supporters, 36
    at Temple fire, 55–6
    'progress' through the west (1680), 69
    at Oxford (1681), 74
    'progress' through the north-west
        midlands (1682), 82
    and the Council of Six (1683), 91–2
    in Holland (1685), 124
    in rebellion (1685), 127–32
Montagu, Sir William, 133, 141
Moyles' Court, 134–7
Muddiman, Henry, 145
    J. G., 142, 198
Muggleton, Lodowick, trial of, 24–6
Musgrave, Sir Christopher, 143

                    N
Neesham, Sarah (Jeffreys' first wife), 21, 33
Nelthorpe, Richard (trial of Alice Lisle),
    134–5
Nevill, Sir Edward, 147
New Martyrology, The (1689), 185
Nipho, Ieronimo, 143
North, Roger, on Hale, 20–3
    on Chiffinch, 27
    on the Popish Plot, 41, 43, 47
    on Scroggs, 48
    on Bethel, 69
    on Oxford parliament, 75
    on the City elections (1682), 81
    on Saunders, 87–8
    on the Rye House Plot, 92–3
    on Charles' advisers, 110
    on Taunton, 130
    on Jeffreys, 22–3, 109, 111, 148, 151–2
    general, 140, 147
Norton St. Philip, 131
Nottingham, 107–8
    Earl of, 87

O

Oates, Titus, early life, 40
  and the Plot, 41–2
  and the early trials, 44–7
  and the Wakeman trial, 51–3
  begins to be discredited, 53–4
  witness at the trial of College, 77–9
  own trial and sentence, 117–23
  at liberty again, 179
  part-author of attacks on Jeffreys,
    187–8, 191, 195
  death of, 191
Oxford parliament (1681), 74–5, 77

P

Papillon, Thomas, 79, 81, 111–12
Paschall, Andrew, 130
Paul's Meeting House, 130
Peachell, Dr. John, Master of Magdalene,
  73–4, 162–3
Pemberton, Sir Francis, 84, 87, 92–3
Pembroke, Earl of, 159, 172
Penn, William, 165, 178
Penny Post, 86–7
Penruddock, Colonel (trial of Alice Lisle),
  134–6
Pepys, Samuel, on Cromleholme, 19
  his clerk on Jeffreys, 70
  on the Popish Plot, 72
  Dr. Peachell writes to, 74, 163
  on Tangier, 132
  concerning the transportation of
    rebels, 144
  guest of Jeffreys, 151
  on Dr. Peachell, 162
  concerning attack on the Spanish
    ambassador's house, 177
  John Evelyn writes to, 178
Perjury Punish'd, or Villainy Lash'd (1685),
  123
Petre, Father, 153, 176, 192
Pickering, Thomas, 40, 47
Pilkington, Sir Thomas, 85–6, 89–90
Pitt, Moses, 161
Plymouth, 104, 108
Pollexfen, Sir Henry, 125, 133, 135, 139,
  151, 175, 181
Poole, 131–2, 140
Popish Plot, Oates' story, 39–41
  Sir Edmund Berry Godfrey, 42–3
  trials, 42–53
  referred to, 54, 57, 64, 72, 76, 78–9
Portsmouth, Duchess of, 57, 68, 172
Price, Captain John, 143
Prideaux, Edmund, 129, 143
Pritchard, Sir William, 111–12
'Protestant flails', 43, 74
Protestant Martyrs, The (1689), 185
Pym, Lt.-Col. Charles, 143

Q

Querouaille, Louise de, 27
Quo Warranto, 80–1, 87–90

R

Ranke, on Macaulay, 196
Reresby, Sir John, 72, 110, 151
Rich, Peter, 81
Richardson, Captain, 50, 53, 106
Ringwood, 134
Rising, the northern (1569), 199
Rochester, Earl of (Laurence Hyde), 58,
  110, 153, 155, 161
Rose, 'Pascha', 140
Rosewell, Thomas, 111
Rumbold, 'Hannibal' (Rye House plotter),
  91
Rumsey (Rye House plotter), 92
Russell, Lord William (Rye House plotter),
  72–3, 91–2; trial of, 91–4
Rye House Plot, 74, 85, 91–100, 180

S

St. Mary's Aldermanbury, see Alderman-
  bury
St. Omer, 118
St. Paul's School, 19
Salamanca Doctor's Farewell, The (1685), 123
Salisbury, 139
Sancroft, William, Archbishop of Canter-
  bury, 155, 168–70, see also Seven Bishops
Saunders, Sir Edmund, 80–1, 87–90
Schmidt, Father Bernard, 160
Schofield, S., on Jeffreys, 197–8
Scroggs, Sir William, 27, 30, 46–8, 51–4,
  60–1, 66, 70
Sedgemoor, battle of (1685), 55, 85, 131–2
Settle, on Jeffreys, 107
Seven Bishops, trial of the (1688), 168–70,
  175, 180
Seymour, Sir Edward, 144
Shaftesbury, Earl of, and the Whig party,
  37–9, 59, 70, 73, 75
  and the Popish Plot, 41–2, 45
  imprisonment, 76, 79
  death, 88
  on Charles II, 89
  on James II, 113
Sharp, Dr. John, 156–7, 180–1
Shorthand, 67, 86
Shrewsbury, 18–19
Shute, 89
Sidney, Algernon (Rye House plotter),
  91–2; trial of, 95–100
Six, Council of, 91–2
Smith, Francis ('Elephant'), 60–2, 68–9
  William, 119–20
Somerset, A School History of (1906), 197
Somerset, Bygone (1897), 197
Somersetshire, The Story of, 196
South Petherton in the Olden Times!, 196

Speke, George, 37
  Hugh, 102-4
Stafford, Lord, 44, 73
Stapleton, Sir William, 143
Stayley, William, 45
Stephen, Sir James, 67, 98, 138
Stringer, William, 166, 181
Sunderland, Earl of, and Tory party, 57, 110
  connections with Jeffreys, 58, 95, 139-41
  connections with James II, 114, 153, 171
  and Lord Guilford, 116-17
  and the Bloody Assize, 139-41, 144
  and the Commission for Ecclesiastical Causes, 155
  and the second Declaration of Indulgence, 161
  flight to Holland, 175
  restored to favour, 191-2
Swift, on Burnet, 93

                    T

Tangier, 132
Taunton, 70, 92, 128-30, 141, 143, 172, 197
Temple Church organ, 160
Thurloxton, 129
Timewell, Stephen, 130
Tonge, Israel, 40
Torbay, 175
Transportation, 142-3, 199-200
Trenchard, John, 70, 73, 92, 172, 191
Trevor, Sir John ('Squinting Jack'), 20, 35, 101, 124, 147, 173, 181, 192
Trinity College, Cambridge, 20
Trumbull, Sir William, 151-3
Tunbridge Wells, 133
Turberville, 79
Turner, Mr., 84-5
Tutchin, John, 147, 185, 187-8, 190-1

                    V

Venn, Thomas, 129
Verney, John, 68, 107, 164

                    W

Wakeman, Sir George, 40, 51
Wall, Ellen, 68
Wallop, 101, 103
Wapping, 54, 74, 88, 108, 160, 177, 191
Ward, Sir Patience, 69, 86
Wells, 131, 141-2, 144
Wem, and Loppington, 116
West, Robert, 91
Western Martyrology, The (1705), 185-91, 196-7, 201
Westminster Hall, 15-16, 170
Westminster School, 20
Weston, Richard, 64
Westonzoyland, 131-2
Wharton, Thomas, 115
Wheeler, Adam, 132
Whig party, composition, 36-7, 88
  origin of name, 56
  tactics (Popish Plot, and Exclusion, Ignoramus endorsements, and City elections), 45, 56-7, 69, 74-5
  Royalist tactics against (trials and Quo Warranto), 88-91
  Jeffreys on, 105, 112
  view of Jeffreys, 193-6
  suppression of rebellions by, 199-200
  Sir Compton Mackenzie on, 200
  see also Court and Country parties, Rye House Plot, Shaftesbury
White, Dr. Thomas, Bishop of Peterborough, 175, 180-1; see also Seven Bishops
White Horse Tavern, 41, 59, 117
Wilcox, Alderman, 78
William of Orange (later William III), 57, 74, 128, 142-3, 150, 173-6, 179, 187, 192
Williams, William, 61-2, 70, 82, 89-90, 101, 108, 165, 170, 174, 191
Winchester, 105, 133-8
Winnington, Sir Francis, 46
Wright, Sir Robert, 133, 141, 147
Wythens, Sir Francis, 62, 70, 97, 99, 119, 122, 133, 141

                    Y

York, Jeffreys at, 110
York, Duke of, see James II